Empowering Women Through Literacy

Views From Experience

A volume in
Adult Education Special Topics:
Theory, Research, and Practice in Lifelong Learning

Series Editor:
Kathleen P. King, *Fordham University*

Adult Education Special Topics: Theory, Research, and Practice in Lifelong Learning

Kathleen P. King, Series Editor

Empowering Women Through Literacy

Views From Experience

edited by

Mev Miller
WE LEARN

and

Kathleen P. King
Fordham University

Information Age Publishing, Inc.
Charlotte, North Carolina • www.infoagepub.com

Library of Congress Cataloging-in-Publication Data

ISBN 13: 978-1-60752-083-2 (pbk.)
ISBN 13: 978-1-60752-084-9 (hardcover)

Photo and Art Work Credits
Cover: Rosa's Woman with Water Jar; photo by Deborah Wilson
Part 1 Divider Photo: Marta & reference book; photo by Deborah Wilson
Part 2 Divider Photo: Ana Maria at Graduation, Voice from the Earth; photo by Deborah Wilson
Part 3 Divider Photo: Guadelupe Glazing Rose Platter; photo by Deborah Wilson

Chapter 2.13 Figure1. WE LEARN Logo, Designed by Mev Miller
Chapter 2.13 Figure 2. Threads of Experience: 2007 Conference Art; Artwork by Sally S. Gabb
Chapter 2.13 Figure 3. WE LEARN 5th Anniversary Celebration Calendar Cover; Artwork by Sally S. Gabb; Design by Mev Miller

Printed in the United States of America

CONTENTS

SECTION II: LEARNING COMMUNITIES

DEDICATION AND ACKNOWLEDGMENTS

We, the editors, dedicate this volume to all those who actively vision, create, and support the mission of WE LEARN. We believe in your commitment and principles, we applaud your courage and persistence, and meaningful resist stance, and we cherish your respectful hearts that continue to reach out to empower other women. Thank you for who you are and what you do.

There are so many people we want to recognize, yet space is short. However, please know that on behalf of all 49 contributors to this volume, we thank each of you who has supported us though our journey of learning and empowerment.

In bringing this book to the public there are three essential acknowledgments we must explicitly note for this first volume of the planned biennial series.

In creating a volume of practice and experience of this measure, the contributors are indispensable. Their work makes this volume the treasure of insight we believe it has become. We are deeply indebted for the quality and honesty of your reflections, essays, research, poems, art and life-sharing. Thank you for your willingness to make your work visible in this community endeavor.

In addition, we greatly appreciate the skillful eye and style of Seamus King in copy edit and style edit work. Thank you, Seamus, for tackling a large task with your commitment to scholarship, empowerment and gender equity, and your good humor!

We also greatly appreciate the vision and commitment of our publisher, George Johnson and Information Age Publishing, for recognizing the need and value of this volume.

INTRODUCTION

Mev Miller and Kathleen P. King

To build awareness of and support for women's literacy issues, WE LEARN (Women Expanding Literacy Education Action Resource Network) addresses several key groups, including (but not limited to) the general public unfamiliar with basic literacy/education needs of adults, community and/or feminist activists who may not recognize how literacy needs impact organizing efforts, and educators or researchers who may not be knowledgeable about women-specific learning styles. *Empowering Women through Literacy: Views from Experience* was developed not merely as an opportunity to build this awareness but also as an assertion for visibility about the many creative and innovative practices already in use by everyday adult educators, and their successes. This volume includes the voices and experiences of practitioners who conscientiously and thoughtfully construct supportive and meaningful learning environments for women learners, specifically those participating in adult basic, literacy, and developmental education (ABE) services or programs. More than half of the contributors to this volume have been long-time members or supporters of WE LEARN.

As seems fitting, ABE educators tend to focus on the needs and goals of their students. They prioritize their time developing productive lesson plans, curriculum, and educational opportunities for student achievement. They are occupied by discovering best practices, meeting educational standards, and honing their professional skills in order to assure the success of students. Women literacy educators are overworked, underpaid and sometimes stressed-out yet they remain deeply dedicated to their students. While teachers receive professional development related to academic standards and content (cognitive aspects), they rarely have time to reflect on what they are doing or to replenish their hearts and souls as women and as professionals. They receive little encouragement or support for addressing the more affective dimensions of women's learning, namely, those dependent on building relationship and community. Many of these educators, especially those addressing women's literacy issues, work in isolation and have limited (no) opportunities to discuss and evaluate their work with other like-minded educators. These reflective practitioners desire space and time for reflection about the work they are doing, and want support for renewal and rejuvenation. With this volume, we seek to directly acknowledge the work of each contributor and integrate each voice into the big ABE picture. We want this volume to extend the dialog about what we are doing, to build community from our experiences and to dissipate our feelings of doing this work in isolation.

VISION AND NEED: VISIBILITY AND EMPOWERMENT

When we first conceived of this project, we hoped for an emergent volume that could take the first steps towards broadening the visibility and discussion about women's empowerment through literacy. When we developed the call for proposals, we had no idea what to expect. But the response soon became overwhelming and we had many more proposals than we could handle. From this experience, we have made at least two observations.

First of all, WE LEARN members and ABE teachers who address women's literacy issues need a public forum in which to share and discuss their work. Because we sought the experiential and inventive, we have uncovered many voices that don't typically have an opportunity for publication through standard educational venues. We received writings from long-time professional academics, career classroom teachers and administrators, graduate students, tutors who were formerly adult literacy learners, researchers, professional developers and trainers, peer groups, counselors, and poets.

Here you will not only find research-based essays, but also poetry, a letter, a graphic novel, artwork, journal entries, stories, conversations, and theater. Educational locations include immigrant learning centers, GED classes, homeless and transitional shelters, alternative programs serving teens, corrections, university settings, workplace collaborative, disability services, and community-based projects. The 47 contributors reflecting on their experiences with critical topics of adult women's literacy practices include those from Australia, Belize, Brazil, Canada, Cypress, Dominican Republic, Germany, and several regions across the U.S. They represent a diversity of racial, ethnic and cultural, ages, sexualities, educational backgrounds and experiences.

Secondly, we discovered how strongly the affective aspects of women's learning form the centerpiece of these contributors' experiences. Each one unapologetically and without pause discusses the relationships they build with learners and among colleagues in their teaching/learning situations. In this volume you will not find techniques on the best ways to teach the content of writing or reading or pronunciation or grammar or math. What you will find though, are the ways in which building relationships, creating safer learning spaces and allowing for holistic possibilities to integrate spirit, body and emotion creates critical paths to reaching women's learning minds and supporting their successes, not only for students but also as professional educators. It is our (not so) quiet hope that this volume creates one step towards reconsidering the policies about and research strategies for students in ABE, especially women.

REVEALING STRUCTURE OF THE BOOK

We have organized the writings in *Empowering Women through Literacy: Views from Experience* into three sections: Reflections, Learning Communities, and Explorations of Practice. While all the writings in this volume include personal reflections from the writers, Section I, Reflections, includes some of the clearest voices of introspection, expression, and insight into how and why adult educators consider themselves and their students as women in a variety of educational settings. These writers reflect on their own vulnerabilities (Becker), and consider how their own lives and learning experiences not only affect their capabilities as teachers but also provide insight for empathy towards their students (Horsman; Rivera; Spilvoly). Others talk about their transition from their personal struggles as students who suffered depression, health issues, or racial discrimination to their currents roles and teachers and tutors (Diaz; Arrindell). They share some of their specific strategies for inviting women into the learning environment (Milheim; Chlup; Evans). Creative writers explore their own understanding of their craft as they bring opportunities for students to voice their own experiences and realities (DiMarzio; Gover) while poets tell the stories of their students and themselves in the artistic ways that poetry brings unusual dimension to the telling (Childress; Holland; Shoemaker).

In Section II, Learning Communities, writers highlight and identify the various types of learning communities practitioners have fostered in order to support women's literacy empowerment. We invite you into this section through a graphic novel depiction of the ways in which some women are welcomed into a co-learning environment (Gabb). In "Learning Communities" you will find a variety of settings (hidden curriculum) that support individual and groups of students. These include book discussion groups on African American women's literature (Jones), empowerment messages hanging in the classroom (Reid), or prioritizing student-centered content (Gruver; Bennett). Additionally, these learning communities can be understood through dialogue (Donnelly) and through artistic expression (Ben-Yosef). They involve building collaborations in the program context across all participants, teachers and students alike (Aggarwal; González; Nevel & Placencia) or as teacher-student mentors and coaches (Miller, G. & Makinen; King). This section also provides practitioners the opportunity to explore how they can build their own professional development and support communities (Bradshaw & Matheson; Silver-Pacuilla, Lantz-Leppert, Porfirio, & Anders). It closes with more information about WE LEARN and the ways in which we can take our smaller individual and program-based practices into a larger (inter)national reflection and action context (Miller, M.)

Section III, Explorations of Practice, provides essays that more formally address evidence-based practice through inquiry, action research and theory supported reflective practices. The reflections and essays in this section weave personal experience with more research-to-practice support. This section challenges you to consider the dissonances between evidence-based practices and your own personal wisdom and reflection (Rivera). These essays consider the ways in which addressing fear and trauma sometimes contradict what we think we should do (Robertson; Zabitgil) while keeping in mind the ways in which persistence and resistance complement each other (Boden). Essays in this section articulate the ways in which empowering women's literacy involves challenging programmatic, professional, and policy barriers (Ramdeholl, Evans, & Gordon; Bridwell; Alfred; Addy). Finally, the closing essays in this section, and volume, encourage you to consider practices that push us to consider women's literacy empowerment through expanded approaches using technology (King), theater (Schaedler), community-organizing (Strohschen) and pottery (Redfield Shakoor & Wilson).

OUR COMMON ORIENTATION FOR EMPOWERING WOMEN

This book specifically evolved from the WE LEARN conference of 2008 but included global invitations to other contributors as well. Although the entry writers were not instructed to include the WE LEARN mission and indeed some are probably not conversant of the principles, it is still compelling how fully the authors articulate values identified by WE LEARN.

Realizing this dynamic, we believe it helpful to outline briefly these principles as an introduction to the perspective of this volume. We realize many of you might or might not have articulated such values/guides/principles for yourself previously, but we ask you to join us in reflecting upon them and considering in what ways they match, and mis-match your own consciousness, perspective and practice. Such reflection, literary exchange and consciousness-raising are the foundation of women's critical inquiries for their lifelong empowerment (Belenky, et al., 1986; Hayes & Flannery, 2000).

Purpose

Our efforts (strategy) for building inclusive movements are focused in education, specifically the basic literacies women need to gain access to systems of power and to achieve personal and community empowerment. Women as learners gain positive benefits from creative, accessible, and meaningful basic literacy materials that look critically at women's issues such as violence, poverty, and the silencing of women's voices. These materials, especially when based in participatory education contexts, give visibility to their experiences as women, support their on-going desire to learn, encourage critical thinking, and provide the support and information necessary for reflection, understanding, and action to change their current situations (Miller, 2002).

Movement building for change. Movement building involves creating critical learning environments that make use of these materials and methods, foster learner leadership, involve learners more directly in the development of theory and action related to women's political movements, and provide a catalyst to transform women's lives. Additionally, literacy workers that have access to women-centered curriculum materials are better supported in creating relevant learning contexts and possibilities for all their learners, both women and men. WE LEARN seeks to encourage teachers to create holistic women-supportive learning environments in spite of restrictions placed by the National Reporting System (NRS) and state/federal assessment and accountability policies. We challenge activists from every social movement to consider the literacy proficiencies of all people and to consider how print-based information and privileged language continues as a barrier for access of the people to people's liberation causes.

For WE LEARN, movement and movement-building means interrupting and ending systems of oppression. We challenge anti-oppression movements (especially those addressing sexism, racism, heterosexism, and classism) to consider basic literacy/education as a factor for full participation in movement building.

Principles to Consider

In discussion with our members, WE LEARN's Board of Directors has started to articulate principles to help identify their position in the world on key issues related to gender, oppression, education, and equity. Reflect with us upon the following principles to consider your perspective and experience. We are certain you have your own stories, experiences and recommendations regarding their occurrence and challenges. Indeed, this activity may be used to prepare individuals and groups of readers to consider stories and views of the contributors in this volume. Readers and group leaders might use this as a discussion prior to reading the volume, with each chapter or at the conclusions of parts or the entire book. This suggestion leads us to our first principle.

- **Feminism/womanism/woman-centeredness**: This principle refers to valuing women's voices and experiences; women's ways of knowing that nourish the mind, body, and spirit; sharing stories/experiences and using these as a basis for learning and action, learning that involves more than the mind; supporting and celebrating women's successes. We focus on women because women are still excluded from making decisions about their lives, still isolated without the opportunities to talk about their common experiences. We recognize that learning happens in every aspect of women's lives, not just in the classroom (Cox & Sanders, 1988; Laubach Literacy Action, 1995; Miller & Alexander, 2004; Miller & Peters, 2004).
- **Social Change**: This refers to access, acquiring skills, and internal transformation, both individual and societal/systemic change; individual and collective empowerment and action; the ability to see, connect with, and act upon a bigger picture; beginning where people are at; literacy as one tool/means to change; not reproducing the status quo; revolution! (Brady & Hernández, 1993; Weiler, 1988)
- **Social Justice**: This refers to our humanity, how we treat each other; about larger systemic change; about sharing power; equity; having a collective, shared sense of responsibility for each other. (Freire & Macedo, 1987; hooks, 1994)
- **Participatory practices**: This refers to collective thinking, shared power, and being part of a whole; about doing with rather than doing to; being responsible for others and needing self-care (without emphasis on individualism); collaboration rather than competition; working together and hearing each others needs and perspectives in order to reach a shared vision of social justice for all people (Campbell & Burnaby, 2001; Nash, 2000).

INVITATION TO EXPLORE EXPERIENCE

With this brief overview of the text and theoretical foundation revealed, we invite you to join us in the empowering experience of exploring this volume. Indeed, while the stories themselves are about radical change, new possibilities and overcoming severe obstacles and oppression, the experience of reading it will most likely raise a new sense of empowerment within you as well.

We firmly believe that in order for us to be effective as adult educators, change has to happen within us first. Consider yourself and your colleagues or learners' needs as women learners, envision them as you read these pages. Realize the situations of people around the world, striving to overcome and create to spaces for themselves and their self worth.

Then ask, what has this meant in your life journey? Where are you in the process? If you have not reached that confidence and empowerment yet—let this book lift you up to new possibilities. If you are seeking to share that gift with others because you know the deep impact it has had on your life and work, experience and extract everything you need today and for years to come form this myriad of stories and recommendations to help the vibrant variation of women you will serve.

We count it a great privilege to have so many talented educators respond to our call and to then edit such a book of import. We invite you to continue the conversation with us through the WE LEARN website [http://www.litwomen.org/publications/empower/] and by using the book resources posted there.

REFERENCES

Belenky, M. F., Clinchy, B. M., Goldberger, N. R., & Tarule, J. M. (1986). *Women's ways of knowing: The development of self, voice, and mind.* New York: Basic Books.

Brady, J., & Hernández, A. (1993). Feminist literacies: Toward emancipatory possibilities of solidarity. In C. Lankshear & C. McLaren. *Critical literacy: Politics, praxis, and the postmodern* (pp. 323-334). Albany: SUNY Press.

Campbell, P., & Burnaby, B. (Eds.). (2001). *Participatory practices in adult education.* Mahwah, NJ: Lawrence Erlbaum Associates.

Cox, R., & Sanders, L. (1988). Women & literacy. *Canadian Woman Studies/les cahiers de la femme, 9*(3 & 4).

Freire, P., & Macedo, D. (1987). *Literacy: Reading the word and the world.* Westport, CT: Bergin & Garvey.

Hayes, E., & Flannery, D.D. (Eds.). (2000). *Women as learners: The significance of gender in adult learning.* San Francisco: Jossey-Bass.

hooks, b. (1994). *Teaching to transgress: Education as the practice of freedom.* New York: Routledge.

Laubach Literacy Action. (1995). *By women / for women: A beginning dialogue on women and literacy in the United States.* Syracuse, NY: Laubach Literacy Action.

Miller, M. (2002). *Women's literacy power: Collaborative approaches to developing and distributing women's literacy resources.* Retrieved November 28, 2008, from http://www.litwomen.org/Dissertation/dissindex.html

Miller, M., & Alexander, I. (Eds.). (2004, Spring). *Women and literacy: Moving from power to participation. Women's Studies Quarterly - Special Issue.* New York: The Feminist Press at CUNY.

Miller, M., & Peters, C. (Eds.). (2004). *Women & literacy. Special Issue of The Change Agent* (19). Boston: New England Literacy Resource Center.

Nash, A. (Ed.). (2000). *Civic participation and community action sourcebook: A resource for adult educators.* Boston: New England Literacy Resource Center.

Weiler, K. (1988). *Women teaching for change: Gender, class & power.* New York: Bergin & Garvey.

SECTION I

REFLECTIONS

Workshop presenters, JacLynn Stark & Wyvonne Stevens-Carter, "Learning Stitch by Stitch: A Quilting Curriculum," 2007 WE LEARN Conference.

Photographer: Beatriz McConnie-Zapater

CHAPTER 1

ENRICHING LIVES

Geraldine Cannon Becker

My job isn't easy, but I wouldn't have it any other way. Risk-taking is nothing new to me, because I became motivated to take charge of my education in my last couple of years as a high school student, long after I had been labeled as an "at-risk" student. Fortunately for me, I was able to work closely with a couple of educators who really believed in me. However, my life was changed forever when I enrolled in college and those blue horizons continued to expand.

It is amazing how life can be improved just by someone else taking an interest, and taking the time to exchange ideas. But this can be a challenge in itself, when the "at-risk" student is afraid to open up and share aspects of life that may have been closed off to prevent access and injury. Sometimes the walls are too high, and sometimes they fall too hard.

The walls can be mental or physical or even a strange combination of bricks. Because I had so much trouble in high school, I often find myself tensing up as I walk toward academic buildings, especially high schools. Even though most of the time I teach small classes on a small college campus, I do occasionally have to brave larger crowds. The hardest thing of all for me can be walking into a high school building or an office of some authority figure, like a principal. I know I'm no longer that "at-risk" kid, but feelings of inadequacy stemming from a label like that can linger. Now

Empowering Women Through Literacy: Views From Experience, pp. 3–6
Copyright © 2009 by Information Age Publishing
All rights of reproduction in any form reserved.

that I have earned my own degrees, I challenge myself to volunteer to help people overcome literacy obstacles, to better communicate their ideas with others, and to develop themselves to the best of their abilities.

I practice deep-breathing and relaxation techniques and I try to keep the oxygen flowing as I sign in and make my way to the Adult Basic Education (ABE) Lab. On the first day of the first meeting with my new learners, I always open up and tell them a bit about my past. I have to admit that I was afraid to do this at first, because I had fought to try and fit in with similar types of learners in high school. I would put on my "brave face" and while I may have been great at building walls (sometimes using chips knocked off others' shoulders) I rarely shared my true feelings with anyone—especially on the first meeting. I was an "outsider," a "misfit," or a "loner." I missed a lot of school, and was in the ninth grade three times. I was "weird," but I preferred the word "unique." I was a writer, but not everyone knew that. I loved to read, but I didn't tell everyone that, either.

In the ABE Lab, I am a "humanities scholar," and I volunteer to lead a reading circle for the Maine Humanities Council's New Books, New Readers Book Discussion Program. All the participants are going to read the same books and we are going to talk about them together, sharing our thoughts and feelings on the content of the books. Each set of books is built around a central theme, like freedom, journeys, differences, and so forth. I remind myself that the learners will probably be more comfortable with someone who is more like them. I try to relax, but I am still tense and I will feel this way until I get to know them better. When I hear them tell their stories, the focus is no longer on me, and this is why I am here. I want to help them learn. When we talk about the books, I invite them to make connections between the content of the books and their own lives, so it helps to try to get to know a little bit about each participant before the book talks begin.

So, we start by talking about each other, but we also talk about the broad theme of the book series. The last theme we worked with was "freedom" and we each tried to come up with a good definition. We thought about all the things freedom could mean to us. We each wrote the word "freedom" on a page and wrote acrostics that we shared with one another. We discussed a few broad questions about freedom that we would return to session after session, with more and more insight. Questions suggested by the Maine Humanities Council, like "Do we have to fight for freedom?" "Is it a right?" "Do we have to give up anything in order to have freedom?" "Is freedom for a group of people different from individual freedom?" We brainstormed ideas for a hands-on activity that we could use to open each of our sessions, and we came up with the idea to let freedom fly by making kites.

One person in our group made her kite and then wrote on it while it was upside down. She didn't want to show anyone, at first, because she hadn't realized that it was upside down while she was writing. It turned out to be a happy accident, because on the front she had written "Freedom: Against All Odds…" I was able to assure her that the accident corresponded with our content well. Honestly, I think it helped reinforce not only the main idea of our theme, but also the idea that we were learning together and communicating our ideas against all types of odds. The form fit the function. That kite would fly. Having a corresponding hands-on activity seemed to help locate the theme in the body as well as in the mind. It brought the group together to work on something that was visual and physical as well as mental. We called the activity "Freedom Takes Flight," and we hung our kites on the wall when we finished making them (see Figure 1.1).

I usually like to go to each session early, so I can talk to the participants and get to know them better, but we also talk while we do our hands-on activity. While we studied "Freedom" we talked about how we may not always really know what freedom entails, for there are usually responsibilities involved. We may not always know exactly what it is that we want and we may not always like it when we get it, so it is good to have someone to

Photo by Becker

Figure 1.1. Freedom Kites.

count on for an open door and the comforts of home, or someone who will understand our fears and encourage our independence—even so.

We talked about how important it is to try to know what is out in the world before setting out, and how important having an education is to assist us in this research. We discussed what it takes to find our strengths. We talked about the importance of building upon those strengths and helping others. These discussions were connected to those broad questions we kept asking ourselves about freedom and rights. These thoughts connected to the story I shared with them when we first met and highlighted my reason for being there to help them in the first place, so we came full circle with our last session. They saw how my experiences as an "at-risk" student helped me connect with them, helped me to gain their trust and helped garner their interest in the broad topic of freedom.

No matter what the topic is, brainstorming for hands-on activities that correspond to the literature we plan to discuss helps to assure that we are all on the same page and that all of our voices are heard. Through our exchanges, lives are enriched for everyone, including me. These experiences are truly empowering. Yet, for me, the greatest satisfaction comes from getting an invitation to a graduation/awards ceremony and being asked to present certificates to the participants. I know horizons are opening up for these learners, and that some of them will go on to college. Yes, I may have to struggle just to begin my job, and there may be some "tough" patches here and there for me to contend with, but I'm a risk-taker, and I love my job. I really wouldn't have it any other way.

REFERENCE

Maine Humanities Council, New Books, New Readers. (n.d.) *Series for use in New Books, New Readers Book Discussion Programs*. Retrieved October 13, 2008, from http://www.mainehumanities.org/programs/books.html

CHAPTER 2

FINDING COMMON GROUND

Fostering Positive Relationships Among Women in the Literacy Classroom

Karen L. Milheim

I remember when I first started in the field of adult literacy; as part of my training, one of my colleagues conducted a brief reading lesson with me in Russian. The point of the lesson was to provide me with an opportunity to experience the inability to comprehend the written word and, as a result, have to learn the language from an elementary level. I still can remember the lesson; I felt nervous, embarrassed when attempting to say the sounds aloud, and constrained by not being able to look beyond a poster board with pictures and foreign letters.

Women with low-level reading and writing abilities face similar feelings every time they enter the classroom. In addition to being a student, they must successfully fulfill many roles, including mother, caregiver, worker, and head of household, all while balancing the feelings and inhibitions often experienced by those with poor literacy skills in everyday life situations. As organizations such as ProLiteracy Worldwide describe (ProLiteracy Worldwide, n.d.), fulfillment of these roles must also be in

Empowering Women Through Literacy: Views From Experience, pp. 7–12

spite of a myriad of negative factors which have shown, in women in particular, to result from having poor literacy skills, including individual and family health issues, poor self-esteem, exposure to violence, loss of self-identity, and low wages and viable work opportunities.

Because of the unique characteristics and barriers facing women in literacy, when I started in the field as a teacher, I immediately knew that, to be effective, I had to begin to develop an understanding of women students' everyday roles, lives and, more importantly, how illiteracy was affecting them as individuals. To do this, I began to find a common ground from which to foster successful relationships.

STARTING ON THE RIGHT FOOT

As obvious as it may seem now, one of the first lessons I learned as an adult literacy teacher when attempting to find common ground with women students was that starting off on the right foot with a student is critical to setting a positive tone for future interactions in the classroom. I remember, early in my career, sitting down for a one-on-one discussion with a young woman right before she joined my advanced literacy class. I began by asking her questions, and after about five minutes, she looked at me (quite annoyed, I might add) and asked: "Why are you asking me all of these questions? I thought I was here for class, not counseling!" That student taught me a valuable lesson: most adult students are used to a traditional classroom where they are not typically asked to share personal viewpoints or general information about themselves. Opening up discussion about personal viewpoints and feelings is not typical in other types of classroom situations; from that point forward, I knew I had to alter my approach.

Now, when I meet a new student, I still never have them join the group without first having a one-on-one discussion. However, to better prepare myself and them, I simply let them know that I would like to learn a little bit more about them before having them start in class in order to make them more comfortable. In doing so with women in literacy, in particular, I make a point to tailor my questions to be inclusive of some of the challenges they face as a woman to help foster discussion surrounding these areas. Some examples of topics I typically cover include: life goals and their link to improved literacy skills, challenges and strategies to overcome barriers, expectations, preferred methods of learning, prior positive and negative classroom experiences, and specific issues related to illiteracy and their role as a woman in society.

The initial discussion is a welcome opportunity for them to learn about me, my teaching style, and how I structure the classroom. More importantly, it is a chance for me to learn about the student and her interests, experiences, and reasons for being in the class. Keeping in mind some of the life situations many women face, my questions often acknowledge the fact that the student comes to the classroom with their own unique story. Our discussion brings their situation to light so I have a foundation from which to probe into areas where, as their teacher, I might be able to accommodate or better understand the impact illiteracy has in their life. In a broad sense, the initial one-on-one discussion serves as a platform from which to build good rapport and relationships with students.

GETTING TO KNOW THE COMMUNITY

Another approach towards finding common ground is by getting to know the community I am serving. Literacy programs are typically serving a larger community; therefore, I find it important to become involved in the community, or, at a minimum, understand what is happening daily which might affect students. Women in literacy are often mothers as well; therefore, a continued awareness of current happenings in the local schools, how the family structure is supporting education, and general community issues become very important.

Many women students' goals are to better educate themselves so they can set good examples for their children. As a mother, I definitely have a great appreciation for the value of education, how our school systems operate, and the safety and effectiveness of our communities. Often, these commonalities allow me to open lines of discussion surrounding these important topics. Beyond that, particularly when I was working near the Philadelphia area where most of my students' children went to a poor, low-performing school district, I kept attuned to what was happening in the schools. Daily lessons and discussions which led to practice writing focused on the community newspaper or Internet articles about school administration, the district, or current events.

There are endless opportunities for instructors to open discussion regarding community interests, particularly for women students. Several other approaches I have found to be successful include:

1. Using course materials that are relevant to the lives of women in literacy;
2. Holding discussions surrounding community events specific to women's interests;
3. Having guest speakers from the community speak about topics which are of interest to women students;

4. Providing an opportunity to collaboratively work on a community project that is worthwhile to them;

5. Going on a "field-trip" to explore a local art exhibit or museum.

One of the most valuable and effective ways I use to determine some of the interests of the group is to invite students to share suggestions with regards to their interests in the community, or particular events they may want to attend as a group. While I found that students are often receptive to one another's suggestions, it is also important to recognize that not every person may want to partake in discussion, go on a field-trip, or listen to a guest speaker. Allowing students to make their own choices with regards to these types of activities not only shows that you, as the instructor, value their input, but also avoids any conflicts or within the group.

Of course, this list is only a brief glimpse of the possible avenues which can be taken when planning educational activities for women in literacy. The best ideas typically emerge from the discussions you have in the classroom, allowing students to embrace their own learning with activities of interest.

LOOKING FOR SILVER LININGS

Before engaging students in any of these activities, I learned that it is important to not assume certain outcomes of a particular approach. I had a professor in college who started each class with a brief, informal chat session where we, as students, could share stories about anything that happened during the week that were either cheerful or concerning. It was a nice opportunity for us to all catch-up on what was occurring (both good and bad) in the lives of our fellow classmates. I naively thought this type of session would be effective with my adult literacy class; at the time, I was teaching four women, and felt it was a nice opportunity for them to get to know each other and begin to build rapport.

The first chat session turned into a discussion about the welfare system and the lousy job market; it was quite a dismal and depressing conversation. When I went home, I felt like the session was a failure. In college, we typically took this time to talk about who was going on vacation, how far along we were in writing our dissertations, and promotions at our jobs; far more joyous than what had occurred in the literacy classroom that day. I assumed that the discussion in the literacy classroom would be just as joyous, yet, it wasn't. In time, I learned this was okay; the women in the class still had opportunities to discuss common issues and concerns, and the session helped open up dialogue on several topics.

As instructors, ideas may not always turn out as planned; I learned that if I assume a certain outcome of a project or new idea will be a specific way, it will most likely be the complete opposite. I now take the time to look for silver linings; a path I started walking may just lead me in another direction, so I adjust to it. This may mean finding alternative course materials, developing new approaches toward learning, and being flexible in my classroom approaches.

FINDING COMMON GROUND AND EMPOWERMENT OF WOMEN IN LITERACY

The ability to read and write signifies opportunity for empowerment. For women, in particular, we must often strive much harder in the workforce to earn equal wages and opportunities when compared to our male counterparts. This struggle requires us to be empowered to take responsibility in numerous areas, including parenting, politics, health, technology, and the workforce. To that end, facilitating opportunities for women to participate in their own empowerment, beginning in the classroom, is another key to finding common ground.

As an instructor, I make it a point to bring awareness of the benefits of educational empowerment, and offer women an opportunity to engage in discussions that allow them to communicate their goals, think positively about being a woman, and understand the doors a better education opens for them. In the past, discussion has included topics such as candidates' viewpoints during political elections; current, prominent female figures; involvement in local organizations benefiting the community; and male-dominated careers and options for women in those roles. As a teacher, I experienced first-hand the impacts of fostering the commonalities discovered among women in the literacy classroom. As a result of these discussions, opportunities for writing projects, community involvement, and other literacy-related activities emerged. Students have been prompted to vote in elections, write to their state representatives, obtain their driver's license, explore new job opportunities, and become interested in higher education, among other positive actions.

FINAL THOUGHTS

Some individuals working in the field of adult literacy education may not agree with the approaches I take as an instructor. In the past, I was perceived by other instructors as being too lenient with students, allowing them to go off-topic, straying from lesson plans, and not focusing strictly

on literacy-related activities. Perhaps there is some truth to these perceptions; however, the approaches I presented in this chapter led me to
retain students, see improvement in literacy skills, and, most importantly,
respect women in literacy for who they are, who they want to become, and
the value they bring as individuals to the classroom. While I may stray
from sequential lessons, allow students to listen to their iPod every so
often, or practice typing if they don't feel up to being in the class on any
particular given day, I feel, as an instructor, women who have taken my
classes have benefiting from the flexibility, understanding, and empathy I
have for them as women.

Finding common ground with and among women students has led me
to discover new approaches toward learning, mutual respect, and, most
importantly, opportunities for empowerment through education.

REFERENCES

ProLiteracy Worldwide (n.d). *Women in literacy: Critical issues in literacy series*.
Retrieved July 28, 2008, from http://www.proliteracy.org/NetCommunity/
Page.aspx?pid=359&srcid=319

CHAPTER 3

THE LITERACY OF BEING

Denise DiMarzio

I am.
You are.
He is.
She is.
It is.
We are.
You are.
They are.

I exist.
You symbolize.
He represents.
She signifies.
It occurs.
We stand forth.
You live.
They endure.

A common verb, commonly used. Monosyllabic and yet incantatory. An irregular verb chanting out in regular time and regular beat, a heartbeat, perhaps. A difficult verb to teach, such infinite nature held inside two and three letters. The nucleus of an atom. What does it mean to be in the world? What does it mean to be a woman, learning, a woman, teaching?

What happens in a literacy classroom? Shapes called letters on a piece of paper dance together in ways that form words. These letters and words speak certain sounds, and those sounds in turn have meaning. Those words and that meaning can be held, in the mouth, in the mind, in the heart. They take root in the spirit, sometimes cradling our hearts in warmth and sometimes clenching until we think we will die from their might. A woman learns to write. One tiny word, two letters, "b" and "e," be. Two words, a total of three letters. If she prints, three strokes of the pencil to form the capital "I." A single fluid wave-like motion for the lower case

Empowering Women Through Literacy: Views From Experience, pp. 13–18

"a." A kind of jumping of the hand to make the twin hills of the lower case "m." I am. Uncountable small actions every day change the world. Actions that have no visible consequence at the time, but are as powerful as the wind created by a butterfly, and as far reaching. Breath in, breath out. A woman moves her hand purposefully towards her child, a spoon, the bed sheets, her lover's face. A woman takes up a pencil, cradles it in her hand, commits point to paper, and writes. I am. A powerful action, an action that grounds a woman fiercely in her chosen place, a place of focused attention, a place to be.

The modern English verb "to be" takes its roots from Old English, an ancestor of our Modern English in use roughly from 875 C.E. to 1100 C.E Douglas Harper (2001) describes the verb "to be" as "the modern verb [that] represents the merger of two once-distinct verbs, the 'b-root' represented by *be* and the *am/was* verb, which was itself a conglomerate." That "b-root" verb can be traced back to the Proto-Indo-European (PIE), that true mother tongue spoken six or seven millennia ago, which means that homo sapiens sapiens somewhere in the Copper Stone Age had the language and the mind to consider the issue of being in the world. From today's existing words, linguists can build backwards to ferret out the oldest words in human vocabulary. From the PIE base, *bheu-* and *bhu-* meant to "grow, come into being, become" (Harper, 2001). It also has intriguing connections to the Sanskrit, fourth century B.C.E: "*bhavah* [becoming], *bhavati* [becomes, happens], *bhumih* [earth, world]" (Harper, 2001). *To be a world.*

The Old English form, present tense (Harper, 2001):	
Singular	Plural
ic eom	*we sind(on)*
ic beo	*we beoð*
þu eart	*ge sind(on)*
þu bist	*ge beoð*
he is	*hie sind(on)*
he bið	*hie beoð*

For the last seventeen years, I have worked with students to figure out the English language, to navigate its rules and exceptions, to rein in the estimated quarter-million words to a manageable size, to fashion its gifts of language and form that language into a comprehensible means of relating to the world. I think perhaps I have met as many as 1000 students in classrooms in Connecticut, Massachusetts, and Rhode Island. There have been literacy level classes and freshman composition classes. There have been college students and adult learners, native English speakers and non-native speaking refugees, women and men, aged from late teens to adults aged sixty and more. But most, usually 2/3 of every class, have been women from other countries reading and writing at a low literacy level. Of all of these people a few of the women in particular remain fixed firmly in my memory.

Like thousands of others, Vsna grew up in Cambodia, coming of age just as the Khmer Rouge rose up in their destruction of a world. The fine details of her story are lost to my memory now, ten years after I first heard it in a dislocated workers' beginner ESOL class. How is a life unrecognizably altered compressed to such few words, a summary beyond comprehension: *my mother died there. The man who was to become my husband disobeyed orders, turned his boat around, and came to get me. We escaped together.* She had a pronounced stutter, showed signs of dyslexia. It was her first experience of a formal school as an adult. She had had little schooling as a child. She suffered from debilitating headaches, migraines that came frequently and lasted many hours. I often wondered if these headaches and even her learning disabilities stemmed from her terror. In 1994, Alec Wilkinson wrote "A Changed Vision of God" for the *New Yorker*. It is an article that discusses the curious blindness of Cambodian women survivors of the Khmer Rouge, women whose blindness had no medical origin. Wilkinson implies that the women's blindness was a result of not wanting to see anymore, of a stupendous act of self-preservation.

In our ESOL classroom, Vsna sat at the head of the table, directly across from where I stood at the board. A line connected us, filament invisible. She dutifully copied verb conjugations, attempted dictation, wrote in her dialogue journal, volunteered to read despite her stutter. Her hand gripped the pencil. She came armed with school supplies arrayed around her and with gifts for me—persimmons, squash filled with a sweet custard, and wry comments. She read with difficulty the simple sentences about the blue-collar Everyman Joe Johnson, a character in the beginner's text *Personal Stories*: "I am Joe Johnson. I am single. I am 21 years old" (Koch, Mrowicki, & Ruttenberg, 1985. p. 2). She offered her usual realistic but funny take on things: "What's wrong with Joe, anyway? Joe is kind of boring!" I offer her Joe Johnson when she has seen what she has seen. I think of the little I know of her and write a poem, which I don't have the courage to show her. Who am I to extrapolate her experience?

Maria Lourdes is from the Azores, mid-fifties, with little native language literacy and minimal English skills. She could write English only with great effort. I'm not sure she cared about the benefits of improving her literacy. I soon learned why. In this intensive 20-hour-a-week ESOL classroom for dislocated workers, students wrote in dialogue journals for about one hour a week. Not knowing them well yet, with no background information to go on save that they were all dislocated workers, the first question I posed in each student's journal was, I thought, innocuous, broad and simple. The question was something along the lines of, "Dear _____, please tell me a little bit about your family." Maria Lourdes began to cry when she read these words. Her grown son, in his late twenties, had died of leukemia the previous year. *My son, he is die.* Her life was colored by grief after his death—it pervaded her every moment and rendered all else meaningless. Was it right to ask her this question? Is it part of the teacher's job to accompany people through their darkness? There are no innocent words, but I believe words, spoken and written in compassion, are the raft that saves us, and the lines that tie us together, the filaments of numinous experience.

I am where you are. Did you know that long after birth, cells shed from the fetus circulate in a mother's bloodstream for the rest of her life? (Angier, 1999). We are each other. In the Quaker meeting, a woman speaks a message: our task is to love. To be is to love. Ic eom. Ic beo. We sind(on.) We beoð.

"April 1975: Dream of a Cambodian Woman"

My sister says she knows
where our mother is buried,
but she cannot identify her bones
among the hundreds.
They are
somewhere.

I see the skulls lined up in rows,
a million gone,
gone to ground where the rubies and sapphires
wait for the sun to light their sleeping hearts.
You are
nearby.

My sister runs her hands across and around
the smooth interiors of the skulls,
begging her hands to listen
for our mother's memories.
She is
not here, but not gone.

Black and white ibis look on,
unblinking, mangoes rot in the hot
sun. My sister moves her hands as a new dancer.
Bones speak a silent message.
Our task is
to love.

Whitman wrote "A Noiseless Patient Spider" in 1868. One hundred and forty years ago. I copy it here in full (see figure next page), because it speaks to the human condition, and it also speaks to the microcosm of a classroom.

In a Frierean reading, the teacher and the student are interchangeable, flinging the fine threads of information back and forth, giving, receiving, both staving off loneliness in the face of being on this blue earth. The English language classroom is content and form, parts of speech and idiomatic expressions, proper usage and audience. It is survival language: hungry, police, bathroom, doctor, no, help, mother, child, thank you, love. It is more—the crisscrossing of filaments, nearly invisible lines, one being to another.

A Noiseless Patient Spider

A noiseless patient spider,
I marked where on a little promontory it stood isolated,
Marked how to explore the vacant vast surrounding,
It launched forth filament, filament, filament out of itself,
Ever unreeling them, ever tirelessly speeding them.
And you O my soul where you stand,
Surrounded, detached, in measureless oceans of space,
Ceaselessly musing, venturing, throwing, seeking the spheres to
    connect them,
Till the bridge you will need be formed, till the ductile anchor hold,
Till the gossamer thread you fling catch somewhere, O my soul.

Mai, a Hmong woman, is more educated than her peers, maybe in her mid-fifties. Quiet and contemplative from an animist culture. Another woman on the earth who held the nightmares of what she had seen close to her, spoken perhaps only in the silent stitchings of the traditional story telling cloths, the *paj ntaub*. It was an ESOL literacy classroom in the early 1990's, and there was a cosmic event about to occur, a full solar eclipse visible from the northeast. She had heard something about it from a news report and questioned what this event was going to be. It was my first or second year of teaching, but I am grateful that I had been taught to drop my lesson plan and follow the impromptu lesson wherever it turned out to lead. I drew a simple representation of the solar system on the board, explained that we were here on earth, that the moon would pass between the earth and the sun, and that day would become like night for a short time. She listened very politely, nodding her head. Then she raised her head, looked into my eyes and said, "you believe that?" All the gossamer threads I felt between myself and what I knew to be true shimmered. The earth spun around me, now a planet, now the back of a turtle. The sun and the moon dipped in amusement, Mai's sage face infused with the light of things I could never know. I could have fallen to my knees. Living goes on. The word is the teacher. *O my soul.* The word is to be.

I exist.
You symbolize.
He represents.
She signifies.
It occurs.
We stand forth.
You live.
They endure.

REFERENCES

Angier, N. (1999). *Woman: An intimate geography.* Boston: Houghton Mifflin Co.

Harper, D. (2001). *On-line etymology dictionary.* Retrieved May 30, 2008, from http://www.etymonline.com

Koch, K. D., Mrowicki, L., & Ruttenberg, A. (1985). *Personal stories: A book for adults who are beginning to read*. Palatine, IL: Linmore Publishing, Inc.

Whitman, W. (1995). A noiseless patient spider. In X. J. Kennedy & Dana Gioia (Eds.), *Literature: An introduction to fiction, poetry, and drama* (6th ed., p. 1010). New York: Harper Collins College Publishers.

Wilkinson, A. (1994, January 24). A changed vision of God. *The New Yorker,* 52-68.

CHAPTER 4

AN ONGOING JOURNEY

Beatrice Arrindell

Growing up in the 1970s, I did not know much about racism. To be honest, I never knew that there was a deep hatred amongst races. I was raised in an area that was predominately Black, and the whole block raised all the children from the neighborhood. There was nothing but love and respect amongst the young and old. There were a few White families on the block, but the Blacks never associated with them. To be honest, I never felt any anger or bitterness over the fact that the White families did not want anything to do with us. To me, the White people were like aliens: they were pale, had funny looking hair, and they smelled bad when it rained. Therefore, it was perfectly fine with me if they did not want to associate with me. Little did I know that these people not wanting to associate with the Blacks were much deeper than it appeared.

I grew up in a small household in East New York in Brooklyn. It was only my brother and me. I have two sisters but they were already on their own before my brother and I came into the picture. My brother and I were adopted because our biological parents were drug addicts. I remember the day when I got my name changed from Phifer to Arrindell. I was six years old. It was the happiest day of my life, and I felt as if my life was complete. After the judge made the adoption final, my mother took my brother and me out to dinner and a movie. It felt so good to finally have

Empowering Women Through Literacy: Views From Experience, pp. 19–23

the same last name as my foster parents. Before we went through the legal adoption my mother used to make my brother and me write Arrindell hundreds of times just to make sure we knew how to spell our name.

I never knew my real parents. I was only a year old and my brother, Odriesse, (we called him Ozzie for short) was a newborn when we were taken away. All I knew was Julia Arrindell was my "real" mother and she loved Ozzie and me as if she birthed us herself. Although she showed us love, she was also very strict, especially when it came to our education. She always taught us that we were just as important and special as any other children. At the time, I did not understand what she meant by this, but I would hear this same thing as I entered junior high school.

I went to George Gershwin Junior High School, which was located in East New York in Brooklyn. I did not have to commute to school because the school was within walking distance from my house. I was comfortable with my school, my friends, and my teachers. The year that I started the ninth grade, an incident erupted that would change my life forever. The classroom that used to hold 30 students was now holding 50 students.

In 1980, two years before I started junior high school, a development was being built in East New York. It was called Starrett City, and it was to become a city within a city. There would be co-ops, schools, libraries, and shopping malls, and everyone wanted to move there. This was a wonderful opportunity because it meant more jobs for the people of Brooklyn. Unfortunately, the jobs were only available to White contractors. In order to rent or buy one of the co-ops, the applicant had to fill out an application and pay a fee. When the Blacks tried to get an application, they were told that there were no apartments available. That was my first lesson on redlining. Mother tried to get an application, which I did not understand because we owned our own home. Why would she want to give this up for an apartment? I could not for the life of me understand why mother and other African-Americans were trying to live in an area where they were not welcomed. Now I realize that by her going down to the realtor and asking for an application, which she knew she wasn't going to get, she was helping in the fight for equal rights for her children. She had always instilled in us that we were just as important and special as the next child. When she went down to the realtors, her actions were telling those realtors exactly what she used to tell her children: that her children deserve the right to go to a new school and live in a new neighborhood.

My mother was not an educated woman, but she knew that she wanted a better life for my brother and me. She was raised in a racist state, Virginia. Mother knew the pain that racism caused and she tried to protect her children from it. I guess she figured since she owned a home and had a husband who worked for the city, that this would shield us from being judged by the color of our skin. Unfortunately, it did not, and as a result I would see the strength and dedication of an uneducated woman.

The year that I entered junior high school, Starrett City was completed and people started moving in the neighborhood. The only people that moved in the "city" were White people, especially those few Whites that lived in my neighborhood. They had apartments for the families to live in but the schools were not built yet. That is when the nightmare began because these children ended up at our school until their school construction was finished.

One day we came to school and our desks were not arranged the way they usually were. The room looked crammed because there were so many desks and chairs in the room. Remember, this room could only hold 30 students now it was trying to hold 50 students. However, that was not the worst part; the worst part was when those that were seated in the back were the Black students.

Just when I thought that the humiliation could get no worse, it did. The teacher asked for us, the Black students, to return all our school-books. We did what we were told and were issued used and ripped up books. I cannot explain in words how angry and humiliated this made me feel. I immediately hated the White children who came into our school and "took over our class." I had been raised all my life that I was no different than the next child, and here I had to give up my desk and my books.

I went home that evening crying and upset. My mother thought that I had had a fight with one of the students at school. When I told my mother what happened to me, she became furious. She wanted to know why the principal did not contact her, and she immediately put on her clothes and marched me right back to the school. While I was growing up, all of the parents got involved in their children's education. Many of the parents made it their business to participate in parent/teacher conferences. When my mother and I arrived at the school, there were other parents there as well. They all were furious about the sudden change in the school. The parents wanted to know why the school did not inform them and why their children had been put in compromising situations. That evening there had to be about 400 to 600 parents out there demanding changes.

The next morning there was a community meeting and the parents were still riled up from the night before. They wanted some answers and they wanted them quickly. Some of the parents even took the day off from work to attend this meeting. The only answer they received was that the situation would be looked into. When asked by one of the parents about the mangled books, the school commissioner told them that the books were only temporary until new books came in. When asked why the new students did not receive these books instead of the Black children, the response was that this has nothing to do with Blacks or Whites, this is about children getting an education. Yeah right, this would not have gone down the same way if it were Black children that needed a school. We could not go into Bensonhurst or the Upper East Side and try to take over their school and demand that they let the Black children in because we need an education.

The parents and school commissioners finally came to an agreement: as soon as the schools in Starrett City were ready for occupancy, the Black children would be allowed to enroll in those schools. Everyone else seemed elated with the idea, but for some reason the students did not feel that way. We did not want to go to their school. I wanted to go to George Gershwin and be with my own kind. I could not relate to the White children. We did not have anything in common except the hate that we had for one another. However, being a child from the 70s, I had no voice and I did what I was told. My mother tried to explain to me that this would be the beginning of a change for Black people. I saw it as ruining my life. I wanted to say to my mother if she was so excited about going to the White people's school then she should take my place. Of course, I would not have said that aloud because if I had I would not be alive to tell the story.

It took Starrett City two years to finish their schools and by this time, I was in the ninth grade so I did not have to go to their school. Unfortunately, my brother had to go, and he was not happy about it. He had a hard time adjusting; he fought everyday until they threw him out of school and he wound up going back to George Gershwin.

Maybe my parents did have a point in trying to get their children in the best schools. However, what my parents along with other parents failed to realize is that the children did not feel honored in going to a school were they were not wanted. I believe in change and equal rights, but to what extent was I willing to fight for these rights? My brother used to come home angry. He hated White people. He never wanted to discuss exactly what he went through, but I knew it was something that would eat at him for years.

As for me, I ended up not trusting White people because of what I went through in junior high school; I did not want to live around them or associate with them. I lost many jobs because my bosses were White and I felt that they were going to fire me anyway so I gave them a reason to. I believe that if therapy were available for me when I was in J.H.S., I probably would have learned ways to deal with my anger. Again being a child in the 70s did not give me a right to feel anything. I was supposed to do what I was told and that is it. It does not matter that Ozzie came home everyday angry or that I stuffed my feelings until I exploded. We were participating in the fight for equal rights and that was all that mattered.

Today I am sitting in prison with a 16-life sentence. Do I blame my incarceration on the incident when I was in junior high school? In many ways I do because I have never dealt with my anger. It was instilled in my heart not to trust White people; I believed they would always try to hold me back. I started fighting back, but unfortunately not with my voice, with my hands. It was not until I came to prison and enrolled in college that I became educated about my race and myself. I stopped being the victim and became wiser and stronger. I finally understood what my mother and all the other African-Americans that fought for equal rights were trying to teach me: not to get so mad about my history that it made me ignorant.

Today I am a peer tutor in the college program at Bedford Hills and this also makes me a role model. I help women of all races and nationalities. When I help the women here in prison, I do not see color. Instead, I see women like myself, who now want to learn, who want to make up for past mistakes, past insecurities, past injustices. I have experienced first hand what racism can do to a person, and sometimes I see this reflected in the women who come to the learning center for help. In some cases, it is difficult for them to even admit that they need help. I was like that once, but no longer. I am stronger and wiser now, and I try to help them become stronger and wiser. Today I realize that we are all equal, especially in prison.

I have learned that I am not alone in this fight for respect and dignity. Today I have new heroes and friends in my life, both Blacks and Whites. Heroes like Dorothy Day, Melba Patillo Beals, Madam C.J. Walker, and Fannie Lou Hamer. Friends like Helen Lester, Tonya Bolden, Professor Jane Maher, Susan Kulkin and Jason Low. These people have taught me the meaning of self-worth. They have made it in life through education. Now it is my turn.

CHAPTER 5

BECOMING A LADY OF LETTERS

For Cherie

Cindy Childress

Cherie stood next to me and line by line,
she spoke and I wrote,
then read back to her
the young woman's first poem
and so she composed spontaneously
poetry into the air
writing onto our imaginations
how incarceration feels
on days perfect for the beach.

She'd always had a heartful of words
but no use for letters
until letter by letter she wrote
her spoken poems and read them
aloud sounding word by word,
her fellow inmates and I
offering occasional associations, sound clues,
we acted as bumpers

as she navigated the obstacle course
of language going from oral to textual
back to oral
at age fifteen she sounds out her words
from her journal
emanating satisfaction of so simple a power—
to create the taste of one's own poetry
on the tongue.

BRIEF DESCRIPTION OF EXPERIENCE

I served as Poet-in-Residence at the Pinellas County Girls Correctional Facility 2002-3 in Florida, which gave me a unique opportunity to bring creative writing to at-risk young women. Our weekly classes began with the girls taking turns reading what they had written since we last met, then I would give them handouts of poetry or let them listen to CDs of spoken word, which we would discuss, and from that discussion would spring a new writing assignment. The thing about my job was that it assumed a level of literacy that not all the girls possessed, and Cherie was the most extreme of these. She was articulate, but barely able to write her name. The poetry my students wrote was not necessarily great literature in a large sense, but the writing had powerful effects. When one student read a poem about a friend gunned down, it elicited tears from others who'd experienced the same. A poem about wishing to awaken as someone who'd never done drugs spawned a series of similar poems from others.

Cherie wanted to participate, so she triumphed over embarrassment and fear to ask for help. We began with her telling me what to write, and then I would show the poem to her and help her read what she'd just composed orally. As we progressed, she and I both had pens and paper. She told me what to write, and then asked me how to spell everything so she could literally write each word for herself. The other girls would also help her with spelling and reading aloud, so that her work became a group project whose ultimate goal was to include Cherie in the poetry class.

I do not know how this young woman had fallen through the cracks of public education. The institution discouraged me from asking the students about themselves because they were minors and many had court cases pending. I do know that the desire to write and be part of a writing community was in this instance a powerful motivation toward literacy.

CHAPTER 6

THE RIGHT TO WRITE

Teaching Creative Writing to Women Inmates

Dominique T. Chlup

We are given a shot at dancing with, or at least clapping along with, the absurdity of life, instead of being squashed by it over and over again. It's like singing on a boat during a terrible storm at sea. You can't stop the raging storm, but singing can change the hearts and spirits of the people who are together on that ship.

—Anne Lamont (1994)

I struggled to pick up the few pieces of paper my students were turning in to me as their first writing assignment. I tried to quiet my hands, so the women would not see them shaking. Nine of the twelve women enrolled in my class sat sobbing quietly into their shirtsleeves, some using the back of bare arms to wipe their runny noses. When I asked the correctional officer in charge of overseeing our basement classroom about getting some tissues, he said one word to me before fixing his gaze back on the women students sitting on the other side of the room.

"Contraband."

I had expected teaching to be tough but not this kind of tough. This work felt raw, and I often found myself reflexively covering my heart with my hand like I had been shot, the words of the women opening from inside of me a deep wound. I had arrived at the Valhalla Jail for Women in New York as a young, very young, graduate student prepared to co-teach a creative writing and literature class. The number of women, who signed up for the classes, far exceeded the number of classes we planned to offer, so those of us who were scheduled to co-teach unpaired and took on classes of our own.

I naively expected to run my classroom the same way I had been taught. Read a piece of great literature, discuss what the writer had done to make it great, and then have my students write their own poems and stories. I quickly learned that prisons and jails are not the most conducive spaces for teaching, learning, or for that matter writing. Writing is not an easy task even for seasoned professionals. Couple that with the fact that I had several students who could not read above a sixth grade level and even more for whom English was not their first language. So it was my privilege to have worked with women who could write lines such as,

> As I stand here in this cage feeling trapped, not only with my body but also my mind with no place to go I wonder what has become of my life and myself.... I am like a bird waiting to fly, but my wings are clipped. (Betancourt, 1997, p. 5)

Or find the strength to write about unimaginable forms of abuse all from within the confines of a ten by ten foot cell:

> I was hoping I was going to be raped and that afterward I would be able to leave.... I bit down hard on my tongue to relieve the pain, but it did not work. The pain did not stop, even though the cutting did, and I felt like I was going to pass out again. But before I had the chance to go back to sleep the cutting started again at the upper part of my chest. I felt an arc being 'drawn.' Then to my horror my nipples were removed.... With each movement of the knife across my flesh I felt that much closer to unconsciousness. At this point, I wanted to be dead. (Fraley, 1997, pp. 13-14)

With these types of stories lurking beneath the surface, it is no wonder that pain, truth, and suffering became a constant companion in that first writing workshop I taught.

My first night of teaching I brought Jamaica Kincaid's fiction piece "Girl" to class. The warden had approved it, and I felt the language of the piece was innocuous enough for a jail setting, so when the first woman began to cry I passed it off as an anomaly, but as the entire group dissolved into tears, a tremor started in my hands and rose to a spot just above my heart that made it feel like it was fluttering.

I abandoned my lesson plan as I knew I could not talk about dialogue or the use of narrative description with everyone sobbing. I learned my first lesson that night: *teach the writer, not the writing*. It was my women students and the hurt behind their erupting emotions that mattered. Kincaid's one sentence, 650-word narrative explores the sharp, critical, admonishing dialogue that occurs between a mother and daughter, where the mother does most of the talking. Representative of a torn mother-daughter relationship, these women, who were disconnected from everything in their outside lives, when reminded of their own mothers, were like seams that had unraveled, half of a whole.

I wish I could say it was my love of teaching that drew me to the jail, but that would be a lie. I was young, unseasoned and had not yet had the pivotal experience that would call me to make teaching my profession. Rather it was my love of the written word that brought me there. In the end, it was the exposed, vulnerable, rawness of my students that kept me returning to class week after week. It was also witnessing firsthand the power of Freire's vision that champions the theory that it is through education that oppressed social groups learn to read the word in order to read the world (Freire, 1970). Accordingly, it was the learners' own life stories that became the primary material for our learning processes. As such, "literacy in these terms is not so much about focusing on the need to read as attending to the needs of people who cannot read" (Collins, 1995, p. 60).

The statistics gathered each year by the Bureau of Justice (2007) indicate the overwhelming need for literacy and numeracy education for women incarcerated in our nation's jails and prisons. Nearly half of all women inmates (42%) have not completed high school or taken the GED tests (General Educational Development tests), sometimes referred to as the General Education Diploma. And according to the 2003 National Assessment of Adult Literacy (NAAL) report Literacy behind Bars, which assessed the English literacy of 1,200 incarcerated adults in the United States, nine percent of incarcerated women perform at the below basic level when assessed on prose literacy (prose literacy examples include the ability to read and comprehend editorials, news stories, brochures, and instructional materials). Fifteen percent perform below the basic level on document literacy (document literacy examples include job applications, payroll forms, transportation schedules, maps, tables, and drug or food labels), and an alarming 47% perform below basic on quantitative literacy assessments (quantitative literacy examples include balancing a checkbook, figuring out a tip, completing an order form, or determining the amount of interest on a loan from an advertisement) (Greenberg, Dunleavy, & Kutner, 2007). [For additional background literature on women in prison, see Chapter 35 (Addy) in this volume.]

The statistics were as disheartening when I entered my first corrections classroom over a decade ago. So why do I continue to encourage literacy education for women inmates?

Stanford (2004) describes writing in a correctional setting as "an exercise of power in a place that attempts to deny power to those who are imprisoned there" (p. 278). Given the transitory nature of jails, women, from the beginning, get down to the act of writing "it." Whatever that "it" may be, stories of abuse, love, hate, acceptance. The women's writings breathe from way down to way up. Knowing that I might not have much time with a student, sometimes they were only enrolled for a class or two before they were sentenced and sent home or more commonly sentenced to a longer term in prison, I asked my students from the first night to start by writing down the lines, writing down the lines to their story that is.

Writing is a learned experience. As Steinberg (1991) explains, "poetry does not just come to you—but neither does a Bach 'cello suite when you first pick up the 'cello. Poetry evolves into a medium of artistic expression as you learn and grow" (p. 29).

Many of my students did not view themselves as readers, much less writers, so before we could arrive at the place where pen meets paper and the rhythm and blues of their stories began to pour out on the page, I allowed them to experience reading and writing through the words of others. In this way, they become immersed in literacy development, the same way a student of a foreign language studying overseas becomes immersed.

The first exercise in my class was entitled "A River Runs through It." In this assignment, a student takes a piece of text that we have been reading in class and tilts the page to find the natural white space running through the text and uses her pencil to mark the "river" running along the edges of the words (Padgett, 1997). Those "rivers" contain the text that became the student's first poem. Example of texts used for this assignment include Langston Hughes' poem *Mother to Son*, Aurora Levins Morales' essay *Puertoricanness*, Pablo Neruda's poem, *La Palabra* (both the Spanish and English translation), Audre Lord's poem, *Black Mother Woman*, Alice Walker's short story, *Roselily*, or Ethridge Knight's prison poem, *The Idea of Ancestry*. Each student's white space lines were always different; therefore, their poems differed.

The following week, I brought the same text back to class this time cut up into pieces. I distributed the words in a haphazard fashion and the women worked in small groups to co-author poems. Since the same text is used repeatedly, the women practiced not only their creative writing skills but what Padgett (1997) calls "creative reading." He argues, "We are rarely, if ever, taught that printed words might be changed, played with, bounced around, or cut in half; in short, that we could read as actively as we write, that we could read *creatively*" (p. 5).

By playing with words in this fashion, my students unlearned the stead-fast rules from grammar school that there is always a right way and a wrong way when it comes to language expression. Many of my students tried for years to please teachers that cared more about grammatical correctness than they did about voice or the writer's craft. One of my students, who had left school in the seventh grade, thought that all authors with published books were dead. She never imagined that a writer could be a living, breathing soul. Others believed that writing was reserved only for the most educated and privileged of individuals.

As Tannenbaum (2000), a former poet-in-residence at San Quentin writes,

> people on the suffering end of most economic and social scales—have grown up believing that what they have to say is unimportant or will not be valued. In order for speech to occur, a person must not only recognize his or her own unique voice and particular thoughts and feelings, but also believe that he or she has the right to express these perceptions. (p. xi)

In my class, my students learned from the beginning that they, too, had the right to write. I did not pretend that this would be an easy task by any means, for as sportswriter Walter Wellesley "Red" Smith so aptly observed, "There's nothing to writing. All you do is sit down at a type-writer and open a vein" (Smith in Orr, 2004, p. 7).

I reassured my students that even practiced writers experience the bloodletting that comes from telling one's story. Writing is an act of witnessing where, "We write to expose the unexposed. If there is one door in the castle you have been told not to go through, you must" (Lamont cited in Lamb, 2003, p. 7). The notion that writing can lead us to understand not only ourselves better but also the haunting incidents that shape our lives is not news by now, but to the individual writer the revelation may be one that is experienced again and again as she goes through the writing process (Root & Steinberg, 1996).

In addition to printed text, I used with my women students visual imagery such as photographs or artwork they produced. I asked them to reconstruct stories using the images they selected. In one poignant instance, a student chose the pen and ink sketch she had drawn the week we had read feminist fairytales or women-centered re-conceptions of traditional fairytales. She used her native Spanish to recreate the story of *Beauty and the Beast*, recasting the story as the *Beautician and the Beast*. The narrator in the role of beautician stumbles across a young woman, "the Beast," being taunted by others, and there is

> something about this person the people called "Beast" that made the beautician feel the need to reach out. It saddened her deeply for what she saw.

> She took the Beast home where she got fed, bathed, napped. While the Beast was asleep, the beautician looked her over very carefully. Now she thought this woman has potential. (Torres, 1997b, p. 18)

The author writes how the beautician is able to "transform this Beast into a Beauty Queen" (p. 19). When my student explained her story, most of the class assumed she would self-identify with the beautician as this had been her job prior to her incarceration. My student, though, described how in her narrative, she was playing both the role of the beautician and the Beast. She was reconstructing a feminist narrative where she could be both the agent and the object of transformation. In this instance, the author was writing against the official discourse where women are stereo-typically the victims "saved" by princes. She unmasked the singular, gendered identity of hero and heroine to re-conceptualize multiple identities of self and agency. In this masking and unmasking of self, my student engaged in the powerful act of writing as resistance.

Dooley (1995) discerns,

> In composing the text, we compose, as well, the self. To rethinking the act of teaching writing, the feminist movement's revisioning activity can make a radical contribution ... the intersection of women's arts and theories encourages us to rethink the ways we read and write and the ways we teach students to do both, as well. (p. 6)

With the dehumanizing acts prevalent in jail, writing becomes an empowering act of resistance. New ways of reading and writing texts allow women inmates to engage in radical acts of re-visioning that offer insights into the relationship between reading and writing, writing processes, and the very act of teaching writing. Students when encouraged to manipulate both their reading and writing of language are able to "discover new forms to reconstruct meaning from brokenness" (Dooley, 1995, p. 7). The brokenness of their lives, the brokenness of their dreams, these fragments become manageable, transformable texts that are privileged and valued in the writing classroom.

As Stanford (2004) has noted in her own poetry classes at the Cook County jail,

> The writing is dangerous because it proclaims a making and remaking of selves despite state attempts to confine, fix, and stabilize identities as *inmates* (compliant, unruly). It is also dangerous because it proclaims a "we" within the confines of the razor wire and disrupts the individualistic discourse and practice on which any system of oppression is dependent. (pp. 277-278)

The writer's job is to turn her unspoken truths into words that reverberate with the rhythm of life. A rhythm that when we recognize it we shake our heads in agreement and say, "Yeah, that's it. I've felt that too."

Writers have an invaluable function: to use their words to speak for those who cannot. Scheffler (2002) in the highly acclaimed anthology of women's prison writings, *Wall Tappings*, explores women's prison texts as political entities that speak "uniquely for silenced women behind bars and prison walls" (p. xxi). She observes the fact that, "Today women prisoners increasingly use their own voices to testify to their experiences and to affirm their continuing humanity in literary creations" (p. xxi). While she argues that women prisoners have been writing a narrative of their own for hundreds of years, "It is now time for women *outside* prison walls to listen" (p. xl). Lamb (2003) referencing the multiple ways that women are schooled in silence from abusive partners to parents who threaten, "What goes on in this house *stays* in this house!" describes his own student inmates' published essays as "victories against voicelessness—miracles in print" (p. 9).

The process of moving from the shadows of silence and invisibility to witness and testifier is one of agency and empowerment. In the jails and prisons that I have taught in, I have found, women are not allowed to keep journals or more than an allotted amount of paper in their cells. Keeping more than one week's writing assignment at a time was forbidden, and if correctional officers believed an inmate did have more than the allowed paper in her possession, her cell could be subjected to an unsettling search and punishment could include time in solitary confinement. In this way, writing to each other, loved ones outside the jail, and to me was a subversive act.

The women wrote as a way to resist the system. As prisoner 20257 expresses,

Sitting in this cell/ wild thoughts racing through my mind./ My heart beats fast,/ pressure rises./ Too overwhelmed to think clearly/As I think, what if?/ What could have been?/Anxiety kicks in./ I speak to myself./ I answer myself.... /No, I'm not insane. (Torres, 1997b)

The poem's speaker resists the label that is cast so easily on many women inmates. She refuses to accept the systemic belief that women criminals are mad, bad, or some combination of the two. Instead, her words offer a disruption to the dominant discourse surrounding women prisoners. They force us to reconsider the stereotypical perspective of the woman inmate as unthinking, unfeeling, and unimaginable.

Walker (2004) in her prison teacher's memoir echoes what many of us who have chosen the path of teaching behind bars hopes is true, "Education opens locked doors" (dedication page).

Trounstine (2001) similarly believes that "While it is true that prison is a repressive environment, the one who offers hope in the classroom has the potential to effect change" (p. 9). Education, for many of the women I encountered, offered hope. But I would argue education is not the singular, monolithic answer to overcoming the challenges faced by women inmates. In fact, I believe that it is often not the inmates who need educating the most, rather it us, the outsiders and colluders with the system, who need to be educated. "There are misconceptions to be abandoned, biases to be dropped" (Lamb, 2003, p. 17). We need to read these women's words and learn of their critiques against a system designed largely to punish rather than rehabilitate. Their words give a human face and powerful voice to otherwise uninspired statistics. It is us who must move from teacher to learner to learned individual. There is much educating of closed hearts still to be done.

As a teacher there will always exist the problem of collusion and the need to understand/dissect one's privilege (in its various forms). This privilege is acute in the case of working with inmates. My freedom to come and go, my racial and class privilege were markers that never left me. The challenge of working with students who came from such diverse backgrounds, cultures, socio-economic levels, and possessed an array of abilities, talents, and values also stayed with me. Despite the constant challenge my students and I faced to communicate across these differences, the women all shared one thing—they were all incarcerated.

So why then does creative writing matter to the woman inmate? It matters because of the heart. As Lamont (1994) explains, "Writing and reading decrease our sense of isolation.... When writers make us shake our heads with the exactness of their prose and their truths, and even make us laugh about ourselves or life, our buoyancy is restored" (p. 237).

It matters in the face of the uncertain questions women inmates encounter each day, "When will I get to go home?"; "How long will my sentence be?"; "How will I make it through today?" These women, despite the never ending list of uncertainties, still laugh and sing and breathe and inspire.

In the corrections classroom, above the clatter of voices, as the discussion escalates, there is always a tale waiting to be told. These women's voices will be carried through the blare of trumpets, the shake of tambourines, the lilt of the opera singer, the shout of the drill sergeant, the blast of a machine gun, and rather than allowing the absurdities of life to wash over them again and again, they choose to rise each day and demonstrate their courage in the act of writing. Each day they face the lonely, empty white page that intimidates so many writers and express their right to write.

REFERENCES

Betancourt, D. (1997). *The dark room: An anthology.* Unpublished, Valhalla Women's Jail. Valhalla, NY.

Bureau of Justice Statistics (2007, Dec.). *Prisoners in 2006.* Retrieved September 15, 2008, from http://www.ojp.usdoj.gov/bjs/pub/ascii/p06.txt

Collins, M. (1995). Shades of the prison house: Adult literacy and the correctional ethos. In H. Davidson (Ed.), *Schooling in a "total institution": Critical perspectives on prison education* (pp. 49-63). Westport, CT: Bergin & Garvey.

Dooley, D. A. (1995). *Plain and ordinary things: Reading women in the writing classroom.* New York: SUNY Press.

Fraley, L. (1997). A second chance. *The dark room: An anthology.* Unpublished, Valhalla Women's Jail. Valhalla, NY.

Freire, P. (1970). *Pedagogy of the oppressed.* New York: Seabury Press.

Greenberg, E., Dunleavy, E., & Kutner, M. (2007). *Literacy behind bars: Results from the 2003 National Assessment of Adult Literacy Prison Survey* (NCES 2007-473). Washington, DC: National Center for Education Statistics.

Lamb, W., & The Women of York Correctional Institution. (2003). *Couldn't keep it to myself: Testimonies from our imprisoned sisters.* New York. Regan Books.

Lamont, A. (1994). *Bird by bird: Some instructions on writing and life.* New York: Anchor Books.

Orr, A. (2004). *No more rejections: 50 secrets to writing a manuscript that sells.* Cincinnati, OH: Writer's Digest Books.

Padgett, R. (1997). *Creative reading: What it is, how to do it, and why.* Urbana, IL: National Council of Teachers of English.

Root, R. L., & Steinberg, M. (1996). *Those who do, can: Teachers writing, writers teaching, a sourcebook.* Urbana, IL: National Council of Teachers of English.

Scheffler, J. A. (2002). Introduction. In J. A. Scheffler (Ed.), *Wall tappings: An international anthology of women's prison writings 200 to the present* (2nd ed., pp. xxi-xliv). New York: Feminist Press.

Stanford, A. F. (2004). More than just words: Women's poetry and resistance at Cook county jail. *Feminist Studies, 30*(2), 277-301.

Steinberg, J. W. (1991). To arrive in another world: Poetry, language development, and culture. *Harvard Educational Review, 61*(1), 27-46.

Tannenbaum, J. (2000). *Disguised as a poem: My years teaching at San Quentin.* Boston: Northeastern University Press.

Torres, M. (1997a). Beautician and the beast. *The dark room: An anthology.* Unpublished, Valhalla Women's Jail. Valhalla, NY.

Torres, M. (1997b). No, I'm not insane. *The dark room: An anthology.* Unpublished, Valhalla Women's Jail. Valhalla, NY.

Trounstine, J. (2001). *Shakespeare behind bars: The power of drama in a women's prison.* New York. St. Martin's Press.

Walker, J. (2004). *Dancing to the concertina's tune: A prison teacher's memoir.* Boston: Northeastern University Press.

CHAPTER 7

BUT HOW CAN I TEACH HER IF SHE CAN'T GET HER BUM ON THE SEAT?

Jenny Horsman

I signed up for a Japanese drumming course a few years ago. I had been fascinated by the physicality of this drumming when I'd watched and listened to a woman's drumming group years before. As someone who had learned to survive by being quiet, avoiding being noticed, and dissociating frequently—separating body and mind—I think I yearned to bring my whole being together in these intricate patterns of powerful reverberating sound.

The first class was wonderful; I was startled to find myself making such a huge noise. I left exhilarated, drumsticks in hand. But by the next week it was getting hard. I had such terrible trouble learning the rhythms. Uniting body and mind to let the patterns we were learning sink into my being seemed impossible. The feelings and thoughts that went through my head each class as I felt more and more stupid, more and more incompetent, were all but unbearable. I wanted to master it, but I despaired. I could still imagine how good it would feel if the patterns of drum beats rolled off my sticks with a sure beat, but I just couldn't believe it could ever happen. The teacher could not have been kinder: he gently pointed

Empowering Women Through Literacy: Views From Experience, pp. 37–43

out to me that each week I was a little better than the week before, inter-rupting my continual comparison with the better students in the class. He showed me the patterns again and again without one iota of impatience, but it didn't matter. Every week as the harsh monologue went on in my brain I would get more and more inept. I would want to avoid going, but I had paid my money and I was determined not to quit. I watched myself every week try hard to be on time, or even early, yet every week I would be just a little late. I was relieved when I got a slight cold, and couldn't possi-bly go! I knew it was easier not to miss a class, to arrive on time, yet some-how I just couldn't do it. I found the experience of learning too tortuous, I felt so bad during the class, that it was a huge battle with myself to get there at all. Finally at the end of the first term I quit, telling myself and the teacher that I would be back to start at the beginning again the next year. But somehow I signed up at the very last minute! The class was full. I was disappointed, a little mad at myself for leaving it so late, but oh so relieved. Of course I told myself that next year I really would sign up early. A few years have passed now. I think of it every fall, but I haven't signed up again. I still might some day when I can bring myself to do it—just not this year!

As I lived through this experience, watching myself, wondering at how this course I had been so eager to do had turned into such a nightmare, I found myself thinking of many literacy students I've worked with. I was fascinated (although it drove me crazy) by my total inability to arrive on time. However hard I thought I was trying to leave early and make abso-lutely certain I would not be late, I seemed to be utterly incapable of it. Once I'd stopped attending I just couldn't convince myself to go again.

My own experience led me to a new understanding of an intensive course I had led. I remembered the women who tried it out and didn't come back, and one woman who arrived late for a month or more—so late that the class was ending—and that even after a long period of not arriving at all. But let me start at the beginning.

The women's course had been running for a week or two. It was a three-month course, meeting three afternoons a week with special fund-ing. We called it the Women's Success Course. Women were still gradually deciding whether to join the class, turning up one day and not the next, but Susan hadn't shown up once. I was disappointed as I had imagined the class would be ideal for her when I wrote the funding proposal.

The course was designed for women "who have been through tough times and want to move on," a course that would take into account the violence in so many women's lives and the ways those experiences might have affected learning. I planned that it would help women to assess and strengthen their supports for learning, including their own belief in themselves, and develop their ability to draw on their whole selves, body, emotion, and spirit, as well as mind, to help them learn effectively. It would be a chance to begin to plan the changes they wanted to make in their lives. After the initial three months, we would continue to meet once a week for another three months or more to support that process of change—whatever form of change the women wanted to work towards.

Susan hadn't joined the group. I assumed it must be because the timing wasn't working for her: perhaps she couldn't get after-school daycare for her daughter, or may be she was working, or perhaps enrolled in another course. Then I started hearing from the literacy program coordinators that Susan loved the group, that she thought it was very important, that she was really glad it was running. I was puzzled. It didn't seem to make any sense; I hadn't seen her in the classroom, not even once.

Other women had attended once or twice, then disappeared, then returned again, although some came only occasionally. I had watched this pattern, fascinated, wondering what was happening. Drawing on what I knew about the impact of violence on learning, the importance of control, and the challenge to believe in oneself and the possibility of learning successfully, I began to think this starting and stopping might be an important learning process in itself. Perhaps women were plucking up the courage to attend, perhaps they were struggling with their fears of failure, perhaps they needed to stop and start in order to take control in a stressful situation. I had learned that learning situations, however relaxed they are, can bring up anxiety and fear, and can evoke memories of violence and the terror and loss of control experienced during violence. Taking control and stopping and starting might be vital for some women to create safety in the learning situation. When I heard from my colleagues that Susan found the class valuable, she didn't seem to fit that pattern, and I could not see how she could be learning anything. I found myself thinking and joking to friends that I really couldn't teach her if she couldn't get her bum on the seat, at least once or twice!

Eventually I learnt how wrong I was. After another week or so she did start to appear—just as I was finishing teaching the class and women were settling in to write in their journals. Each day I welcomed her with enthusiasm. I gave her her own journal. She wrote. And she cried; the tears often poured down her face. I asked her what she needed, asked her whether she wanted to talk. Women in the class pushed the box of tissues closer. She didn't talk with the other women, or with me. She kept coming back. She continued to write and to cry.

I worried. What should I do? What could I be doing differently to support her? She wasn't talking to me. Didn't she trust that I wouldn't judge her? I didn't push; I just waited and wondered. She came day after day, always at the same time. As I remember it, it was weeks before one day she handed me her journal to read. What I saw saddened and horrified me. It was a torrent of invective about how worthless she was: how she couldn't learn because she was stupid, how she didn't deserve to have her daughter because she was a bad mother, how she was waiting for me to throw her out of the class because she didn't deserve to be there if she couldn't get there on time.

I was amazed. I had had no idea what she was thinking. How could she be so cruel to herself? I believe on some level she was waiting and looking for me to confirm all her harshest judgements, her self-hatred and self-doubt. I am horrified to think how easily I could have done exactly that! I believe it would have taken so little. I probably needed only to have told her quite kindly that she was too late, that the group was now closed, that she needed to be on time. In the gentlest of criticism she would have heard exactly what she expected to hear. She would have understood that what I really meant was that she WAS worthless, could NOT learn, should NOT be in that class, did NOT belong, and probably even that I believed her daughter should return to the foster family assigned by child protective services.

Don't get me wrong! Of course the last thing I would have wanted to do was confirm even her gentlest criticism of herself. But if program rules about attendance had meant she was automatically excluded.... If funders had been breathing down our necks demanding that women show success as defined by them, that they obtain jobs at the end of three months.... If I had let my own frustration show—frustration that I had done so much work to get the course started, a course that I thought would be perfect for her.... If I had let myself believe that she simply wasn't making the effort to get there at the start of the course, or on time, that she just wasn't motivated enough to study, or didn't care enough to try to make changes in her life. If I had blamed her for my frustration and disappointment rather than owning it myself.... If that frustration had shaped my actions, or even colored the sound of my voice when she arrived.... I am certain it would not have taken much to send her running, to lead her to give up her studies, perhaps forever. In any case, it would have been a long time before she would dare to pluck up the courage, to risk, to try again.

Fortunately this was a special project, an exploration of a new approach; there were no rules about attendance, and no funders demanding a particular level of achievement. I can't say there was no frustration—there was. I worried often about why women weren't there, what I could do differently, whether there was going to be enough change to be recognized as success to write about at the end of the project. I did give myself the space to notice my frustration, to wonder what it said about me and my fears, my hopes, my expectations, and I worked hard at observing myself and the women with curiosity, rather than letting my judgements shape what I believed, what I did, or what I said. I tried not to allow myself to think I knew anything about WHY the women were behaving as they were. I asked questions and I kept watching.

After the profound shift when Susan showed me her writing and I didn't judge her, she started to arrive a little earlier. Often she was in time to join the work of the class. But I noticed that she frequently stayed on the edge, observing rather than participating. One day, for instance, an Anishnawbe Elder led a workshop, with traditional ritual. She invited women to speak, passing her own sacred deer-antler talking stick to each woman to speak about the woman they most admired, and then to describe the ways they too are like that woman. Susan would not join the circle. I tried to invite her in, to ask her what was wrong and why she would not participate, yet could not really learn why she was staying on the outside. I worried whether she felt a conflict between her own strong Christian faith and the traditional beliefs that were being introduced. I watched her carefully during the afternoon. Susan seemed to show reverence for the process, a certain awe of the elder, and I wondered what was leading her to stay on the margins. Later I asked her about the workshop and she said, her face radiant, that it was one of the best classes she had ever been part of. She couldn't or wouldn't tell me why she didn't join in. I wondered whether she preferred to watch, to see at a distance and take it all in, whether she still didn't feel she really belonged, whether she still didn't feel worthy to be a full member of the group, or to take part in such a sacred process.

Over the months she did begin to participate more and more. She seemed to appreciate the help of other members of the group when she had a health crisis and was able to get support when she went into hospital so that her daughter would be safe and avoid being taken permanently into child protective services custody. Later Susan applied for a care worker course at the local community college and was accepted. After a time she acknowledged that she had a problem with alcohol and signed up for a rehabilitation program.

I have told this story many times in workshops and presentations. I like the shock value when participants see that most of us might have contributed to this student's (and of course others like her) sense of failure and worthlessness if the circumstances had been just a little different. Some literacy workers have worried about attendance policies and whether creating space for attendance like Susan's gives a message that "anything goes" and would encourage other students not to attend regularly. Other workers have told me more stories of students who have stayed on the outside observing before they eventually chose to join in. I heard from one worker about a lesbian student who worked in the computer area listening to a group from afar for several weeks until she was ready to join herself. We wondered whether she was observing the safety of the group, fearful that homophobia might go unchecked. Perhaps, like Susan, it was important for her to follow her own process, to join when she was ready, with no pressure from staff to join earlier. Yet it is so easy to make judgements about the seriousness or the motivation of a student who seems not to "commit" to her studies. Attendance policies are often designed to encourage regular attendance and may help some students push themselves to get to class. Yet such policies will surely make it impossible for others to explore healing possibilities and gradually get to a place where they are ready to attend.

I notice as I tell stories about Susan I am tempted to create a simple recognizable success story. She completed her college training, she got a job, her life was transformed, her daughter is happy and doing well in school. Yet I know success is not as simple as that, particularly if we pay attention to the complex process of healing from trauma and violence and the powerful role that exploring education can play in the process. As I write, several years later, Susan is getting ready to go back to college again, she has started and stopped many community college courses, yet she still returns to the literacy program and continues to explore new possibilities. To me she appears to be on a wonderful journey of healing, learning to be much less hard on herself, recognizing how much she has learned, and making important changes in her life. Yet life is still extremely hard for her, and for her daughter. She still struggles enormously to believe in herself. She still finds it hard to complete a full program and get decent employment.

But perhaps this story is not so much about Susan as it is about me and other literacy workers, about my/our challenge to notice our own patterns, to be curious about our own frustrations, to wonder why each student is behaving as they are, without judgement. Perhaps it is about my desire that as educators we can make connections with our own experiences as learners. I believe we must question what will support each student and begin to reflect with students about what will help them get through some of their emotional barriers to learning. We need to learn to offer a far greater variety of models to help students attend classes in a way that works for them. We need to be allies, not judges or critics, on this challenging path. Some students may find that pressure to attend regularly will help them; others may be defeated by it. One challenge is for educators to own our own frustrations and not to blame students for causing them. I feel bad when a student doesn't show up, when I've worked to prepare for her, but that does not mean she is not working just as hard to get to the class, even if I can't see that struggle.

I am left with my desire, not so much to change Susan, as to change the educational structures that give teachers few alternatives to enforcing attendance policies and imposed measures of success. I want to ensure that teachers all enjoy the "luxury" of enough time, support, training, and freedom to stay open and observe our own and our students' behavior without judgement, to question concepts of success, and to avoid strengthening students' own harsh judgments that can so relentlessly block possibilities for creativity, learning, and change.

CHAPTER 8

FRUSTRATED

Laura Holland

Preoccupied
Difficulty paying attention
Expecting too much
Wasting time

"Ma'am, please!
I hear your lesson on geometry
But it's far too deep for me
Don't you know I have failing short term memory?
Too much alcohol, weed, and ecstasy"

Focused on what concerns me
Like…
What time is commissary?
Will my man still want me?
Will my children remember me?
Who's gonna come visit me?

8:30 a.m.
Just too early
Is this essay really necessary?

Empowering Women Through Literacy: Views From Experience, pp. 45–46

Tired and depressed
Can't get no rest
Stressed
Not believing I can pass the GED test

Should've done this sooner
Was focused on other things
Now....questioning
"Will this manifest into a reality"

How did this happen?
Why am I here?
JUST FORGET THIS!
Going back to the past
Doesn't matter

Too old to learn
Too late to make a difference ... anyway

CHAPTER 9

NO OBSTACLE FOR LEARNING

A Learner's Story of Overcoming

Ana Bertha Diaz

OVERVIEW

Learning is something that we should do no matter what. We might need to overcome many kinds of obstacles in life and one of the hardest things to do is to move to a new country with a different language. In addition, it is hardest when we have other kinds of problems or are depressed also.

However, we can use those problems and depression to create a goal by pushing a little bit and focusing on learning. In my case, I focused on learning English because I understand that when one comes to a new country the first thing one should do is to learn the language. That was my situation. I was going through a very bad depression and I made something positive of this terrible feeling. In summary: I learned English, I got a degree, and now I'm teaching others to learn English.

Empowering Women Through Literacy: Views From Experience, pp. 47–52
Copyright © 2009 by Information Age Publishing

BACKGROUND

I came from The Dominican Republic to the United States April 2, 1992 with no English skills and in the middle of a terrible personal depression. In the beginning, everything looked good, visiting friends and family. They had presents for me and everyone wanted me to stay in their homes. However as time passed I started seeing the reality. Even though I didn't have to pay for rent and food, I had to work to support myself.

At that point, I was afraid to go out in public by myself because I thought, "If I get lost, how would I get back if I could not ask any question in English." To get to the point where I could take the subway by myself took years.

Also, I tried to get a job; however, all the places I went to people told me, "You need to know English to work here." I became so frustrated. After a while of looking for a job, I found one in a factory packing tea. It was an easy task to do, but demanding. I had to pack tea very quickly, and I wasn't fast enough so I got fired.

Then I found a few jobs one after the other in the same category. All those jobs meant the difficult aspects of the word work. I had to work very hard to earn minimum wage because I didn't know English. I didn't have another option at this time.

I received the smartest advice from my brother-in-law. He told me, "You should go to college, get a career and learn English at the same time. If you don't want to finish a degree, just learn English." He helped me complete all the steps in filling out the applications, etc. Nonetheless, I was so tired of every thing in America I just wanted to go back to my Dominican Republic.

I went back to my country, but all my applications for college were still on file waiting to be, or not to be accepted. A year later my sister called me at home in the Dominican Republic to tell me that I was accepted to college. I came back to the United States with more depression, but having decided to go to college and learn English.

COLLEGE - ADJUSTMENTS

In the midst of the depression, I entered Bronx Community College even though I didn't want to do anything at all. All I wanted to do was sleep or stay in the house. I was afraid to do anything. I just wanted the days to pass quickly. Every day was very painful for me. I hurt inside so much that I felt my head was going to explode. I expected that once I learned English, I would leave college.

I was afraid and yet in some ways also excited to go to school. I said to myself, "Learning the language of the country that I'm living in is the most important thing to become successful." I thought, "I have to do it no matter what and if I want to go back to my country I will have more opportunities to get a good job there too."

I studied business as my academic major. Attending school helped me focus on my books and distracted me from my depression. I also made very good friends and found teachers that helped me to survive, and get to the end of that long journey.

Even so, many mornings I had to struggle with myself to get out of the bed and go to college. At such times, I might have panic attacks and I felt like I had to push a heavy wall to walk. I pushed that heavy wall almost every day. Getting to the classroom everyday was hard but after awhile I was able to focus on my classes.

I enjoyed all the subjects. They distracted me from my depression. When a panic attack came I started to read or do school work. It was hard to develop this change of habit, but it worked.

At the beginning of attending school in the USA, even though I didn't understand the professors when they taught the classes, I found ways to know what they said. I asked someone in class what the teacher said and what the homework was. Or I would go back to ask the teachers questions with some of my friends who understood enough English to translate for me and then I asked them what I needed to know.

I did all my assignments on time; I read all the books that the teachers assigned us to read. I knew it was the best way to learn the most possible. Learning became an effective therapy for my panic attacks.

LEARNING WITH NEW FRIENDS

At the same time, I helped some of my classmates to study and learn. I understood that teaching is learning twice. I felt so proud when many of my classmates asked me for help and I could help them. My best friend changed her major to study with me. I helped her to study and I inspired her to continue until the end.

She helped me also with her easy disposition about life. She also inspired me to be freer. She helped me to laugh again; she was very funny. It was a good trade for us; we were a good team. I learned how to pull the good things out of bad and difficult moments.

However, one year later I wanted to quit school. I was tired and I didn't want to continue my business major. A nice teacher suggested that I should change my major to something that I liked better. That teacher knew I liked art and suggested that I should be an art major. It gave me a new direction and motivation, and I started a new major in Computers and Graphic Art. That change was wonderful for me in many ways. I enjoyed each subject and every project. I graduated with honors even though English was my second language.

SHOWING PEACE - ART AND LIFE

In my time in school, I participated in an art contest for peace. The contest was very interesting and I decided to do it. I thought intensely about what I could create. I finally decided and painted a white pigeon, a dove injecting a dose of peace in our planet. (See Figure 9.1.)

This piece of art illustrated a lot of power. It reflected my feelings at that time. I was desperate for peace in my soul just as we need it in our world. In addition, it reflected my great need to learn English and to pursue what I wanted and needed. The confusion of not knowing the language had been killing me, pushing away the peace I needed. I earned first place in the contest for the artwork.

GIVING PEACE TO OTHERS - TEACHING

In the reality of life, to teach others is a way of giving peace. If teachers inject a portion of knowledge to those who need it, they give many good things to students. Learning starts to bring peace into our lives because

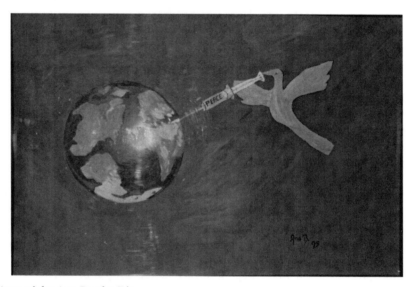

Artwork by Ana Bertha Diaz

Figure 9.1.   Peace Poster, 1995.

we can find better jobs, and that satisfies many of our necessities and removes many worries.

A short time before I finished my degree, I found a job in a high school in New York. That job was very different from my previous ones. Due to what I knew of English I made more money, I had medical insurance, and the work was more pleasant. It brought some peace and more tranquility to my life. After one year, I started teaching in a classroom.

I had learned from this experience that to be educated is very important to be successful. This was the beginning of my new journey as a teacher. I taught elementary and high school level for a few years. I saw that being a teacher offers you important life rewards. When children began to change their lives from being on the street doing wrong things to getting a GED and going to college it made me feel so happy.

One day I was teaching art and I told my students, "To be an artist you need to be neat and organized." The next day one student told me, "Miss Diaz I organized my room and I made it look neat because I want to be an artist. You told us in class that an artist had to be neat." It surprised me in a good way. It was good feedback as a teacher and at the same time so genuine. It is wonderful when you touch a life.

I also taught adults English as a Second Language (ESL). It was a terrific experience. I really loved to teach them. It was similar to when I was learning English. I truly understood and "fit in their shoes."

I wanted to teach these ESL learners what I needed when I was at that same place. I wanted to get inside of their minds and give them my spirit to not give up. I wanted them to understand that if I could do it, they could make it. I also advised them how important is to learn English and how much more successful you can be in America when you speak English.

For this group of learners, my example was a good one. Like them, I came here with no English, with problems, having a minimum wage job and working at a job I didn't like, but I changed my life just by going to school and learning. I shared with them that they could do the same thing.

I had pushed a heavy wall every day trying not to give up. I told them, when you feel that you don't want to go to school say, "No, I have to go. I need it for my future and my children."

ALMOST GONE

After getting my life on track, I had a brain aneurysm; I almost died. I was unable to teach for a year and half. When I came back to my *new* life to teach, I chose to teach adults. I started with new energy. I share my experiences and the new life God gave back to me with my students. I say to them, "No matter what happens in your life don't give up."

It feels so rewarding when I hear about the real life and meaningful progress of my students,

"Teacher now when I take the train I can understand the announcements."

"I made a doctor's appointment for my child."
"I can communicate better with my boss."
"I can help my children to do their homework."

All these stories inspire me to continue teaching. Now I believe that many people need me out there in the world and in their classes.

CONCLUSION

To be successful in life we have to work hard and take our time. We need to always remember that time passes, and it is good that if when it passes we have done something positive with it. If we are going to school, we should not let a problem or circumstances stop us from being successful. When something bothers us, we should not settle for an excuse to leave school. Being educated is the key to finding our dreams and reaching our goals. Learning is something we need to always do. When we go to live in a new country to have a better life we need to do the most important thing, which is to learn the language. In order to succeed, we have to be positive about learning. Even if the problems we have don't let us move forward, we can push that heavy wall and gradually move ahead.

It is important to get something good out of our problems. We can feel the satisfaction at the end and be proud of ourselves. This approach brings us much peace in life because when we find a good job, it helps us meet our necessities and have more freedom. In addition, we can also better help others from this position.

There are many people who need us here on earth. It is very satisfying when we are responsible for helping someone succeed. It provides us much happiness. Remember we can plant a good seed in people's lives that can grow later. This approach is a good reward.

CHAPTER 10

DEAR MARY

Lorna Rivera

Mary Chatman was one of my favorite students when I taught GED classes in the Adult Learners Program at Project Hope in Boston, MA. I wrote the following letter after she was killed on February 10, 2000.

Dear Mary,

I never got to give you that perfect attendance award. Thanks for coming to all of my social studies classes and for asking so many questions. I know you always enjoyed our classes because you would stay afterwards still talking about whatever subject we had just discussed in class, even though everyone else had already left. I'm sorry if I sometimes rushed out of the room, or kept collecting papers and erasing the board instead of giving you my full attention. Sometimes when you were waiting to see Vera I would sit with the two of you because I enjoyed how you liked to lecture me. "Oh Lorna you're too soft. These women don't need you to hold their hand!" When I told you about how I called Sereta one morning to wake her up for school you said, "No you didn't! Now, now if you need to call someone to get them to come to school, forget it." In class discussions you always gave your opinion, and whenever someone talked, you always listened carefully, and would say, "Now listen if...." You always seemed to "have it together" and you'd tell others, "you got to get it together. How

Empowering Women Through Literacy: Views From Experience, pp. 53–54

can you come to school without tablets?" Sometimes I wondered how you got to be so stubborn? What was missing in your story? How come you didn't want anyone outside of school to know that you were a GED student? I don't blame you for not wanting to memorize your multiplication tables. After all, you ran a successful business without knowing them. But, how did you "pass" for so long? What other secrets did you have? You had dreams of becoming a fashion designer. And when I spoke with Lori's mother about an apprenticeship for you, your eyes lit up as you imagined yourself working as a fashion designer. Later you told me, "You people at Project Hope are making me crazy. I came in here knowing what I wanted to do. Get my GED. Now, I don't know what I want to do with my life!" This was said with a twinge of hope and fear. You were so proud when you gave me your daughter's drawings, and you even brought her over to Project Hope so she could draw the front of the house. You always bragged, "My girls this and that…" You always talked about them. What will happen to them now? Mary, you are the heart and soul of our work. You came into our food pantry and told Sister Anne that you wanted to finish your education, and we were there to help you. You said, "God sent me to Project Hope." Indeed, in this holy place, you were always trying to look on the positive side of things. How can your classmates learn from your example? Maybe someone who is afraid of change will be less afraid? Maybe someone who doesn't quite think she can make it will try a little bit harder because of what you were able to do? Mary can you guide us all? Can you protect other women who are in similar situations like you were? Can you help me tell your story so that others will understand that your life had great value? Mary, what more can I say? I'm shocked that you're gone. I can't believe what happened to you. I am pained that I didn't get a chance to say goodbye. I can't accept that I will never see you again. I am so grateful that you offered me advice. I was looking forward to your membership on the Advisory Council and hoping to read your autobiography. I'm sorry I got mad when you wanted to be paid for the book project, or when you asked us for money sometimes. Now I know that you needed money desperately and it may have saved your life. I know that sometimes you were frustrated with "non-GED" activities, but I'm glad you still kept coming to our parties and wished us all a good time. I once said that you complained too much, and I regret saying that. I really do. I just wish I had asked you more questions. Please forgive me Mary. I wish I had taken more time to find out the source of your suffering.

CHAPTER 11

A CRADLE IN THE CLASSROOM

Creating a Positive Learning Environment for Student Mothers

Tanya M. Spilovoy

INTRODUCTION

Before having my own baby, I had little tolerance for family-child excuses. School was the most important thing. I did not make many exceptions for sick kids, spousal issues, daycare problems, etc. When I had my own son, everything changed. I suddenly realized that while work and school was important, my child was by far the most precious thing in my life. I immediately developed a new understanding and empathy for my student mothers. This essay delves into women's challenges/difficulties/rewards involved in having children while still pursuing their career and educational dreams. It shows practical ways I have made my teaching more child-friendly and how it has positively impacted the educational experience of my female students.

Empowering Women Through Literacy: Views From Experience, pp. 55–58
Copyright © 2009 by Information Age Publishing
All rights of reproduction in any form reserved.

Narrative

Sahel stood at my desk, her eyes barely visible under her tightly-wrapped hajib as she stared down at the floor. "Sorry I wasn't here yesterday, Teacher," she said. "My little boy was sick and I had to take him to the emergency room last night." Her words burned hot in my head ... *another stupid excuse for missing class.* Sahel had given many other reasons for previous absences: a missed bus, an illness, a problem with her landlord. I was tired of hearing them. I didn't care if the excuses were true or not.

Although I knew that life in the United States was difficult for my adult English Language Learners—poverty, difficulty communicating, discrimination, homesickness, culture shock, and post-traumatic war syndrome—I knew that learning English and earning a high school diploma would give them a chance to succeed. Sahel spoke very little English, and her education had been disrupted by the Somalian war and her subsequent flight as a refugee. She didn't seem to understand the desperation of her situation. She had not turned in one assignment, and it was already week three of the semester.

"Well," I said coldly, my disapproval clearly visible, "You are currently failing this class. You are never here. Excuses aren't going to help you get through school!"

Her eyes shot to mine, full of tears, hurt, anger, and indignance. "He *was* in the hospital, Teacher. He is still very sick with pneumonia. I can bring you a doctor's note. School is *not* the most important thing in the world."

The meaning of her words struck hard. School was *my* life. During the day, I taught English as a Second Language in an inner-city grade school. Then I drove through rush-hour traffic to teach another four hours at an all-ESL adult high school for new immigrants. I was working hard to pay off my student loans, a new car, and finally buy the things I had always wanted. But I was also teaching because I loved the work. I felt needed, validated—like I was making a difference in the world. And there stood a young mother with completely different priorities, telling me that I was wrong.

"Well, just try to be here. You can still turn in your assignments for partial credit," I stammered, uncomfortable, trying to quickly remedy the situation. But it didn't help; Sahel never came back to my class. I saw her in the hall a few times throughout the semester. I asked about her son and when she was coming back, but she was evasive. I found out later that she had transferred to another English class.

At a young age, I was aware that boys had more opportunities than girls. Education was not offered freely to the women in my family. My uncles were given cars and tuition. My mother got a sewing machine and was encouraged to get married. At age twenty-eight, she went to back to college while working and taking care of a family. She knew that education was the way to independence and self-fulfillment—and she drilled that concept into my head. I wanted to seize every advantage for myself, but I also wanted to empower other women to follow the same path. For me, school had always been the most important thing, until the day my son, Dakota Sky, came along.

I taught twelve hours the day I went into labor. At 3 am, on the way to the hospital, I called my principal's voice mail and listed all of the things that needed to be finished in my absence. I had this baby "thing" all planned out. The baby would just have to fit into *my* busy schedule...little did I know that he had a completely different plan. Somewhere between diaper changes and watching his little eyes flutter to sleep at nap time, I realized that nothing else in the world was as important as this precious, helpless, brown-eyed boy. My priorities had to change.

At the end of my maternity leave, I reduced to part-time employment and quit my night teaching job. I gave up the $20,000 in lost wages because taking Dakota for walks, to baby yoga, story time, and cuddling was more important than money.

Dakota is two years old now. I'm currently teaching English at United Tribes Technical College—a cultural, community, and family-centered Native American Tribal College. The majority of my students are parents. Most are also employed. And I realize that school is not the most important thing to them either—the welfare of their children and families comes first. So I have adapted my teaching philosophy to make education work for them by making my classroom a child-friendly environment. My office phone rang while I sat reading student essays last October, and a quiet, worried voice asked, "Hi Tanya, this is Cree. My baby Nayln is sick today, and his daycare wants me to pick him up. What should I do?" Instinctively, I said, "If he's not too sick, you can just bring him to class with you." And she did. I taught a short lesson; then I held Nayln and gave him a bottle while Cree finished her final project with her collaborative group. Cree didn't miss her class, and the other students enjoyed seeing the tiny visitor.

Since then, other students have also occasionally brought their kids to class in an emergency. A few times, parents have had to take their children out of the class for a short break. But most of the time, the kids have been hardly noticeable. I now keep a basket of crayons, toys, fruit snacks, and Play-doh right by my office door to encourage parents to come to me for help—even if they don't have a babysitter. My students know that they can also call ahead and get assignments, attend other sections of the same class, or submit assignments by e-mail in a crisis. One student, Jackie, had her baby mid-semester and still got a B+ on the final test because of the afternoons I spent tutoring her. She now comes every few months to visit and to show off her beautiful baby girl.

I know I can't go back and change what happened with Sahel. But I can make sure that the women who walk through my new classroom door feel empowered to achieve their educational goals without neglecting their families. As a result, I have enjoyed increased attendance and retention rates as well as better rapport with my students. There are definitely times when my office looks more like a daycare than a college, but I'm happy to pick up the toys when they leave, knowing that their mothers will be back to learn again tomorrow.

CHAPTER 12

TELLING OUR TRUTHS

Tzivia Gover

When I first started teaching poetry to teen mothers in a GED program in Holyoke, MA, I lived in dread of the questions I would inevitably get from my students: "Why are we wasting our time on this? I just want to get my GED and get out of here!"

Back then I said the same thing I say now, eight years later: "Because when you get your GED you'll be what, 18-, 19-, 20-years old? Then what? What about the next 80 years? The GED will help launch you into higher levels of education and job growth, but poetry will be with you and serve you for the rest of your life."

I gave grantors, who supplied the money to pay my salary, a slightly different story. To them I would describe the grim statistics of my students' lives: In Holyoke one in four adults lacks a high school diploma. The young women at The Care Center, ranging in age from 16-21, live below the poverty line, are raising children and have low educational attainments. Then I would explain how poetry and the arts have been shown to help students fare better on standardized tests and that poetry offers an opportunity to approach spelling, grammar and literature in a non-threatening way.

But the truth was, I had my doubts. The stories and situations that at first shocked me, then became commonplace but no less wrenching,

Empowering Women Through Literacy: Views From Experience, pp. 59–63

included students dealing with the murder of a brother, parent or best friend, students who dozed in class because they'd stayed up all night in an emergency room with a child suffering from asthma—one of the many side-effects of living in poverty; students who came to class with a black eye or with stories of the indignities associated with living in shelters; students living with the fear that the electricity was going to be shut off because a boyfriend had just landed in prison and now there was no way to pay their bills. In the face of all of this, I'd wonder: Was I really serving them by spending a precious hour of their 6-hour school day reviewing the rhyme scheme of a Shakespearean sonnet, or memorizing the syllable count for Haiku, reading Lucille Clifton's homage to her hips, or laughing with them over Martín Espada's poem "My Cockroach Lover?"

I didn't set out to use poetry to help combat poverty or put an end to teen pregnancy. Nor did I theorize that it would boost test scores and therefore should design a curriculum to bring verse to the world of Adult Basic Education. In fact, I began teaching poetry to students in under-resourced schools and neighborhoods more or less by accident.

At the time I was a graduate student at Columbia University in New York, studying non-fiction but sneaking in poetry workshops every chance I got.   I needed a work-study job when I saw a notice tacked to a bulletin board in a student lounge: "Poets Needed" it read. The successful candidate would teach poetry at P.S. 75 with Teachers & Writers Collaborative. Only problem was, from my point of view at that time, I'd have to teach children and teenagers. Teaching was the last thing I wanted to do; I wanted to write. Period. Besides, the idea of a room full of teenagers scared me. On the other hand, the money was good and the hours fit my schedule, so I applied. I could put up with anything for a semester or two, I reasoned.

Then, I fell in love. I didn't care whether the kids needed poetry. I just knew I needed the kids – and I needed their poems: direct, honest and unexpected. Their words fueled me.

After graduation, when I returned to my home in western Massachusetts and my job as a newspaper reporter and editor, I realized I missed teaching. So, I volunteered during my lunch hour at The Care Center. Soon after I became a consultant at the school offering afternoon poetry workshops. Then I became a part-time employee, and finally I was hired full-time to teach, organize a visiting author program and edit a student literary journal.

Meanwhile, over time, the students' resistance to poetry receded. And in many cases, true poets emerged.

Gladys, a soft-spoken young woman who is pregnant and raising a 2-year-old boy, described her feelings about poetry this way:

... Poetry is like the eyes of my son.
Poetry is a book with a lot of writing
that makes you feel new.
Poetry is like eating a banana.
Poetry is what I see and hear.
Poetry is like a waterfall.
Poetry is like a cell phone
ring, ring, ring and it won't stop
ringing until you pick it up....
[From "Poetry Is" by Gladys Ruiz, 2008]

For Gladys, poetry is all-pervasive. It's what she sees and hears. It's in nature and it's in the eyes of the person she loves most. It's as insistent as a cell phone; it demands our attention.

For another student, Sharika, poetry is as necessary as air. Recently, Sharika sat in my office and told me about her struggles with the GED exam, and her frustration about her slow progress toward her goal of passing the test. "Honestly," she told me, "if it weren't for poetry I'd have dropped out already. I know wherever I go after this, there won't be poetry there."

Poetry proved to be a way for Sharika to express on paper her feelings about her struggles with learning, her confusion about relationships and her complicated emotions about her father's death from AIDS, among many other things. After reading a poem by Mark Doty, in which the poet describes how he was haunted by dreams of his lover who died from AIDS, Sharika wrote her own poem, and dedicated it to Doty.

Poetry has also been a way for Sharika to grow and blossom as a young woman. When she is frustrated with math, or down on herself for not understanding a lesson in social studies, she pulls out a piece of paper and writes a poem.

For her teachers, poetry has become a way to more deeply understand Sharika's struggles, and to have more compassion for her.

In her poem (Look!), Sharika describes her frustration with not being able to learn as quickly as she feels she should be able:

(Look)

Look   at me
What do you see?
I am sad because things won't go how I want them to be.
For some people
they learn quickly
but not me.
Look at me
once again

Try to see my pain.
I keep trying so hard
but still I feel like I have no brain.
Look at me. Tell me what do you see?
Damn, I feel like about anytime
I will fall on my feet.
Life's so hard.
How do people keep up?
I wonder   sometimes if I won't wake up.
Look at me.
Stare real hard.
Tell me what you see,
'cause sometimes
I start to think this is all a dream.

Like a button in my mind
is broken. Then I ask myself,
can it be fixed?
Is there any way it can be repaired?
But right when I am about to say I can do it,
instead I just
wander away.
[Sharika Rivera, 2008]

The poem itself is moving and revealing. But by sharing it, Sharika received support and encouragement—better yet understanding. Sharika posted the poem to a poetry blog we launched last winter. She received comments from staff members and students. This one, from one of her classmates, summed up the responses: "Sharika, you are a strong person that knows what you are doing. I love this poem a lot. It got to me."

What gets to me is how when a student shows herself through her poetry, the tide of answering voices floods in.

Another student, Monica, wrote a poem about what it was like to grow up without her mother, and what it felt like when, as an adult, her mother finally tried to come back into her life.

Three Girls Without a Mom

There are three girls without a mom.
They wonder what it is like to have a mom.
Three girls without a mom
to know what it's like to have a mother and daughter relationship.
Three girls without a mom
to have girls night out and have fun.
Three girls without a mom
to talk about boys and how to plan a wedding.

Three girls without a mom.
Then you call, almost twenty years later.
Three girls without a mom.
[Monica Rodriguez, 2008]

Monica wrote the poem quickly, nearly tossed it off, and when it was selected for our student poetry journal, she expressed surprise. But what surprised her more, she said later, was that other students approached her to tell her they'd experienced the same thing. "I was just trying to write about myself," Monica told me later, "and then I realized other people had been through the same thing, too."

I often try to explain to students that poetry is a conversation, across generations and across time. When we read a poem by Emily Dickinson, then write our own inspired by her words, we are opening the door for the next generation of poets to respond to our words. By not only writing poems together, but reading them aloud, publishing them online and in our journal, we have discovered that this conversation nurtures us and our readers in the present, in our classrooms and our communities.

Is poetry essential in the classroom? It is difficult to offer easily quantifiable reasons to justify it, and perhaps more difficult to rationalize the pursuit according to state-mandated curriculum guidelines. Even as a poet and a teacher I have had my moments of doubt. By my students have shown me that the answer is clear and simple: Yes. Absolutely.

REFERENCES

Rivera, S. (2008). *Look at me.* Unpublished poetry.
Rodriguez, M. (2008). *Three girls without a mom.* Unpublished poetry.
Ruiz, G. (2008). *Poetry is.* Unpublished poetry.

CHAPTER 13

LAUGH, LISTEN, AND LEAVE THE DOOR OPEN

Working With Teen Women in Adult Programs

Stacie Evans

"What did you mean by that," Sandy asks. "What boy frightens you?"

Nia looks surprised, almost shrugs off the question, then tells us about the boy she's been talking to, the "boy" who is really a 33-year-old man who won't accept that 17-year-old Nia isn't interested in dating someone so much older. He looks for her at her job, sometimes waits outside her house. "I talk to him," she says with another shrug. "I don't know what else to do. I thought if I didn't talk to him it'd be worse, he'd get angry. But he wants more than talking, and he's getting angry anyway."

We are working with Denise Duhamel's *1,001 Feelings*, (2005) a book-length list poem with provocative lines like: "I feel like faces betray us," and "I feel tortured by the memory of our last fight." We have been reading groups of feelings, discussing them, writing and reading our own lists. Buried in Nia's list was one line: "I feel frightened with this boy." It went by fast, very nearly swallowed by all the things she felt about the death of

Empowering Women through Literacy: Views From Experience, pp. 65–71
Copyright © 2009 by Information Age Publishing
All rights of reproduction in any form reserved.

her grandmother, all the things she feels when she's dancing, when she's out with her friends, when she imagines her future. The line surprised me from Nia, who never talked about herself. I wondered if anyone else noticed, wondered how I could swing us back around to it without the segue being too heavy-handed.

Needless worry. Every girl in the room zeroed in on that line. Sandy just got the question out first.

I teach a low-level Pre-GED class for Out-of-School Youth, kids who used to be called high school drop outs. Students in my class read and do math at about sixth grade level. The majority of my students are sixteen to twenty-five, and most are women.

Years ago, I taught in a college prep program at City College in Harlem. I taught twelfth grade English to kids who were so into school that they spent their mornings in their high schools then trekked to City for more school all afternoon. They were kids who wanted to be doctors, who (mostly) had parents backing their play, who could see themselves working in hospitals and private practices. That was all I knew about teaching teens before my current job.

When I left that program, I interviewed at public high schools. At an alternative school, one of the teachers asked: "What would you do if a student called you a 'ho'?" Before I could answer, the principal kept it going: "Or a bitch, a dyke, a nigger or a cunt. What would you do?" Good question. I was naïve enough to think they were crazy. This was *me* we were talking about: I'm incredibly nice ... people always say so. No one would *ever* talk to me like that.

Fear of abuse didn't turn me away from public school teaching, though. It was the number of students I'd be expected to manage. I was leaving a program in which I'd had a workload of 45 kids. In the public schools I'd have had 150-175 kids. I was pretty certain I wasn't up to that challenge. I moved to adult education (adult ed), where I've been ever since.

In recent years, the "adult" in adult ed has gotten considerably younger. A concerted (and largely illegal) effort to push low-performing students out of city high schools has left GED programs facing the need to serve more and more young people. The state defines "adult" as anyone sixteen and older, but adult ed programs that accept 16-18-year-olds tend to lose most of their real adult students. As a result, many adult programs make the decision *not* to enroll younger teens, leaving these kids few options once they leave high school.

I teach in Brooklyn, New York in one of the few adult programs in the area that accepts 16-year-olds. Finding ways to teach this population has required what often feels like a shift in my center of gravity. These aren't the kids I taught at City, and they aren't the adults I'm more accustomed to. My empathy, my sense of humor, my ability to think on my feet and to plan lessons are all skills I bring to this younger classroom, but I've had to jettison much of what I thought I knew: about teens, about managing a class and making room for the work that has to happen in our room beyond the five subjects of the GED.

The girls in my classes are all the girls you know: the cute girls, the sexy girls, the wild girls, the tough girls, the meek girls, the loner girls, the keep-my-head-down-and-study girls, the clique-ish girls, the boyish girls … They are all sizes and colors and ages. They are gay and straight. They are there by choice and mandated by courts. At first glance, they have nothing in common beyond gender. But each is a girl the schools couldn't manage—she slipped through a crack, walked out, was invisible in the back of a room, had to juggle classes and childcare. Each is a girl who isn't quite in love with herself and isn't sure why anyone else should be, how anyone else *could* be, if anyone else ever *will* be. Each is a girl who isn't sure the path she sees in front of her is the one she wants to be on. Each is a girl who wants to be in Level 2 already, in Level 3, holding a GED in her hands five minutes ago.

Given the differences in our ages, I am definitely a mother to some of these girls. And I *act* like a mother with them a lot of the time. But I am also girlfriend, confidante, and giant-listening-ear. I am a referral source. I am a liaison between them and the social service and legal systems, between them and their parents. Sometimes, the most important thing I am—even though they would never articulate it this way and might not even be fully aware of it—is a fat, black woman with kinky hair and a decent job who gets a fair amount of pleasure out of life. I represent a lot of things that it's important for them to see as possible.

On the first night of class I have students write three questions for me that aren't about school, without their names so everyone can ask what they really want to know. I stress that the unrelated-to-school part because I want them to know it's ok to ask anything (though I *do* reserve the right not to answer!). It always leads to some quick laughs that put the group more at ease, and then there's the cruel writing assignment—an essay about me using info learned in the Q&A—to help them see they should pay attention even when it seems that we're just messing around.

A few things always come up … and in almost always the same order: how old am I, how many children do I have, how did I learn to talk the way I do, where am I from, am I married. This is another reason for the exercise: to get all the juicy tidbits out of the way on the first night. Well, *almost* all—my raging vanity means that I never tell my age.

It's interesting that students assume I have children before they wonder if I am married. Shows how old-fashioned I am as much as it tells me anything about my students. I am also interested in how they interpret the way I speak. I have either learned it and am choosing to speak a certain way for them, or I am from somewhere else – California, maybe – or somewhere foreign. We have the "acting white, talking proper" conversation, and it always gets heavy in the end: do I look down on them because of the way they speak; do I think they are 'ghetto' or ignorant; am I going to be correcting every word they say? (No, no, no and no.) And that tells me a lot more about teachers they've had in the past than it does about them.

In another group, we stop for our break. Max and Eugene, the only guys in the class, go to the store. They walk out and Tanya closes the door behind them.

"It's nice like this," she says. "Just girls in here." She pulls her chair closer to Dana and sits down. "Let's talk about stuff," she says.

"Tell us about your baby," Caroline invites.

"Which one?"

"You *got* more than one?" This is from Dana, in typical Dana fashion. We've all heard Tanya go on and on about her baby girl. We've seen photos and heard her cooing from Tanya's voicemail. Last week I got to meet her one night after class. Everyone laughs at the question.

"I *had* more than one," Tanya says. "My first baby, my son, he died."

(It's the start of term. We've been in class together a couple of weeks, fewer than twenty hours.) Tanya tells us how her baby never came home from the hospital, how she moved into his room so he would know she was there for him, that he wasn't alone, how he managed to hold on for eleven painful months before his heart failed.

"That's why I got pregnant the second time," she says. "I wanted a baby right away."

"The first time was an accident though, right?" Dana asks.

Tanya shrugs. "I guess it was. I was only fifteen, so I probably wouldn't have done that on purpose." She shrugs again. "But this time was no accident. I *wanted* a baby."

"Everything comes out with you in that classroom," my supervisor says. And that feels true, but I have to wonder *why*. The "why" seems almost impossibly easy: my students talk, and I listen. I was shocked that they opened so completely and quickly. I was glad for it but couldn't figure it out. At my students' ages, I was sealed like a vault. The idea that I would have talked in class—and to one of my *teachers*—about any of the real things in my life was laughable. But again and again my students talk. Even the ones who hold their doors tightly shut tell so much.

Our classroom is part of the 'why.' I am certain Tanya wouldn't have told us about her son if our class was held in one of the other rooms. The Ed Center has three classrooms—first floor, basement, second floor. The first and basement rooms are large, and both are almost public space. The school supplies storage closet is in one room; the director's office and both first floor restrooms are in the other. Our class is held in the tiny, almost-hidden second floor room, an awkwardly-shaped yet cozy and intimate space that can only fit about a dozen students. We are physically very close. We are behind closed doors. Our intimacy is almost—*almost*—a given. It closets us away from the rest of the Center, and Tanya took advantage of the cocoon-like space of our room to introduce us to her son.

As she talked, the classroom was utterly silent with all of us feeling through that sad story. Our thoughts may not have been the same, but our attentiveness to Tanya, the way we wrapped our hearts around her. That was the same. That was no accidental telling. Tanya *wanted* us to know she had had a child before, wanted us to know what had happened to him and what that had done to her. And she wanted to tell *us* – the girls – and not Max and Eugene, wanted to have this information included as we developed our perceptions of her.

I am working on a project my third term in the program. The students who are researching STDs have just discovered that Google is awash in utterly gruesome photos of variously diseased genitalia. Valerie finds a truly horrific image of a man in the late stages of … I don't *know* what. That first day, everyone is so excited about finding photos that no one remembers to note which disease is responsible for which resulting horror. They just know that this man's penis was clearly a source of great pain for him. After everyone has been appropriately grossed out, Valerie says, "If you can look at these pictures and not wear a condom, you are *crazy*." Jeovany says the picture is making him think twice about having sex at *all*. All the photos are taken after the people have been sick a long time. "You'd know something was wrong long before any part of you started to look like those pictures," I say. "Wouldn't you go to the doctor sooner?"

I asked the question, but I wasn't really prepared for everyone to start telling ugly stories about their experiences with the health care system. I had no idea how badly kids get treated by people who are supposed to take care of them. And this is, apparently, true much more for the girls. The guys had problems, but they confirmed that the girls had it worse.

"They're afraid of us," Jeovany said, "so they don't talk to us the way they do females."

And how do they talk to females? Apparently it's standard practice for medical providers to treat young women as if they are having non-stop, porn-star sex with every man in the City.

"They talk real loud," Nia said. "They let everyone hear your business."
"They talk nasty with you about sex," Valerie said. "Like no *way* you're a virgin. One nurse grabbed my belt and pulled on my pants asking me how many boys had been in there."

When Sandy got pregnant, her first pre-natal visit turned out to be her last. "The nurse kept telling my business to the receptionist and everyone in the waiting area," she said. "Oh, she's pregnant. Oh, she's only fourteen. Oh, can you imagine how she's breaking her father's heart. Oh, her mother must be so ashamed to have a daughter like this. Oh, maybe she'll have a miscarriage and she can start over again, almost clean." She shook her head. "Can you believe that? Can you understand why we don't go to doctors?"

My students talk. I talk, too, but mostly I listen. My students open up because they want and need to, and they open up because the space for that is always left open, because they know I'll listen. That's the main 'why' for what happens in our room, for the attention and the *retention*—the ones who talk most are the ones who *stay*. Listening is, maybe, the most important thing I give my students. Their thoughts, ideas and experiences all have value, are all funny or interesting or painful or powerful or true … or all of those things at once. And few people in their high school lives acknowledged or believed that. And few in their lives since leaving high school acknowledge or believe it. Helping them see that there's nothing 'wrong' with their thoughts or feelings helps them trust themselves in other ways. My listening lets them put on the table all the things that get in the way of their concentration on schoolwork.

It isn't always easy. I have to forcibly hold my tongue. Often. I've always been a fairly good listener, but I've had to elevate my game. The ways I want to interrupt would shut them down. And if I did that, so much of what they need to say would be lost. Being the giant listening ear guarantees that they have at least one adult they can say these things to. If Nia hadn't told us about the man who was harassing her, would she have told anyone? And how might that story have ended if she hadn't talked?

I think about the interview I had at that alternative school years ago and the questions that seemed to promise abuse from the students. The implication was that such behavior was the norm, that I hadn't been teaching real teens. The kids I teach now would most definitely register as "real." Many have up-close and personal experience with the juvenile justice system. All have difficult, painful, or horrific family histories. Some are actively self-medicating with drugs or alcohol. All have vocabularies straight out of *The Wire*. Never has one of them treated me with anything but respect and kindness. They are, in fact, so funny and sweet and charming as to be utterly winning despite the tough facades they throw up for protection.

I don't accept everything they say. When Reina urged me to have a piece of fried chicken at a class party because, "We know your people love fried chicken," we had a … teachable moment. When Tatiana insisted dressing provocatively was the only way to get a good job, we had another.

I am their teacher, after all. But even when I challenge things they believe, I listen, I leave room for the conversations that need to happen if I hope *they* will be able to listen, if I hope they will make themselves vulnerable enough to learn, to make change.

REFERENCES

Duhamel, D. (2005). *Mille et un sentiments (1001 Feelings)*. Danbury, CT: Firewheel Editions.

CHAPTER 14

IT HAS BEEN A PLEASURE

Sharon L. Shoemaker

It Has Been a Pleasure is a collection of four reflective poems expressing my experiences as an Adult Education and Literacy teacher. The piece documents the struggles of both the students and me. The poems speak of how adult education has changed the students, and how working with them has changed me. All of the students' names have been changed.

Empowering Women Through Literacy: Views From Experience, pp. 73–77
Copyright © 2009 by Information Age Publishing
All rights of reproduction in any form reserved.

IT HAS BEEN A PLEASURE

On the first day I entered the classroom, I didn't know...
  much about adult education
    how I would like this new job
      if I could persist
        if I could handle those so unlike me.
I had finished school
  Followed the rules
    Avoided trouble
I was soft spoken and sometimes studious.

I fell in love with the job
  The people
    The sense of purpose
      The teaching...listening...caring
        Knowing that my actions impacted others for a lifetime.
This displaced homemaker flourished.

I still have doubts;
  I wish I could help everyone I meet.
    I'd love to tell them all I know...how to succeed in 500 words.
  But I quietly model and teach
    I care for these people with broken lives and hearts
      I see beyond the indecorous behaviors, to the souls
        Trapped in protective armor.

I am stronger and more assured.
My students have given me more than I've ever given them.
Yet, still, *they thank me* for helping them.

If they only knew the truth....
  It has been a pleasure!

SHE IS LEARNING

It's wonderful to see CeeCee learning.
She is sitting quietly before the math page.
I've worked with her for over an hour …
         ….and….
         ….She's learning!

Do you how many times we've gone over these concepts?
Do you know how little she retained?
Do you know how many years it has been for this thirty year old
woman…?
          ….how many fruitless attempts to obtain her treasured GED

Then…
         She walked into my classroom after a long absence
               And announced…
         "I'm on medication."
She is actually learning now.
The coveted prize is in her grasp.

My heart is filled.
I feel gratitude—for her
   For me.
Thanks and relief flood my mind
She is finally able to learn.

NELLIE

When Nellie walked into our class
With pain-wracked body on meds
    We decided to nurture her.
She learned very little through the fog that kept her in comfort,
      But she could soak in our care and concern.
        Sometimes the soul has to be mended before the mind can
        learn.

Her daycare followed a very structured timetable.
      Sometimes Nellie was late;
        They asked her to leave.
      No one could convince them to bend a little.

Nellie, dejected and hurt, went on her way.

I picked up the paper today.
      Nellie was in there….
        ….in the obituaries.
The 35 year old mother of two had given up on life.
      She had chosen suicide.
The scarred young lady was at peace…
      Now her children can carry her scars with them.

Oh, I wonder….
      ….What we all could do if we would show more compassion?
Nellie will never know.
      May death bring peace to this precious soul.

PACKING

This is the last day.
As I pack up the books that represent nine years of educating adults
I reminisce.

The awkward, beautiful souls of hundreds of Adult Basic Education
 students
       Have filled my life with so much loveliness.
These humble people who felt like failures
       Because they could not read
         Or did not finish school
Know how to say thank you,
       Remember that other people hurt,
         Relish the moment…
           …and know how to live.
After working hard for months to accomplish their goals,
They come to *me* with thanks and adoration
When they should be thanking ***themselves***.

We have laughed, cried, studied, played, partied and mourned.
We have struggled, failed, tried again, succeeded…
       …then we've begun over and over again
Until the goals have been met.

Today I move into administration
And though I will not be able to touch my students personally
       I will still be helping them follow dreams.
I will still celebrate their successes and mourn their losses.

This is a sad and happy,
wonderful and poignant day.
This very last, first day in my life.

SECTION II

LEARNING COMMUNITIES

Ana Maria at Graduation, Voices from the Earth; Photographer Deborah Wilson.

CHAPTER 15

A TEACHER'S VISUAL REFLECTION ON WOMEN AND LITERACY

Sally S. Gabb

In our very visual world of television, film and computer screen, many adult learners have never learned to enter the world of fiction through text, but can relate well to visual narrative. This graphic novella is both an expression of my own early teaching experience with women, and a potential tool for instruction.

Since the 1960's, the terms picture novel or graphic novel have been used to describe cartoon narratives for adult audiences. The term was first used with the complex super hero, mystery and gothic visual narratives of the 1950's and 60's. In 1950, St. John Publications produced the digest-sized, adult-oriented picture novel *It Rhymes with Lust* by Arnold Drake and Leslie Waller (1950). The graphic narrative is a film noir and pulp fiction influenced story about steel town life starring a scheming, manipulative redhead named Rust. Promoted as an original full-length novel by its publisher, this graphic story led to other similar publications, and by the 1970's, the term graphic novel was born (Norman Rockwell Museum, n.d.).

Many adult literacy instructors have utilized comic strips as a tool for developing reading imagination. The story-in-pictures concept can enable

Empowering Women Through Literacy: Views From Experience, pp. 81–86
Copyright © 2009 by Information Age Publishing

newer readers to make the transition from a visual/pictorial orientation to engagement in print narrative. As a new teacher in the early 1970's, I first resisted using what I considered comic books, but found that using picture stories could inspire discussion of such concepts as plot, setting and character development, which I could then apply to narrative text.

In the 1980's, I was a teacher for a women's adult education project at the Providence, Rhode Island Opportunities Industrialization Center (OIC). With other teachers and the women in this program, I developed a curriculum for the General Educational Development (GED) reading test preparation program based on a picture story-to-text process. Using comics, photos or pictures from magazines, the students developed story lines. They presented their stories to the class, describing the story line, the characters, the setting and the conclusion. Each student then wrote out his or her story. This proved to be an exciting sharing and concept development process.

The graphic novella presented here describes my own experience teaching women: how the amazing women in my adult education classes have taught me about both the fears and the strengths of women returning to school for basic education. This story can also can be used in the picture story-to-text process to inspire picture stories among students, or used directly as text. An instructor many eliminate the captions, asking students to insert their own. In addition, students can be encouraged to write out the story as text, describing characters, moods, and events of the picture story.

In our visual world, this medium can be the bridge for new readers, using the strengths of both visual and verbal expression.

REFERENCES

Drake, A., & Waller, L. (1950). *It rhymes with lust*. New York: St. John Publications, Inc.

Norman Rockwell Museum Source Material. (n.d.). *LitGraphic: The world of the graphic novel*. Retrieved October 12, 2008, from http://www.tfaoi.com/aa/7aa/7aa971.htm

Artwork by Sally S. Gabb.

Figure 15.1.   Fabella and Fiona.

Artwork by Sally S. Gabb.

Figure 15.2.   Fabella and Fiona.

Artwork by Sally S. Gabb.

Figure 15.3.   Fabella and Fiona.

Artwork by Sally S. Gabb.

Figure 15.4.   Fabella and Fiona.

CHAPTER 16

READING AGAINST THE ODDS

African American Women, Literacy, and Transformation

Jaye Jones

In describing the inspiration for her poignant narrative *The Bluest Eye*, Toni Morrison once said: "If there is a book you really want to read but it hasn't been written yet, then you must write it." As the largest not-for-profit provider of free adult education services in Illinois, Literacy Chicago was similarly motivated to develop a program that would address the unique and unmet needs of the primarily female and African American clientele it served. Though many of the students were actively engaged in the more skills-based adult literacy classes the agency offered, it had become increasingly clear to both staff and volunteers that something was missing. Students were not showing gains on standardized outcome measures—a situation that left many frustrated and discouraged. And more importantly, the skills centered curriculum didn't appear to be encouraging students to more critically reflect on their learning and their experiences. Indeed, a significant majority of the students were facing personal and emotional concerns that were rooted in negative and demeaning messages that they had received throughout their lives as a result of their

Empowering Women Through Literacy: Views From Experience, pp. 87–95
Copyright © 2009 by Information Age Publishing
All rights of reproduction in any form reserved.

academic struggles and myriad other traumas, including domestic violence, addiction and incarceration. Recognizing the impact that the inter-
section of racism, sexism and classism had had on these women's lives
suggested that a more comprehensive and sensitive learning experience
was required.

The development of a yearlong semi-structured reading discussion
group entitled Reading Against the Odds (RAO) was the outgrowth of this
commitment to an adult literacy curriculum that supported the academic,
personal and interpersonal growth of African American female students.
The narratives of Toni Morrison, Zora Neale Hurston, Maya Angelou and
Gloria Naylor provided the foundation for an innovative learning experience that was challenging, intellectually stimulating, and embedded in
the African American female experience. Involvement in community
activities and critical dialogue around the issues raised by experiences in
the group were also utilized to strengthen learners' skills and facilitate a
shift in their perceptions about themselves as both readers and producers
of knowledge. Though the works chosen are considered difficult for even
experienced readers, RAO was committed to the notion that with
thoughtful supports and accommodations adult literacy students could
capably engage with demanding texts. Indeed, the notion of "reading
against the odds" related to the idea that as learners these students were
challenging conventional understandings about their abilities and also
that they are actively engaging with a body of literature generated by
women whose literary insights have been historically marginalized.

The theories of Paulo Freire (1970/1993) and bell hooks (1994) also
provided a frame for incorporating pedagogical practices that supported
a transformative and engaged educational experience. Centering the
notion of education as a practice of freedom meant that the group not
only honored the learners' narratives, but also actively encouraged them
to reflect on connections between their experiences and the themes raised
in the texts and discussions (Freire, 1970/1993). These dialogical conversations would encourage the women to both unearth and question the
structural bases of oppression; a critical process that would highlight their
own strengths and generate ideas about ways they could collectively
demolish barriers that limited their growth, progress and success.

Literacy Chicago sought support from the American Association of
University Women (AAUW) community grants program to fund RAO.
The grant program's mission to "promote education and equity for
women and girls" meshed with the theoretical foundations of the group
and Literacy Chicago's commitment to utilizing a unique, community-
centered approach with a culturally and socially censured population of
women. Funds from AAUW provided the students with books; allowed the
program to purchase art supplies and audiovisual materials and provided

access to community events that supplemented and encouraged learning and discussion. These diverse activities highlighted the critical idea of literacies—the fact that there are a variety of ways to gain and impart knowledge—while strengthening adult literacy practitioners' knowledge about best practices with this population.

STRUCTURE OF THE GROUP

Reading Against the Odds began in August 2007 and met twice a week for two and one-half hours in a classroom located at the Literacy Chicago main office in downtown Chicago. The first weekly session focused on reading and/or listening while the second session emphasized (a) discussion (b) a creative/written activity (e.g., art project, journaling) (c) cultural event (e.g., museum visit) and/or (d) presentation by an invited speaker that reinforced themes raised by the book.

The literature was thematically arranged across four quarters and the themes and books were reflective of a progression toward increasing awareness and self-efficacy. In the first quarter, *The Bluest Eye* by Toni Morrison (1970) introduced the theme of exploration, which emphasized the impact of childhood trauma on development, and notions of history and memory as they influence the perceptions of individuals and communities. The second book, *Their Eyes Were Watching God* by Zora Neale Hurston (1937/2006) focused on the theme of insight, which highlighted self-reflection as a source of knowledge and the complex often painful emotions raised by contemplative practices. Maya Angelou's (1986) *All God's Children Need Traveling Shoes* introduced the theme of growth and concerns such as taking thoughtful risks to stimulate personal development and diverse experiences of personal and community evolution. The final book, *The Women of Brewster Place* by Gloria Naylor (1983) reflected on the theme of perseverance and issues such as overcoming setbacks and unconventional notions of strength and power. Clearly, the books could be identified with more than one theme; however, the concentration on one central issue provided a useful frame for reflection.

Over the year that it met, RAO served nearly 30 women who ranged in age from their early 20's to their late 60's. An average of 10 women attended the weekly sessions and attendance was quite consistent considering the responsibilities they faced—three women attended RAO for the entire year. The reading level of the women entering at the start of the group ranged from below first grade to 7th grade; with a mean of approximately third grade (which was similar to the average level of all students in the adult literacy program). Two female volunteers of African descent were the primary facilitators of the group; they co-led reading activities and discussions, accompanied students on visits to community events and helped evaluate the impact of the group.

Transformation: Strengthening Skills, Nurturing Growth and Fostering Connections

"Every book I read … inspires me to read": Reading Level & Confidence. Overall growth in reading skills was assessed through administration of the Slosson Oral Reading Test (SORT), which has been used as an evaluation tool by Literacy Chicago for several years. The test is easy to administer and provides evaluators with information concerning a student's word recognition and reading level. As noted earlier, the average reading level of students entering the group was approximately third grade (i.e., 3.0). At three months, the mean reading level had increased to fourth grade and examinations suggest that these changes were statistically significant. Though an examination of the year-end results are still pending, individual students have shown remarkable gains over time. For example, one woman's reading level rose from .07 to 1.2 while another student started at 3.6 and ended at 6.4. Significant increases of this magnitude were not present prior to the implementation of RAO, which strongly suggests that the learners benefited from the educational support the group provided.

Reading confidence was assessed using a 7-item scale adapted from the National Foundation for Education Research (Sharp, Blackmore, Kendall, Greene, Keys, Macauley, Schagen & Yeshanew, 2003). Results indicated that despite expressing some increased nervousness when reading, students experienced an improvement across time in feeling that they were good readers, liking to read by themselves and to others and their belief that they could effectively decode and comprehend reading materials. These shifts in thinking suggested that students were developing a better sense of their abilities and that they were responding positively to the challenges posed by the texts. Students requested that the facilitators develop a list of vocabulary words to help them more effectively navigate the reading passages. Students spent time diligently breaking words down and integrating them in their daily conversations. More students also began to ask to read aloud as they focused less on how they were being perceived. As one student noted, "For one thing, I [used to read] real slow and all of a sudden, I'm reading a little bit!"

Gains in reading level and confidence were associated with an increasing level of engagement in the literary and social world. Several students indicated that they were reading more in general—other books, newspapers and magazines—and were motivated by their success in the group to push themselves harder. One participant proudly declared:

"Every book I read...inspires me to read." Because the students were able to keep their books, they developed an almost emotional connection to the physical text—they wrote and underlined things that were important to them, bought colorful bookmarks, held the books with reverence and described how they would create a personal library. The dog-eared tomes embodied their commitment and follow through, "I normally start something [and] never finish." Said one long term group member, "and [now] I'm finishing."

"I learned some things about myself": Personal Growth & Healing. For many women, profound changes in how they begin to see themselves as women of color, as single mothers, as survivors of abuse, and/or women in recovery occurred as a result of their involvement in RAO. One woman who had overcome substance abuse noted, "If you're really into the class you can grow. I've [grown] since I've been here." Her comments not only illustrated how the women experienced change, but also highlighted how group members utilized the group process. Women in the group were engaged, and their passion and emotional connection to the stories, characters, and concerns resulted in constructive deliberations regarding the African American female experience. For instance, a heated conversation regarding rape in *The Women of Brewster Place* led to a rejection of sexist and racist ideas that make light of the sexual victimization of Black women and provided a space for a more women-affirming notion of sexuality.

As they gained a better understanding of their strengths and limitations, one learner revealed that she was being more "honest" with herself and described feeling less afraid to express how she really felt. In the past, she had kept her feelings under wraps, but through her involvement in the group she had begun to open up more. This movement toward self-revelation encouraged many women to set new goals and take a more active role in their educational and personal development. One woman left the group to enter a community college program, while another developed a plan that would help her pursue a career as a nurse. The texts also provided some women with a way to understand and learn more about themselves and their history. Lessons about the blues, the Harlem Renaissance, the power of the media, and HIV/AIDS not only supplemented the formal narratives, but encouraged multi-layered reflection on the oppression, contributions and resistance of African American women.

The subjects of abuse and trauma—a topic that resonated with many of the women—were central in all of the books read. These discussions were difficult because of the complex emotions associated with issues like corporal punishment, domestic violence and sexual assault. Research on connections between trauma, violence and literacy suggest that literacy workers must be sensitive to how women themselves frame their experiences, and acknowledge the impact of trauma on their educational past and re-entry (Horsman, 1990). Many women appeared to use the characters in the text as a way to both affirm and distance themselves from painful experiences. This process seemed to help some of them begin to sort out and integrate distressing events without becoming emotionally overwhelmed. The pains, joys and triumphs of characters like Pecola Breedlove, Janie Starks and Mattie Michael were a bridge to passionate and healing dialogues about raising children in a racist world, the pressures to conform in romantic partnerships and the anguish of heartbreaking relationships with female family members.

"I love it because we don't look down on one another": Interpersonal connections. The supportive environment of the group allowed many women to feel comfortable and take risks—there was strong sense that others would not negatively judge individuals. One woman, who clearly struggled to read, consistently volunteered to read aloud and other women in the group cheered her on and patiently offered help as she tackled difficult passages. Other women talked about hiding their inability to read for years, and how important it was for them to find others who had similar stories. One woman who had been very reticent to even enter the adult literacy program attended the group for the entire year. She said very little during classroom discussions, but her consistent presence was a testament to the bond she felt with the group. Indeed, this sense of relational connection formed the basis for a camaraderie that often filled the classroom with laughter and tears, as women joked with one another, offered sometimes blunt advice and reveled in a space where they felt valued and respected.

Group members began to develop a more critical, collective consciousness as they used the relationship created by the group to pose thought-provoking questions and build a more global understanding of their experiences. *All Gods Children Need Traveling Shoes* (1986), which focused on Maya Angelou's experiences in 1960s Ghana, stimulated reflection on the historical, macro-level aspects of oppression as well as the power differentials present in intraracial relationships. Though most women did not identify as feminist, they acknowledged a shared experience of sexism within the black community that helped to further illuminate the racism, classism and neoliberalism that also shaped their lives. The cultivation of this cooperative voice was crucial in helping group members outline ways they could take action and confront repressive cultural arrangements. For many, engagement with the campaign to elect Barack Obama as president provided an entrée into a political world that had routinely diminished their concerns.

This strong commitment to one another also resulted in women making sure that their group mates were cared for outside of the classroom. A young woman with special needs was especially embraced and numbers were exchanged so that women could follow-up with one another if they or family members became ill. Older women became like mothers to younger woman, and at times provided soothing comfort when they became frustrated or overwhelmed. This is not to say that no one got angry or upset. However, dissent did not necessarily lead to disconnection; providing a space for all women to articulate their concerns was an essential part of RAO's mission.

Facilitating Relationship: Promoting Transformation

The desire to facilitate RAO was embedded in a commitment to educating women of color adult literacy students and helping them fulfill their dreams. As a college student and a social worker, the facilitators recognized the importance of education, discussion and healing and the need for African American women to experience an environment where their stories were de-marginalized. Significantly, the role of facilitator and not teacher was stressed since it was believed that the women were the experts concerning their needs and situations. Listening was central. And though the facilitators would propose potential links or associations, the goal was to support and build upon the women's ideas. In fact, disagreements often prompted dynamic discussions on meaning-making processes.

The majority of the women expressed appreciation for the work of the facilitators, or described feeling blessed by their presence. One woman highlighted how "[the facilitators] help us a lot in reading and understanding our own culture, where we come from," a statement that suggested that recognizing and exploring culture was crucial. As women of African descent, the facilitators were invested in addressing the intersectionality that characterized the lives of women of color as they raised their families, struggled with addiction and faced unique challenges as adult literacy students who were also women and of color. Many women talked about educators who had given up on them or who had not invested time in helping them learn when they were having difficulties. Their experience with facilitators who believed in their capabilities and encouraged them to challenge themselves resulted in a shift in thinking that altered aspirations.

The Larger Impact and the Future: Expanding the Odds

This woman-centered and women-positive reading discussion group strengthened African American female adult literacy reading skills and commitment to knowledge-building practices while also enhancing their personal growth and fostering affirming relationships with other women. For many women, RAO also cemented the notion that they could critically engage with the world and be *creators* of knowledge. This sense of purpose trickled down to their families, as one participant noted: "I share with my grandkids and I tell them, it doesn't matter how old you are never give up, because you can do anything you put your mind to." This drive to achieve and support the accomplishments of others broadened RAO's impact. As they witnessed the transformations that took place in the lives of their mothers, grandmothers and aunts; daughters, granddaughters and nieces were encouraged to similarly expand their horizons.

Despite fiscal struggles, there are plans to continue and expand RAO at Literacy Chicago. The identified academic and socioemotional gains suggest that a commitment to critical and engaged pedagogical practices can promote agentic actions that highlight the capacity and power of African American female adult literacy students. RAO has also become a vital component of Literacy Chicago's adult literacy curriculum. At a culminating event to celebrate the year, several students talked about how materials and insights from the group had enhanced their individual tutoring sessions, while staff members and volunteers shared how the affirming spirit that sustained RAO had affected the entire agency. "As we keep on coming," one learner optimistically noted, "It will get bigger and bigger." And one day, just like Toni Morrison, they will be writing the books they want to read themselves.

ACKNOWLEDGMENTS

The author would like to acknowledge the support of the AAUW Educational Foundation as well as students, staff and volunteers at Literacy Chicago, especially J. Porter, A. Egwiekhor, V. Hemphill and A. Stoll.

REFERENCES

Angelou, M. (1986). *All God's children need traveling shoes*. New York: Random House.

Freire, P. (1970/1993). *Pedagogy of the oppressed*. New York: Continuum.

hooks, b. (1994). *Teaching to transgress: Education as the practice of freedom*. New York: Routledge.

Horsman, J. (1990). *Something in my mind besides the everyday: Women and literacy*. Toronto: Women's Press.

Hurston, Z. N. (1937/2006). *Their eyes were watching God*. New York: HarperCollins.

Morrison, T. (1970). *The bluest eye*. New York: Penguin Books.

Naylor, G. (1983). *The women of Brewster Place*. New York: Penguin Books.

Sharp, C., Blackmore, J., Kendall, L., Greene, K., Keys, W., Macauley, A., Schagen, I., & Yeshanew, T. (2003). *Playing for success: An evaluation of the fourth year* (National Foundation for Education Research Rep. RR402). Nottingham, United Kingdom: DfES Publications.

CHAPTER 17

COURAGE, CHOICE, CHANGE

Gestalt Therapy Techniques Within the Adult Literacy Classroom

Cheryl Reid

Step inside. The walls surrounding the women's learning space have affirming messages to be taken in, consciously and unconsciously. Learners are reminded, "My best is good enough; I know that I am good at certain things; There are no mistakes, only lessons; I am taking control of my learning," and "I give myself space to dream."

It is fascinating to witness the varied reactions to these affirmations. Learners that come into the program with a personal belief that they are doing great things with their life will nod with conviction when reading the messages. This type of new learner has not been common for me. Much more frequently, I meet learners that have been told they are stupid and won't amount to anything. They tend to initially read the affirmations with hesitation and skepticism. It is obvious in their tone of voice and facial expressions that these positive phrases are unfamiliar and definitely not a certainty to accept right away. In Gestalt terms, I am challenging their beliefs by presenting an alternate point of view to consider each time they enter the learning space (Rosner, 1987).

Empowering Women Through Literacy: Views From Experience, pp. 97–104
Copyright © 2009 by Information Age Publishing

The creator of Gestalt Therapy, Fritz Perls, used frustration to challenge clients.

> The experience of frustration produces mobilization. This will impel the individual to break through his or her phobic and paralyzed behavior and become sufficiently aroused to reach out for what he or she wants. In other words, the client will experience self support. (Rosner, 1987, p. 103)

As both a therapist and a literacy worker, I can trust that on some level, whether wholeheartedly or within a tiny part of herself, the learner that walks into the literacy program with a low view of herself is open to experiencing something different in her life. I trust that we can both allow ourselves to be open to her potential. I challenge myself with assisting women in looking at herself from another point of view. A view that believes she is capable of much more than she may have been told by others in her life.

In the world of Gestalt Therapy, the beliefs and values that we have swallowed without consideration are called introjects. The process is frequently compared to eating. We need to chew on ideas to see if they agree with us.

> If you feel nauseated and allow yourself to throw up, you'll get it out of your system. If not, you will either succeed in painfully digesting it, or it will poison you.... One way to learn to become aware of your introjects is to listen to what you are talking about when you say "I should..." or "I shouldn't..." or "I must" or "I mustn't." (Rosner, 1987, pp. 53-54)

The family environment in childhood leaves most of us overflowing with introjects. Many of the beliefs and values that we pick up serve us well in life. For example, most of us would agree, "Everyone should brush their teeth daily," is a good belief to adopt. On the other hand, "You can't do anything right!" is not such a wise introject. Sadly, for educators in adult environments, it is all too common to see the lasting impact of what can be labeled negative introjects.

Over the past sixteen years, I have observed the harsh and self limiting introjects of countless learners in the literacy classroom. With great interest, I regularly note the impact of introjects on the learners' sense of self. My study and use of Gestalt techniques has made it possible to address the barriers to learning that these introjects have created. As part of our programming, I assist learners with recognizing their introjects and at times identifying where they originated. As well, I provide opportunities for learners to 'try on' different beliefs and values.

To heighten awareness when a learner is being particularly tough on herself, I will ask her to repeat her harsh self-judgments while making contact with another learner or myself. I am interested in the woman's reaction to herself when she makes statements like, "Of course I got it wrong," in full awareness. This is a form of intentional frustration that can lead to a shift. Learners often have a distaste for this critic when it is given the full floor in our learning space. Frequently, they decide that the critic is not always correct and is in fact a voice from long ago. Peers can see how damaging the words are for their friends in those moments. As well, they regularly notice that the critical voice is similar to the one in their own minds. Learners are invited to offer supportive feedback for themselves and peers.

Experience has shown me that the encouraging voice is often unfamiliar to literacy learners. As a result, we build time into our program to learn what positive self talk and feedback to others sounds like. We practice it regularly and find that the efforts are well worth the time. The shift in how they speak to themselves and support each other has a huge, positive impact on both their openness and ability to learn new things.

As one learner wrote shortly after joining the literacy program, "I know that it hurts to say negative things about myself and it does not make me feel good. I made a vow to be nice to myself and not say anything bad anymore." This woman looks physically stronger after several months in the program. She carries herself with confidence—a tall spine and a look of assurance. Not only has her body language changed, her voice has changed. When we met, she often sounded like a timid six years old. Her voice suggested her lack of confidence, and she apologized repetitively. She sounded ready to be wrong. Once in a while, I hear the little girl come back, but most of the time, she now sounds like a woman determined to succeed.

In Gestalt, we highly value honoring the client with where she is in the moment.

> Gestalt theory is focused on the experience of contact that occurs in the here and now. It considers with interest the life space of teachers as well as students. It takes interest in the complexity of experience, without neglecting anything, but accepting and amplifying all that emerges. (Polito, 1997, p. 1)

To tell a learner that she is wrong to have her feelings is not only dismissive, it is potentially abusive. It is my practice to give space first, for what is present. I acknowledge the harshness of the language used by a learner that is feeling low. I show empathy for how painful it must be to carry around such negative beliefs. I may say, "It must be painful to believe that you will fail if you try anything new." I give space for that feedback to be absorbed and accepted by the learner. Having these moments of contact can be extremely healing for anyone. There may be no further work to do.

If it feels useful to take the process further, we might explore if there was a particular person who held this harsh belief about her. This awareness can be useful in separating the present moment from old experiences. The learner often realizes that the opinion of the voice from the past does not always belong with her now. That unsupportive person can be symbolically kicked out of the classroom on days when we recognize his or her unpleasant comments surfacing. Learners are often empowered by telling the person, "Get out of my life! I don't need to listen to you. You were wrong about me." Gestaltists call it a shift when a client begins to change their fixed way of looking at something. Simply identifying the voice can take away some of its power to discourage a learner in the present.

Another approach to potential shifting is to consider the voice of someone supportive and kind in the learner's past or present life. A current learner recalled a sweet aunt with this exercise. We have been able to call on the aunt for words of loving encouragement when harsh judgments show up in the classroom. I simply ask, "What would your aunt say to you right now?" Consistently, the woman smiles and offers a phrase like, "That was a great try. Look at the part you have already learned." It is wonderful to see the softening on the woman's face as she allows the kind words of support to carry more weight than the familiar critic in her head. In time, those warm words and feelings of support may become her own. I have witnessed this shift in attitude towards self many times.

The voice of a kind mother assists another learner when she notices herself being critical and feeling discouraged. She will hear the mother say, "That's OK. You can try again," when she is feeling challenged. The learner shared, "It is much easier to calm down and focus on my learning. I feel so happy about this gentle voice. I have learned to be nicer to me by listening to it." This woman has been able to let go of the harsh introjections and welcome a warm, supportive point of view.

One particular woman has opened herself to the risk of learning through repetition of empowering thoughts. The phrases on the walls of the classroom have helped her so much that she reads them out loud to others in the group when she hears negative self-talk. She will let people know that she doesn't allow those comments in our room. Fortunately, her feistiness is met with amusement and warm agreement in the group.

Our 'affirmation junkie' has taken her positive energy out of the classroom in many ways. She is encouraging a friend to return to school, and she is making sure that she is treated with respect. Recently, she made a formal complaint to her landlord about the condition of her apartment. When he did not take action to improve the building, she reported him and had an inspector come in to ensure that repairs were made for her health and safety. She glowed with pride while sharing her story. This learner said, "In the past, I would have just sworn and given up." She didn't believe that her voice held power. She didn't have faith that she could bring about positive change by speaking up for her herself and writing a letter of complaint. Thankfully, those beliefs have changed. Her experience was a moment to celebrate.

An introject that is particularly common when entering our program is the belief that you shouldn't say or do things to upset others, even when that means personal suffering. As one woman shared,

> Before I came to the learning center, I remember that I didn't have the guts to express my opinion in front of people. I was very concerned what other people thought of me. I was fearful they might laugh at me or they might disagree with me. I just followed what other people were doing. If I was asked for a favor, I would agree even if I didn't want to do it. I felt that I didn't have my own voice.

This woman has had repeated opportunities with classmates and me to practice dealing with the anxiety of disagreement. The group debates hot topics and defends their points of view. The excitement of standing their ground empowers the women to try it outside of the classroom.

The woman quoted above reported a local transportation worker when she was not treated well on public transit this year. Prior to that, she reported a filing clerk to a manager after being treated without respect when she was getting her taxes completed at a community center. She was extremely proud of herself in both of these instances. The woman credits the practice of presenting her own voice in our learning space as giving her the courage to speak out in the community.

Activities such as debating foster the skill of supporting oneself rather than holding silence. Another way of developing self-empowerment has been through the ongoing negotiation of their curriculum. I have noticed that most women are not comfortable telling me what they want when they enter the literacy program. There is the introject that they should do whatever the teacher feels is best for them. At times, I will work with the process of intentional frustration to encourage learners to make themselves heard. I might go along with the request of one learner for a lesson, even if I know that several women may not be interested in the activity. They notice that those that speak up often get what they want in our space. I might drag on with a lesson to see how long it will take for learners to request a change. When a learner reaches the stage that she freely disagrees with classmates or myself regarding the agenda for the day and expresses her personal interests for lessons, I am delighted. We have a clear demonstration of identifying personal needs and requesting that they be filled. I love those moments, and I point them out to the group as something to celebrate.

Since telling people what they want on small day-to-day issues is a huge shift in behavior, it is predictable that many women hesitate to make their own decisions about the big choices in life. Most of the women attending the program that I work within are part of cultures that don't encourage females to make decisions about their lives. I recall asking a woman what she would like to do in the future. The woman teared up and needed a moment before she was able to speak. I asked her if she was OK. She smiled and replied, "No one has ever asked me what *I* wanted." What a pleasure it was for me to open the door for her to even consider that her opinion mattered. That woman taught me to treat questions related to goals and desires with much greater reverence. I'm more aware of the potential impact of asking a woman what she wants, of offering her a choice, of offering her the possibility of being responsible for her own life. It is a precious part of both Gestalt and literacy work.

Learning to listen to our body's wisdom is one of the many ways the women are encouraged to bring their whole selves to the classroom. Women at the learning center are invited to try gentle yoga movement and breathwork as tools for letting go of stress and improving concentration. Gestaltists and Yogis are aware of the wisdom we hold in our bodies rather than our brain. It is touching to see women begin to listen to their bodies and value what it has to say.

We explore how our treatment of our bodies is often a mirror of how we treat ourselves in other parts of our lives: Do we ignore how we feel and do whatever the crowd is doing? Do we rest when we need to? Do we give up quickly? Do we challenge ourselves in ways that are invigorating without being dangerous? Do we trust our bodies to be wise? One particular learner brought to my attention the power of simply inviting people to listen to their bodies. She was feeling very relaxed and content after taking good care of herself in her first yoga class. She told me, "I have never in my life even considered asking me body what it wanted." This possibility was exciting, and it was one that she welcomed.

Over time, listening to the body and giving it what it needs begins to be valued off of the yoga mat. I witness learners taking better care of themselves in the classroom. Thankfully, the introject that they should sit still in their chair and only take breaks when I schedule them begins to fall apart. The women suggest taking a yoga break when they need to release some tension in their body or refocus their mind. Even if the group doesn't follow, many learners will take personal stretch breaks to loosen up, stand when it is more comfortable and take short walks when they need to clear their mind. This development of self-care is a pleasure to observe.

Last year, a learner repeatedly showed anxiety about being seen as untrustworthy to return books from our library collection. Her need to prove her honesty seemed excessive. I asked her what was going on, and she became teary. My hunch was that there was some belief present that related to her past with someone else rather than her relationship with me. I let her know that I trust her with our resources, and I asked who in her past didn't trust her to be honest. It came out that she had frequently experienced prejudice in nearby shops. She shared stories of being watched carefully while shopping in stores. She knotted her bags before entering shops to decrease the chances of being seen as a thief. There were tears of sadness while recalling these experiences. They were followed by tears of relief for the present moment with me when I pointed out that I don't look at her with suspicious eyes. In my opinion, she didn't need to worry about being seen as a thief. It was healing for her to hear those words and trust them to be true. This woman noticeably softened with me that day. In that moment, she gave herself permission to be seen as trustworthy. Gratefully, this shift has lasted.

As learners begin to try new things and experience successes, I make a point of slowing those moments down. My intent is not only to provide a space for the women to feel the experience of success, but to also feel the experience of being seen by others in a moment of pride. Often, the experience is so unfamiliar that many women find it hard to tolerate. Tears of joy are frequent in our learning space. Tears of sadness are also welcomed as part of their healing. I have noticed that as the women's tolerance to be seen increases, their ability to take in positive introjects also increases. The learners expand the possibilities of how they see themselves in the world. Two key aspects of Gestalt work are providing people with the opportunity to be truly seen as well as experimenting with a new way of being. I have found using these techniques in the literacy classroom to be effective and exciting.

As the examples in this paper reveal, Gestalt methodologies complement the world of adult literacy. "Gestalt work discloses irrational introjections that have interfered with healthy learning processes and affords students an opportunity to put their thoughts and feelings in a perspective that is nourishing and self supportive for them." (Wolt, & Toman, 2005, p. 316)

In both Gestalt and literacy environments, the need to meet the client where she is at, to expose her to various opportunities, to remind her that she is in the driver's seat of her life and to encourage her to take control of it are all important pieces in the work. Through awareness and acceptance people are able to grow in many exciting ways.

Like Gestalt work, effective literacy work is about dealing with what is present in the moment. In my experience, having an intimate group of 6-8 women at a time in an environment where the members support each other's growth has been essential for success. Letting learners know that the program is about much more than reading and writing is also key. It is worth noting that Gestalt methodologies are being brought into other programs:

> Principles and techniques derived from Gestalt therapy are being applied in a variety of educational settings internationally. Initial investigations of the results of these applications have noted significant increases in teachers' self-knowledge, sense of personal control, flexibility, and attention to the "here and now." Additionally, students ... have shown significant increases in a number of areas, including self-esteem and self-awareness. (Philips, 1976, p. 1)

For me, it has always been difficult to determine which came first – the self confidence or the literacy skills of learners. It resembles the chicken or the egg debate. Through observation, I have come to believe that they develop in unison. As a result, I am grateful to be able to bring both my Gestalt therapy training and my teaching skills into the classroom.

For literacy programs that are choosing to serve the whole learner, the Gestalt Institute of Toronto has a marketing byline that they may wish to borrow, "Courage, Choice, Change." This phrase lets learners know that they are walking into an environment of excitement; they are coming into a space that presents new possibilities; they are entering a program that encourages empowerment.

REFERENCES

Phillips, M. (1976). The application of Gestalt principles in classroom teaching. *Group & Organization Management, 1*(1), 82-98.

Polito, M. (1997). *How Gestalt theory can facilitate teaching and learning processes.* Lecture at the 10th Scientific Convention of the Society for Gestalt Theory and its Applications. Vienna, Austria. [Abstract]. Retrieved November 21, 2008, from http://gestalttheory.net/conv/polito.html

Rosner, J. (1987). *Peeling the onion: Gestalt theory and methodology.* Toronto: Gestalt Institute of Toronto.

Wolt, A. L., & Toman, S. M. (2005). *Gestalt therapy: History, theory, and practice.* Thousand Oaks, CA: Sage.

CHAPTER 18

PORTRAITS AND POSSIBILITIES

Empowerment Through Literacy

Elite Ben-Yosef

I want a language that I can lean on and that can lean on me,
that asks me to bear witness and that I can ask to bear witness,
to what power there is in us to overcome this cosmic isolation.
—Mahmoud Darwish (Darwish in Rich, 2001)

Hope House is a recovery home for women; a safe space that provides the residents with their physical needs, allowing them to work on recovery through outside programs, meetings, counseling and job training. The women arrive after coming out of mental institutions, as recovering addicts or after incarceration, and their stay is temporary: they are free to leave at will, though most stay for several months or longer, as they work on getting their lives back on track. Most of the women living in Hope House belong to groups on the bottom rungs of the social and economic ladders: women of poverty, released prisoners, substance abusers whose lives and families have fallen apart, women whose children have been taken away by court orders, women suffering from mental illness, abused

Empowering Women Through Literacy: Views From Experience, pp. 105–111
Copyright © 2009 by Information Age Publishing
All rights of reproduction in any form reserved.

women, women of color. These women's voices have long been silenced by personal and social criticism and labeling, and they are generally power-less in defining their own identity and/or as agents in their own lives.

For several years I have been working at Hope House in a weekly liter-acy class. Appropriating a Freirian approach, we critically read the world and the word through dialogues and readings of printed as well as visual texts (documentaries, commercial films, plays, art work) and through cre-ative activities that promote reflection and further discussions (Freire & Macedo, 1987). We question, talk and write about our lives in attempts to "re-vision" them, as Adrienne Rich calls "the act of looking back, of seeing with fresh eyes, of entering an old text from a new, critical direction" (Gelpi & Gelpi, 1993, p. 167). In our discussions, art projects and creative writing, class participants negotiate social positions trying to reposition themselves within their worlds, striving to communicate and connect to "the lost community" which they are trying to rejoin (Rich, 2001). In our work together over time we have managed to create a safe and respectful space where we listen to and support each other and where we all can talk openly about our lives, learn to see events from new perspectives and imagine possibilities of change (Ben-Yosef, Forthcoming).

The circumstances of my students' lives have determined that our classes focus on pedagogy of possibility where "the agenda is to create practices that encourage, make possible, and enable the realization of differentiated human capacities" (Simon, 1987, p. 138). We do this by critiquing and interrogating current realities and existing knowledge, followed by opening up the thinking to expand what it means to be human and to contribute to the establishment of a just and compassion-ate community. Such a pedagogy involves a process of self-empower-ment by allowing voice to those who have been silenced, providing opportunities of sharing authority, at the very least, in their own lives (Simon, 1987).

Raising student voices begins with letting them take authority of their own life stories: becoming aware of the powers they have to define their own reality (rather than allowing social and cultural conventions to dictate it, usually in derogatory terms), telling their own stories (presenting themselves rather than being represented by others), valuing themselves, their lives and experiences (rather than buying into the paradigms of out-siders), and dreaming and expecting better. Much of our work is done by focusing on language and its inherent power as a resource that can work for the students as they appropriate it for raising their voices and stand-ing up for themselves. We aim for rekindling hope and vitalizing transfor-mation processes (Christensen, 2000).

SELF-PORTRAITS

One of the ways we work together toward these goals is through self-portraiture (in a broad sense of the concept): different ways by which our class participants present and represent themselves, their lives and their experiences in writing and in art (some may call this narrative art). Sara Lawrence-Lightfoot wrote about portraiture as a method of inquiry and documentation through which it is possible to gain understanding of the "richness, complexity and dimensionality of human experience" in its rightful context, while "conveying the perspectives of the people who are negotiating those experiences" (Lawrence-Lightfoot & David, 1997, p.3). Rather than mirror the subject (something an outsider might do), a self-portrait captures the person's essence, and this can be accomplished with words as well as with art media. Self-portraiture as a methodology resists generalization and stems from a positive, humanistic perspective, giving voice to peoples' experiences through the medium of narrative. Engaging in self-portraiture in a group is also a community building process, as we come to understand other peoples' experiences (Lawrence-Lightfoot & Davis, 1997).

When we create a self-portrait and tell our own story it is an act of self-representation: *we* decide on the experiences we are ready to expose, *we* illuminate our lives and portray our sense of self and show ourselves as *we* wish to be seen and known. We become the subjects of our own lives (Lawless, 2001). We tell a story of a unique personal experience in an authentic, original voice, a narrative that is intimate and true in the sense of being our own. The process of creating a self-portrait is a learning experience on its own: we learn about the possibility of seeing ourselves from different perspectives and that human beings are multifaceted; we find our power in making choices, and we open up our imagination; we practice using our voice and try out/on possibilities. Telling our own stories can challenge versions told by others, those who don't know or don't care to know us as individuals in both our struggles and in our successes. And by sharing our stories with each other in a space that is open and accepting, we create bonds and cross borders into each other's experiences, growing our understanding of differences and commonalities.

The Work

Dina rarely talked about herself. She had been a substance abuser, spent time in prison and her son was being raised by her sister and brother-in-law. She had trouble patiently working her way toward recovery when she would get her son back, and was thrown out of Hope House twice for breaking her curfew. She was trying hard but was battling many demons and during our classes she was mostly listening, seldom speaking. One day she produced the following self-portrait in the form of a collage which tells the story of her journey from silence to voice (Figure 18.1). It is a self-portrait in the sense that it tells about her unique experience and captures the essence of this experience: a struggle to overcome a personal obstacle with a successful outcome. The narrative aspect of the portrait is a full story with a beginning (silence), middle (a learning process) and end (finding voice); with a character who goes on a journey, finds new understandings and changes her life; building up to a climax ("I learned"), and with great sense of tension between the two sides of the collage in terms of both the written and the visual language; a tension that is resolved by reading the written words. The medium of portraiture has given Dina's voice a stage, illuminating her struggle and newly found personal power. It is a statement of self-worth and self-respect.

Figure 18.1.   Dina's Collage.

Later, Dina wrote a self-portrait that includes a dream of a possible future:

I am Dina. I live in a sober house.
I say to myself every day that
I can live a normal life like

I once shared with my son and family.
I hope my family notices how hard
I'm working to get back their love that
I neglected for so long.
I dream that one day soon
I can have my life back together again.
I am Dina. I live in a sober house.

Dina's voice rings loud and clear in this portrait: she describes past problems, present struggles and her belief in the possibility of overcoming and transforming life. She is telling her version of her life's story, portraying herself as a woman who has taken responsibility for and is actively involved with changing her life ("I say to myself," "I can," "I'm working," "I neglected," "I dream"). This text describes a quest for transformation and the hope it can be achieved through a newly acquired inner strength.

Looking, Looking, Looking **Daughter** working, working Job hunting Car shopping, **Hoping** sweet friendly funny animated best friend **Linda, Linda, LINDA,** Best, Best friend **Flo, Flo, Flo,** sister and buddy! Happiness is **Tracy, Brian,** TRACY, **Brian** Love Cats and Dogs Favorite colors Black and Pink "No drinking 19 months" "Happy 19 months" Can sleep again! No more nightmares! Beach, Beach, Beach! Exercise a l ot! **Brownies,** Brownies, Brownies **Pizza,** Pizza, Pizza! Love my Computer!!!!!!!!! Knowledge is Power! Keep on Learning! Learn new things Hope is getting my own **apartment**! Getting my own car! Miss my mom! Love my two **Dads**! Not lonely anymore! Happy at last! Want my own cat! (Badly) Hoping to stay Happy and content! Prefer cool weather! Love music, especially rock and roll, some heavy metal! Love computer graphics! Can never get enough! **Appreciative** and Humble, finally! Awake from a life that was better to sleep through! Love camping, Hiking, Sea World, Fire Places and being able to gaze at the stars and appreciate them. Best of all I am **grateful!** Being able to live in a world I used to be very afraid of facing! **Life is good**!

Figure 18.2.   Lauraine's Self Portrait.

And then we created another kind of self-portrait: the list. Lauraine's self portrait (Figure 18.2 above) is a combination of print and visual symbols (the original was in color). She describes the present, which is going well for her, with many exclamation marks indicating excitement and strong, positive emotions. Yet she includes hints of her journey and struggles getting to this point ("No drinking 19 months," "Can sleep again," "No more nightmares"). Here too we find a full story in which the difficult beginning is inferred (substance abuse), a trying journey to being able to live in and face the world is mentioned (sleeplessness, nightmares, loneliness, fear) and an end, the present, which is the main focus of the work, where Lauraine says she is awake to life, has close relationships and friends that make her happy and has come to a point where "Life is good." The overall picture one gets is of a woman with a strong sense of self-worth, empowered to face life and do what is necessary to move ahead (job hunting, car hunting, learning). A woman who has found her voice and is unafraid of raising it.

CONCLUSION

"The impulse to create begins—often terribly and fearfully—in a tunnel of silence," writes Adrienne Rich (2001, p. 150). Breaking the silence and energizing a process of self empowerment have been our main goals in the literacy classes at Hope House. Self-portraiture was appropriated in our work because of its flexibility as a tool that lends itself to storytelling from multiple perspectives, gives the artists/writers a vehicle for voice as well as authority over their own narrative, allowing them to reestablish themselves as subjects of their own lives. The ability to review their lives "with fresh eyes" from a new, different and critical perspective that foregrounds agency, self-worth and the possible, infuses power and hope into the process of transformation that the women at Hope House are working hard to achieve.

REFERENCES

Ben-Yosef, E. (Forthcoming). Today I am proud of myself: Telling stories and revaluing lives. In D. Caracciolo & A. Mungai (Eds.), *In the spirit of Ubuntu.* Netherlands: Springer.

Ben-Yosef, E. (2008). Students finding voice in a college classroom: Reflections on a teaching/learning journey. *Curriculum and Teaching, 23*(1), 73-88.

Christensen, L. (2000). *Reading, writing and rising up.* Milwaukee, WI: Rethinking Schools, Ltd.

Darwish, M. (1995). *Memory for forgetfulness, August Beirut, 1982.* Berkeley, CA: University of California Press.

Freire, P., & Macedo, D. (1987). *Literacy: Reading the word and the world.* Westport, CT: Bergin & Garvey.

Gelpi, B. C., & Gelpi, A. (Eds.). (1993). *Adrienne Rich's poetry and prose.* New York: Norton & Co.

Lawless, E. J. (2001). *Women escaping violence: Empowerment through narrative.* Columbia, MO: University of Missouri Press.

Lawrence-Lightfoot, S., & Davis, J.H. (1997). *The art and science of portraiture*. San-Francisco: Jossey-Bass Publishers.

Rich, A. (2001). *Arts of the possible*. New York: Norton & Co.

Simon, R.I. (1987). Empowerment as a pedagogy of possibility. *Language Arts, 64*(4), 370-382.

CHAPTER 19

CULTIVATING INTIMACY IN THE CLASSROOM AT THE KING COUNTY JAIL

Kit Gruver

I am an artist by nature, a teacher by trade. I am always seeking a deeper connection with the significant elements of my life: my relationships, my garden, my work. I think of this as a form of creativity, an act of mindfulness, and a nurturing of intimacy. I believe that magic can grow out of a close examination of the moment at hand. What do I have to work with today? Who is in front of me right now? Where can I take this? I teach literacy and math to women at the King County Correctional Facility in Seattle. I have come to believe that this simple practice of intense focus, of truly paying attention, is the most essential thing I bring to my work. Women thrive on relationship-based learning and this approach nurtures a classroom that is far more intimate than most. Attending to my students at this level empowers them to embrace this educational opportunity and transforms the classroom experience into something that works for them on many levels. It also becomes a deeply personal and meaningful experience for me.

I work part-time and I am the mother of two small boys. I am almost always in motion, so I make it my ritual to rise early and revel in the

Empowering Women Through Literacy: Views From Experience, pp. 113–118
Copyright © 2009 by Information Age Publishing

stillness and solitude of morning. As I drink my cup of coffee and stare out at the trees, I consciously let go of my lists and the clutter of my busy life. I try to quietly gather my energies for whatever matters most that day. This morning meditation brings me to the present and clarifies my priorities before my children wake, or before I leave for the jail.

I am lucky to live on an island and as I board the ferry to work, I actively let go of my family and begin to focus even more on my students. I recall moments from my previous class, the faces of my students, their questions, their passions, and the intensity of their desire for more help, more mentorship. I often read and write in student journals while I am crossing the Puget Sound. It is the perfect place for reflection. Water is a medium that transports my students to me, away from the confines of the jail and it reminds me of the connections inherent in humanity. Some of their journal reflections take me back to times in my life when I felt lost, or they recall a more narcissistic time in my life when I had only myself to worry about. Whatever it is, the process calls forth my own transgressions, my own self-doubt and my own flawed self. I am now in a softer place, which makes me more accessible, more humble, and ultimately, more generous in my feelings towards these women.

When we dock, I leave the boat and turn from the light, the tides, and the smell of salt. I try to carry this opening, where the water meets the city and my own awareness of my place in the world, to my students who reside six city blocks away in the jail. It seems like the most important thing to bring with me. These solitary hours of morning have been more important than any other preparation I will do that day.

At the office below the tower, I go through the motions of copying, e-mailing, and prepping, with a kind of detachment. I find out who has been released and who is still a part of my classroom community. I learn the names of new students but not the nature of their crimes. This part of their history has nothing to do with my work, and I consider it a distraction unless it is offered from the student as part of their story. Finally, the introvert in me takes a deep breath and I remind myself how much I love the company of women. I remind myself that teaching can feel a lot like a really great dinner party.

I have been teaching long enough to know how to hook my students. We read and write poetry in the voices of women who have lived, or survived years of neglect or abuse. We read, discuss, and write on a broad range of topics: motherhood, critical events, addiction, prostitution, materialism, habits, faith, art, incarceration, family of origin, etc. Students practice fluency in their journals as they free-write about their personal history, current struggles, family issues, and plans for post-release. Students often want to explore topics in personal development, so I plan lessons about things that help them clarify and reveal aspects of themselves that they want to tend to. I bring options with me everyday and encourage the students to be assertive in their choice-making. It has been shown time and time again that students need and want relevant, interesting, and applicable material to grapple with as they learn basic skills.

However, I don't believe that it is just the student-centered curriculum that inspires my students to become their best selves in my class. My students, as most women do, respond to authentic relationships and thrive on engagement. I feel scrutinized in this regard and I can't imagine what it would be like in the classroom if I wasn't one hundred percent present. At the same time, my intensity and my focus surprise them. My attention to them has the natural consequence of bringing their attention to themselves and to me. This may be effective, but exposure brings forth its own issues for them. They don't want to continue the life they are living, they don't know how to escape old patterns, and they struggle with more emotional pain than most groups of learners.

At least 80% of my students are here are drug-related charges. When I learn their stories through conversation and writing, I sometimes wonder how they survived this long. The mother in me is still convinced that life is so fragile. But many of these women were groomed for this lifestyle from an early age. Many have family 'in the system' and would have had to beat unbelievable odds to escape the typical trajectory of abuse, abandonment, drug-use, and crime to support a drug habit, or to please a man. There are always a few students who come from a more privileged background, who visited the edge and got hooked on drugs and ghetto culture and couldn't pull themselves out. And there are always a few students who suffer from the shame of a more twisted path.

It is safe to say that most, if not all of these women feel invisible. In fact, they are invisible in the jail. The red uniform of the inmate and their wristband with a number have the immediate effect of stripping one's individuality. So it is not hard to imagine that this small gesture of being wholly present with them has such a profound affect on their sense of self, their trust of me, and their motivation academically. When you can be present you are honoring the sacredness of that person. You are saying, "You are worth my time. What you have to say, or offer here is valuable to me and to this classroom community." For these women, this is no small thing. I believe this is why students behave with respect in my classroom. They know that I am taking them seriously. It follows that they would take themselves seriously as well.

Oftentimes this confrontation of self can be raw and there is such self-deprecating grief and regret in their writing. I remind myself often that my role is a teacher, but I have some responsibility for this layer of emotion. When appropriate, I select readings about forgiveness and the resilience of the human spirit. I also simply offer love, kindness, and a softness that they are sorely in need of. They have such a deficit of this in their lives and this sense of care and safety is an invaluable element in my classroom. I try to protect it by having extremely clear boundaries myself and by counseling students out of the program who are not ready to participate in a productive, respectful manner. If this diplomatic approach does not work, I am not afraid to step up and remove students for inappropriate behavior. While I have never felt danger in my classroom, I have stood shoulder to shoulder with students to assert my presence and dissuade a conflict. There is no space for women who bring negativity and disruption to the classroom. These boundaries serve to help my students take the risks they need to in order to grow educationally and emotionally.

The powerful exchange that happens between my students and I is the hardest to describe. This is the magic. It is there in the room when a woman reads a poem out loud that she has written, stops midway due to the emotion and another woman sitting next to her finishes it for her. We all clap, and we all cry. We are bearing witness to the suffering of the human spirit and remembering our own, claiming the connection between us. It is there again when an older student is preaching to the younger ones about the dead-end of this lifestyle, the preciousness of life lost. "Do you really want to be forty in here?" I step out of the way. This conversation needs to happen. We may have started with the form of a five paragraph essay on the topic of addiction, but I know what the more important piece is here. Best laid lesson plans tossed aside, I try to remember my intent, as I break free and go where this moment is leading me. I know that this unknown path may not bear fruit, but, if it does, there is far more collective brilliance to be found here. This is my art.

For all of our sakes, this class has to be a balance of intensity and lightness. And for all of the drama in their lives, there is so much humor and sass in this group of women. It elicits the same in me and although I am always appropriate, I have to laugh out loud when a student passes a GED test and says with a big grin, "Maybe I won't be a prostitute anymore!" On another day, I good-naturedly remind a student, "No, you can't write your budget on the projected income of a drug-dealer!" Alternatively, there are these poignant moments of celebration and great spirit. Recently, a student who is a musician came to class with a rap inspired by our time together. She let it go rhyme by rhyme, beat by beat, with a huge smile and the moves to go with it. I was amazed and inspired by her life-force. This feeds me, and it's all I can do not to start dancing with her. Maybe I should.

It is not always easy to show up for my students. There are days when I am struggling with despair. There are days when I can't access my natural curiosity and enthusiasm for working at the jail, days when I want to have the kind of job where I can sit quietly, uninterrupted at a computer for several hours and not be needed. I remind myself that I can hold this feeling, that being in the company of women can allow for it, that if I am my whole self, fully present, there is nothing that can go terribly wrong. It is often on those days that I witness the most interesting classes. Perhaps I give more of my control away on those days. Perhaps these women sense my fragility and step up to carry things that day, I don't know. I do know that it is a privilege to wander these places with them and always be aware of my own growth and stretching. And there are always surprises just when I need them the most. A student I have been working with tells me that she is reading *Women Behind Bars: The Crisis of Women in the US Prison System,* by Silja Talvi (2007), aloud to inmates outside of class. To imagine these women gathered around Yvonne, reading a book like that is a beautiful thing. I wish these images counted with the policy makers.

We have a problem with incarceration in this country. Many people think the answer is to build more jails to resolve an overcrowded system. This will not help my students. What they really need, I can't provide. They need good mentors, excellent treatment, and more chances. They need water, sun, wind. They need to get outside of the tunnel they are in and they need selflessness from others who will step outside with them. They need mothers, sisters, good men. This all seems too much to ask for. Buddhist Pema Chodron (2006, p. 36), writes, "to the degree that each of us is dedicated to wanting there to be peace in the world, then we have to take responsibility when our own hearts and minds harden and close. We have to be brave enough to soften what is rigid in our hearts, to find the soft spot and stay with it. We have to have that kind of courage and take that responsibility. That's true spiritual warriorship. That is the true practice of peace." This sounds so simple and right, but much harder work than building another prison.

My students are often seeing clearly for the first time in months or years. They are more open than most and desperate for a new way. There is no better time to delve into the soft places and encourage, among other things, attention, peace, and forgiveness. I can't give them much, so for now we will settle for laughter, visions, rewriting and rewiring, exposure and letting go. Perhaps I can help them become artists of their own life, as they have helped me in mine. When I leave the jail and turn towards the water again, I breathe in the fresh air and I let go of these women for a while. Sometimes, I am aware of a student who will be released before I return. I think of the dysfunctional systems that she will be immersed in and the odds that will be stacked against her. I say a silent prayer and hope that she will find her way. Now, I am bound for home and two small boys.

REFERENCES

Chödrön, P. (2006). *Practicing peace in times of war.* Boston: Shambala Publications, Inc.

Talvi, S. J. A. (2007). *Women behind bars: The crisis of women in the U.S. prison system.* Emeryville, CA: Seal Press.

CHAPTER 20

WOMEN CREATING CHANGE

The Center for Immigrant Families' English Literacy Project

**Ujju Aggarwal, Priscilla González,
Donna Nevel, and Perla Placencia**

WHO WE ARE: THE CENTER FOR IMMIGRANT FAMILIES

In 1996, the Clinton administration enacted three laws that, together, had dire consequences on the lives of poor and working class people of color and immigrants, particularly women.[1] In response, community members, community mental health workers, and activists came together and began a process of exploring the ways in which the multiple impacts of these laws and the country's increasing xenophobia affected not only the material conditions but also the emotional and psychological well-being of individuals and communities. We also believed deeply that those most negatively affected needed to be at the forefront of the responses driving the solutions–not as victims but as agents of change. These discussions laid the foundation for the Center for Immigrant Families (CIF).[2] Recognizing the interconnectedness of the social, political, legal, and

Empowering Women Through Literacy: Views From Experience, pp. 119–129

psychological realities facing our communities, CIF was established in 1997 as an independent organization that would address these multiple dimensions in our struggle for social justice and community self-determination.

In 1999, CIF officially became a collective where poor and working class immigrant women of color could come together and organize for personal and social transformation.[3] Over the past several years, CIF has forged a political analysis and practice that relies on the power and meaning of communal storytelling rooted in the lived experiences of working class immigrant women of color and has developed a holistic approach through which we address the multi-layered impacts of injustice. With a profound commitment to a process based on popular education and Participatory Action Research and drawing inspiration from liberation theology and popular education-based social movements throughout Latin America and the Global South, we work to unlock our collective imaginations and our dreams and visions of the society we want for our families and communities to thrive.[4] Building from an approach that recognizes the intersectionality of oppressions, we locate our most powerful resistance as one that can emerge from the strength of who we are as women, caregivers, economic providers, survivors, and, essentially, as the glue that holds many of our communities together.

CIF's Women Creating Community English Literacy Project

In 2001, we engaged in a community assessment where the development of English language literacy was identified as an issue of priority among immigrant women of color in our community of Manhattan Valley, an Uptown Manhattan neighborhood in New York City that is largely made up of working-class Black and Latino families. The 1996 reforms and the precedents that they set were now combined with a post-9/11 New York where racism and anti-immigrant sentiment had dramatically mushroomed. We found, across the spectrum of needs, dwindling ESL/ESOL services and increasing restrictions on those that were available. Adult education and literacy programs–whose participants are largely immigrants, single mothers, people of color, and poor people—were, and continue to be, severely under funded (Greene, 2006). And those programs that received governmental funding were offering limited access to undocumented immigrants and to women with young children.

Furthermore, many of these remaining programs increasingly subscribed to conservative pedagogical approaches and seemed to conflate English literacy with assimilation and citizenship. Too often, CIF and other community members who had participated in these programs shared with us that, finding themselves approached as blank slates upon whom dominant notions of language, race, culture, and citizenship were to be inscribed, they were subjected to yet another assault. In fact, the discrimination they faced, which was often articulated via language, were reinforced and intensified in many adult education and English literacy programs. When someone did access a program, the treatment they received was usually disrespectful and humiliating to them, for example, casually being referred to as illegal or having their accents or cultural traditions ridiculed.

As a response, in 2002, CIF launched the *Women Creating Community English Literacy Project.*[5] This project is one of the few in our community that is accessible to poor and working class women of color, including those with young children, regardless of immigration status and income.[6] Our literacy workshops place English language learning within a community-building and social justice framework. The situation of working class immigrant women of color learning English within the borders of the United States is, indeed, a part of the legacy of oppressed communities throughout history. As Frantz Fanon (1967) has written, "Every colonized people–in other words, every people in whose soul an inferiority complex has been created by the death and burial of its local cultural originality–finds itself face to face with the language of the civilizing nation..." (p. 18). Thus, the dominant language, how it is learned, and what it enables us to communicate become *political* questions.

At CIF, as we engage in the process of English language learning, we also actively seek to promote the value and sustenance of our own languages, our mother tongues, and cultures. It is in our mother tongues that we convey our deepest sentiments and selves. Our own languages are the expression of our hearts, our families, our memories, and the legacies of which we want our children to be proud. Learning English in this context, we locate the language as a tool of resistance and, sometimes, of survival, one that also has a particular use-value for us. It has a function in our lives. As we consider the significance of learning English in our lives, we focus on our own and our community's reasons for wanting to advance English language skills. For many of us, English language literacy skills mean having a tool to defend ourselves and greater confidence and independence as women. It also means access to jobs, being able to help our children with their homework, and enabling communication and building with people and groups from different communities. We also work to challenge popular and internalized notions of who knows English by promoting the practice of women of color teaching and learning together.

As we engage in our learning together, reclaiming our memories and stories of survival (including, how we become immigrant women in the United States) is, therefore, central to our methodology and intention.

For us, these stories are not mere reminders of when we arrived or of our cultural heritage, but they are also about why we came, who and what we left behind, our expectations for life here, and what we found when we arrived. As we share our migration stories among a community of women whose stories resonate with our own, a generative process of individual and collective empowerment unfolds as we speak and narrate our own lives for ourselves and with each other. Our individual stories, shared with one another, allow us to explore both the similarities and differences among us as we forge analyses of the many profound impacts of migration. Through our stories and the analyses that build from them, we understand the different issues and challenges affecting us within a larger structural and historical context of immigrants' rights, racial justice, and women's empowerment, rather than in terms of personal failings.

Emerging from this process, a community of women with strong ties of support and trust is nurtured. We recognize our power, wisdom, and strength as *luchadoras,* or women warriors. The curriculum is structured to culminate in a final project that draws upon the English language skills participants have acquired as well as their collective reflection and learning that come from the shared stories and realities as immigrant women. The projects that we have developed and engaged in together have ranged from a social justice campaign to a photography and storytelling exhibit to newsletter publications.

Application and Practice

CIF's English Literacy Project has been marked by a process of growth and evolution that is shaped and molded by the courageous women who put their faith in the process and leave their contribution for the next group of *compañeras* to absorb and build upon. The section below outlines some of the ways that our process and principles come to life in our practice.

Facilitating a community of learners. CIF's English Literacy Project works to strike a delicate balance between teaching and facilitating. The facilitators strive to ensure that the sessions reflect the belief that we are all teachers and learners. That is not to suggest that we all exercise the same role. Facilitators locate their knowledge of the English language as one tool to which they have access and can share, while, simultaneously and proactively, making explicit that participants' many different experiences, skills, knowledge bases, and wisdom are equally valued. To that effect, the conscious and intentional role of facilitators is to value each learner's knowledge and not to promote expertise based, for example, on formal education.[7] The intention of this community of support and mutuality is communicated from the outset and in the initial orientation, where facilitators make clear the goals of the project as a process that is about personal and collective growth and learning based on a commitment to one another as individuals and as a community.

Indeed, the facilitators' roles are to find the best ways to bring out what participants already know. Although some participants may locate themselves as Level 1 Beginners, this is often in response to experiences of being ridiculed or made fun of when trying to speak English. Many, in fact, already speak and understand some English. To encourage participants' voices, facilitators make a point of not correcting pronunciation or grammatical mistakes while a participant is speaking. Additionally, facilitators integrate regular one-on-one sessions in which, individually, each learner's particular level and needs are addressed as related to writing, grammar, and conversation. Through this practice, we have witnessed the ways in which learners' confidence, which grows tremendously as the sessions progress, has an immeasurable impact upon their English language learning and acquisition.

Finally, as part of our model, we have co-facilitators for every cycle. Co-facilitation reflects popular education principles, such as building collaboratively upon each other's wisdom and knowledge. Together, the co-facilitators work to ensure that the content connects and builds from session to session; that each member of the group has the opportunity to express herself and share her stories and experiences; and, overall, that a supportive environment is created and builds a beautiful community of learners.

Our Curriculum Themes. Thematically, our curriculum is based on a three-part process.[8] We have discussed how the first part of this process, which begins with our migration stories and all that they encapsulate, creates a framework through which we explore, in the second part of our process, the factors that drive migration, the consequences of migration, and the conditions that we confront as we assume the identify of immigrant. The dimensions of our stories become the actual thematic content that we explore as we build English language literacy skills. For example, as we tell our stories, we discuss how the decision to migrate is often shaped by social, economic, and political conditions and global realities. Themes of globalization and neoliberalism grow from participants' own experiences–many of whom have had experiences working in Free Trade Zones. As our stories continue to unfold, we make connections among the feminization of industrialized labor, the discrimination women face in both our home countries and in the United States, and patterns of migration to the United States. And as we locate our stories in the context of issue analysis, we then move to the third part of the process. Driven by a belief in and recognition of our community's strength and ability to bring about change, we explore possibilities of strengthening communal ties and organizing together for justice. An exercise that we use in the third part involves reflecting upon the many ways we are already organizers in our lives, making our lives and communities more visible, and building upon each other's knowledge, experience, and fortitude.

Mother Tongue Sessions. The Mother Tongue Sessions are integrated into the curriculum approximately once a month throughout each twelve-week cycle and recognize, as we engage in the process of developing English language skills, the importance of valuing our mother tongues as a part of who we are. These sessions, held in participants' native languages, enable us to build a deeper and more trusting community with one another as we explore our experiences and stories around key issues and themes. Through the Mother Tongue sessions, we also create a context and content for the English language literacy sessions that follow, experiencing our own languages as a strength and not a weakness.

For example, sharing our migration stories, often for the first time, happens within a Mother Tongue session. In order to fully communicate our stories, we need to speak the language that really allows us to express our emotions, dreams, memories, and everything we carry deep inside of us. Requiring that these stories be spoken in English can make it too difficult to share many of our experiences or it can make us feel compelled to change how they are told, feeling pressured to be telling the story of our successful assimilation into American society.

As we come back to our English language literacy sessions, our stories are understood as content for learning, and, in that way our own voices and experiences remain at the center. To that end, Mother Tongue sessions have explored the emotional impact of other issues that emerge within the sessions, including violence against women and institutional violence; immigration, such as documentation, raids, fear of detention and deportation; and negotiating language and power, often in relationships with children and their schools as well as with English-speaking family members. Then, in our English language sessions, we build upon the emotional experiences that have been shared without self-consciousness as we begin to build vocabulary and sentence structure in our writing and speaking.

Un-locking Our Political Imaginations and Dreams

Indeed, throughout the curriculum, the themes, specific content of each session, and English-language learning are integrated. For example, as we develop a vision for a just world that is grounded in our realities, we work on being able to express intentions, desires, and needs through the future and conditional tenses. These sessions draw upon resources that include Dr. Martin Luther King, Jr.'s *I Have a Dream* speech as well as Nina Simone's *I Wish I Knew How It Would Feel To Be Free*. We engage in listening and reading comprehension activities, reviewing relevant vocabulary in order to explore the meaning of each piece and examine the particular role that collective visions and dreams have played in struggles for justice. As we highlight the rich legacies of resistance and connect our own struggles as immigrants to those of other oppressed communities, we return to our own stories, which we now understand within a structural and historical context. In the sessions that follow, which focus on addressing change, it is the collective articulation of our vision for a just world—for what we *want, hope, dream, wish, could do* and *would do*—that unites, sustains, and strengthens our ensuing community efforts.

The Impact of CIF's Model

The impact of CIF's English Literacy Project occurs on multiple levels and demonstrates the ways in which personal and social transformations are, indeed, interconnected processes. When reflecting on the project's impact on their own individual lives, many participants have talked about how they have come to view their own roles in their families and communities differently. Some have even taken steps to break the silence concerning domestic violence in their lives. Others have spoken about how much stronger they feel in general, and in particular in their interactions at work, in hospitals, with the police, and in their children's schools. Several other participants have envisioned continuing their education, and many are doing it. The sentiments of two participants echo those of so many others:

> Being here [in the Literacy class] is like therapy for me. I am able to express my thoughts, share my story with other women, and feel support from other *compañeras*. We are all here to support each other.

> Yes, I still feel lost in this maze, but now I have it clear that we have to struggle and fight, it made me conscious to see so many *compañeras* take control of their lives!

As noted earlier, each group of participants engages in a project that applies the English language skills we have built and addresses the themes we have explored together. While the nature of the projects we have engaged in has ranged from social action projects to newsletters, the character of the community that is built is consistent and key to the particular type of transformation that is found at CIF:

I've been to so many other places, and none has ever addressed my concerns or made me feel comfortable. It has also been great to make new friends here and talk about what matters to us. We all agree that we have to be united and support each other in our personal struggles and also in the larger struggle for everyone's survival. I really feel like I'm already becoming a new person, feeling more secure in myself.

Indeed, our own individual strength and growth is valued within a community based on principles of mutuality, justice, dignity, respect, and trust and love. An example of the power of this community comes from CIF's *Project to Challenge Segregation in OUR Public Schools*, an organizing initiative that was founded by English Literacy Project participants. Exploring together how we envisioned life to be in the United States, we agreed that one of our primary expectations was that our children would have access to quality education. As our stories continued to unfold, we discussed our experiences with a different reality that has included limited access to our district's public elementary schools as well as discrimination within many of the schools our children attend. Out of the process of identifying the common threads in our stories and developing an analysis of the structural forces at work, we realized that the discriminatory treatment we experienced in the public schools reflected a pattern of systemic discrimination affecting our entire Manhattan Valley community. Centering our own visions, we recognized that our voices and perspectives—as parents, as poor and working class women of color, and as our children's first and primary educators—are essential in the struggle for equity and justice in the public education system and to create systemic change in our schools and school system.

Together, we committed ourselves to raising community consciousness and breaking what we have come to term the *normalization of segregation*. We engaged in participatory action-research, street theater, community events, media work, and the documentation of our parents' stories in a self-published and widely distributed report, *Segregated and Unequal: The Public Elementary Schools of District 3 in New York City*. As a result of our organizing, our families have felt more empowered to reclaim our human right to a quality and equitable education. In 2005, this shift in power became all the more real when, as a result of our work, the New York City Department of Education was forced to announce the implementation of a policy for the following school year to address the racial and economic inequalities in our schools' admissions process. In retrospect, it is clear that this initiative could never have achieved the same success had our stories, our voices, our vision, and such a strong community of powerful and united women not been at the center of the entire process.

Another example of the particular type of personal-community transformation that is indicative of CIF's process comes a photography and storytelling exhibit, "Luchadoras*Women Warriors*Mohila Joddha" that grew out of our 2005-2006 Literacy Project. Through collaboration with unseenamerica of Bread and Roses Cultural Project Local 1199, CIF had the exciting opportunity to integrate photography into our curriculum, which gave us a creative medium to capture a range of powerful experiences, realities, and emotions. Curated by participants, the exhibit features participants' everyday forms of resistance—to find community and sustenance, preserve and pass on their cultures, persevere for joy, communicate with others, advocate for their children, and support family—and challenges dominant portrayals of immigrant women as victims.

The accompanying texts to each photograph, written in participants' own languages as well as in English, are not direct translations of each other. The two versions of each text emphasize the different role each language plays in our lives and in determining the multiple dimensions in which our stories can be told. Participants from this group also planned the opening reception of the exhibit, which drew hundreds of people, and later went on to travel to Boston and to the U.S. Social Forum in Atlanta.

CONCLUSION

The interconnected process of personal and collective transformation that is at the heart of CIF's Women Creating Community English Literacy Project enables a strong and sustained community of women dedicated to working alongside one another for community and justice. Our project has become a reality because of the profound commitment of participants, facilitators, CIF members, and others who have shared their experiences and wisdom and worked to ensure that English language learning is fully, creatively, and imaginatively integrated and intertwined within our community-building work and struggle for dignity and respect.

ACKNOWLEDGMENTS

While we are writing this article as members of CIF's collective who have helped shape and facilitate the English Literacy Project, there have been many different voices, inspirations, and contributors. In addition to those already noted throughout the piece, we would also like to acknowledge the contributions that Liz Werner, Priscila Torres, Dina Lopez, Prita Lal, and Sarah Eisenstein have made to this project. Additionally, we would like to recognize that some of the sections of this article are informed by the doctoral work of one of our collective members (Nevel, 2004).

NOTES

1. The Illegal Immigration Reform and Immigration Responsibility Act, the Personal Responsibility and Work Opportunity Reconciliation Act, and the Anti-Terrorism and Effective Death Penalty Act drastically limited access to public benefits and legal protections for non-citizens and, in effect, criminalized working-class people of color. The effects continue to be felt today.

2. The roots of CIF grew out of a collaboration with the Roberto Clemente Center. Additionally, the Bloomingdale Family Head Start Program played a significant role in shaping the vision and mission of CIF and of our Women Creating Community English Literacy Project.

3. CIF's collective evolved through a long process of creating and implementing meaningful change within our structure. Becoming a collective seemed to us to be the most genuine way to have a process and structure that reflected our principles and ideology.

4. Popular education and participatory action research are methodologies that emphasize the centrality and importance of people's own histories, cultures, and experiences in their organizing and activism and are based on a profound belief in self-determination.

5. For this project, we have drawn significant inspiration from many places, including El Barrio Popular Education Center, the Bloomingdale Family Program's literacy classes, the Highlander Center, and the work of Ella Baker and Paulo Freire, among others. In addition to visiting El Barrio Popular Education Center, we had a number of valuable conversations with its founder, Klaudia Rivera.

6. Often, literacy programs fail to recognize some of the particular and basic needs of poor and working-class women, such as the reality of childcare and juggling multiple schedules and responsibilities, which reflect the inequalities we face. CIF works with the Regeneración Childcare Collective NYC, a network of organizers that provides childcare to facilitate the participation of low-income mothers and queer parents of color in building movements for collective liberation.

7. CIF has developed an extensive training for facilitators on literacy, popular education, and facilitation.

8. Issues and themes are explored through a wide range of exercises and resources that include poetry, films, and Theatre of the Oppressed. We have found that, in the opening up of our stories, beginning with a poem or resource about someone else's story has been particularly meaningful. This makes it possible for us to first discuss our own lives in relation to others and facilitates a greater depth of sharing and exploration. We choose poems and resources based on their English language accessibility as well as the ways in which they speak to different migration experiences and interweave issues of race, class and gender.

REFERENCES

Fanon, F. (1967). *Black skin, white masks.* (C.L. Markmann, Trans.). New York: Grove Press. (Original work published 1952)

Greene, D. (2006). Against the tide: The role of adult student voice, student leadership, and student organization in social transformation. *Convergence, 30,* 5-17.

Nevel, D. E. (2004). *Popular education and organizing for social justice—The Center for Immigrant Families.* (Project demonstrating excellence, Union Institute and University, 2004.)

CHAPTER 21

TWO VOICES

Maura Donnelly

NOTE TO READERS: This contribution is an amalgam of student voices presented as a dialog poem. Please be aware that rape and incest survivors may experience triggered memories through this poem.

I was a doctor in China.

I was a middle school student in Queens.

I worked for the government.

I lived in a housing project.

I helped people and made them feel better.

I went to class and studied.

One day, a man in uniform came into the clinic.

One day, a man I knew came into my bedroom.

He held a woman by the arm.

He held my arms

She was very pregnant. It was her second pregnancy.

He raped me. I got pregnant.

Empowering Women Through Literacy: Views From Experience, pp. 131–133

He told me I had to perform an
abortion or else I would lose my
license and my family would starve.

He told me not to tell what he did or
else he would come back and
hurt me some more.

The woman cried.

I did not let him see me cry.

I had no choice.
I performed the abortion.

I had a choice.
I decided to keep my baby.

I never told anyone and
I went back to work.

I never told anyone and
I went back to school.

**I could not concentrate
on my work.**

I could not concentrate
on my work

I was afraid that the soldier
would return and make me
do it again.

I was afraid of when the whole
school would find out I was
pregnant.

I decided to leave China.

I decided to leave school.

I lived for 2 months in the bottom
of a boat. All we had to eat was
seaweed and dried fish.

I lived at my mother's house and
she made me eat lots of
vegetables for the baby.

I came to New York and have worked
for five years washing dishes and
cooking in a restaurant.

I had my daughter and have
raised her on my own for the past five
years.

Now, I am in this class.

Now, I am in this class.

I want to learn English so I can be a
medical technician.

*I want to get my GED so I can be a
medical technician.*

**Sometimes I remember the
past and I cannot concentrate on
my schoolwork.**

*Sometimes I remember the
past and I cannot concentrate on
my schoolwork.*

There is this young American
girl in my class.

*There is this Chinese woman in
my class.*

She talks so fast.
I cannot understand her.

*She talks with this accent.
I can never understand her.*

She is so loud and always
talks first. She has no respect
for the teacher.

*She is always talking Chinese with
her friends. Are they talking about
me?*

This country has a free education
system. How come she cannot write?

*She has lived in New York for five
years. Why doesn't she speak English?*

CHAPTER 22

WOMEN AND CONTINUED EDUCATION IN BELIZE

Jane Elizabeth Bennett

BACKGROUND

The hauntingly sad face of a young woman in my neighborhood captured my attention back in grade school, and this picture has remained with me ever since. She was a few years older than I was and she had dropped out of grade school (junior high) to become a mother and a wife. I used to see this forlorn look on her face which seemed to express an emptiness and yearning for something more. It was my assessment of that look which led me to conclude that education was the all important for women in order to achieve and maintain financial independence. This conclusion planted the lifetime seed in my mind which clearly stated that there was a very strong need for women to be financially independent.

The importance and impact of Women's Education for the achievement of financial independence and thereby poverty alleviation is one of the driving forces behind the establishment of Eglah's Training Center (ETC) for Women.

Empowering Women Through Literacy: Views From Experience, pp. 135–138
Copyright © 2009 by Information Age Publishing
All rights of reproduction in any form reserved.

During my adolescent years, I observed and participated in my mother's pioneering of Continued Education activities which were run from our home - this experience nurtured the seed already planted in my mind. During the late 1960s and 1970s my mother (now deceased), a high school teacher of business courses at that time, also taught private classes in shorthand and typing to both men and women who expressed a need for additional or new skills in these areas. Some of her students, mostly women, petitioned my mother to also tutor their children who were attending primary or high school and who needed additional help with their Math and English studies. My mother could not facilitate both parents and children since she was the only teacher, so she turned the tutoring of these youngsters over to her own children. So, it is no coincidence that four (including myself) of my mother's six children have pursued teaching careers.

THE VISION BECOMES A REALITY

In 2003, a house-to-house survey was conducted by ETC in a targeted marginalized urban area of Belize City, Belize. The analysis of this study confirmed the need for Continued Education Programs for women.

Profiles of Women in Continued Education in Belize

Students who undertake literacy classes offered at ETC in Adult Basic Education (ABE) and Computer Literacy (CL) are members of the grass roots as well as of the working lower and middle classes. Among them are single mothers who are head of households who need to improve skills which were abandoned when they dropped out of grade or high school. Some of these women also need new marketable skills, while others seek to improve their language skills via ESOL classes.

Women who come to the doors of ETC have different goals. Some examples include women who wish to become more confident readers in their respective churches where they hold positions of responsibility. Although they are in their mid to late thirties they are unable to spell proficiently even though they do read daily (their Bibles and other religious publications). They do so merely from memorization but expressed a need to improve this skill. One woman wished to return to a job with a hospital but needed to improve her spelling skills in order to accurately capture patients' requests for special meals based on their medical condition. Another woman wanted to improve her skills in math to effectively and profitably manage a small grocery shop in her neighborhood. She and her husband had been forced to close down this business having recognized that her deficiency in this skill was having a negative impact on the profitability of their business which she managed. Two other women who hold positions with supervisory responsibilities and who have vertical career aspirations sought ESOL classes to build their self esteem and also to obtain the respect of peers, supervisors and supervisees. A retiree sought classes in CL to improve her computer technology skills for self-actualization as well as for other projects planned for her retirement years. The most significant story for me is that of a woman in her late forties who is almost totally illiterate. I was touched beyond words when she interrupted one of her ABE classes to ask me for "a favor." She wanted me to teach her to sign her name so she could withdraw her salary from a local credit union where her wages for cleaning services provided had been deposited. I felt humbled to be able to help another human being with such a basic skill often taken for granted. I got goose bumps and felt like I had won the lottery for being given the opportunity to make such a basic but profound difference in this woman's life.

Challenges for Women Engaged in Continued Education in Belize

These are not isolated cases and there are countless women in the Belizean Society in similar situations that can and should be engaged in Continued Education to elevate their socio-economic status. However, there are many obstacles preventing them from making this leap. Firstly, there is the psychological block expressed in denial of the real need to become literate. Secondly is the shame of admitting this incapacity to someone else. Thirdly is cultural complacency—the tendency to accept one's status in life as it is without making any conscious effort for development and sustainability. Other challenges include family and financial situations, but in many cases these are used as crutches for not committing to the long stretch in pursuing/completing Continued Education programs like those offered at ETC.

Role of ETC in Women and Continued Education in Belize

My life and work experiences have contributed to my belief that women still are, in many societies, the under-privileged gender. ETC seeks to level the playing field for women in the Belizean Society by allowing them to be empowered with life skills through Continued Education programs.

ETC's mission is:

> To facilitate professional, private and progressive continuing educational opportunities to women who wish to enhance or acquire life skills. To empower women in this way in order to strengthen them as individuals and subsequently their families and the community at large. To reach out to the Belizean community through partnerships with the Government of Belize via its ministries of Education and Family & Women's development, and other groups and organizations for Women's Interest, Youth, Male Interest, Religious, and the Private Sector as well as with local and international development and funding organizations.

ETC maintains a learning environment that is both professional and private. This is not prevalent at other NGOs (non-profits) involved in similar type of work. ETC has been networking with the Government of Belize, the private sector and other NGOs in mutually supportive activities. The Ministry of Education has endorsed the work of ETC and the need that it is addressing for women within the Belizean community.

ETC endeavors to achieve its Mission and Vision by continuing to provide the type of programs that will help meet the community needs of Women through Continued Education. It is envisioned that in the very near future ETC will be able to record an increase in the number of successes for its efforts in Women's Continued Education in Belize.

CHAPTER 23

BREAKING THE SPELL OF DYSLEXIA

A Retrospective Dialogue Between Student and Teacher

Gail Wood Miller and Susan Makinen

Susan Makinen is a brave, persistent, creative, intellectually-gifted woman, whose dyslexia was not diagnosed until she was 35. Shortly after, she began to be tutored. This retrospective presents an overview of her work (1987-2002) with her then-tutor, article author Gail Wood Miller, in learning to spell on her own. Susan Makinen's story appears below as quoted text.

It was Fall 1987. I just began directing the English learning center of an open-admissions college in a large, public, urban university. I don't think I was there a week when Susan walked into the large room divided into tutoring and office spaces. She passed the front registration desk, continuing past my assistant's desk, to my cubby in the rear. She seemed close to me in age. She introduced herself in polished English. She clearly was not a typical student coming for tutoring.

Empowering Women Through Literacy: Views From Experience, pp. 139–145

Susan: I told Gail I had dyslexia and that I had worked with the person directing the center before her. I told her she could read my file, and that I knew
the "Words in Color" charts (1977). I was very good with the charts. I told her
I liked to write poetry, and had made poems using words from the charts. I
asked her if she would help me, which, of course, she said she would. I
explained how hand-waving can make me dizzy to the point of needing to lie
down because of my dyslexia. To me, letters dance on the page.

Coincidentally, I had studied, written, and taught poetry. I was intrigued
with Susan. She had a dual major of biology and art. She loved to paint—
often using tertiary shades, like mauves and greens—semi-abstract designs
in oils, sometimes on large canvasses. We began meeting weekly in one-
hour sessions. I was moved that she had the persistence and motivation to
come regularly for tutoring. Susan showed the "unique" commitment Mellard et al. refer to in the adult learner who chooses to attend a program to
further develop their literacy (Mellard et al., 2007, p. 188).

Thomas Hehir describes dyslexia as the "phenomenon" of "intellectually able" students who have "marked difficulty learning to read" (Hehir
2005, pp. 27-28). It's not the reading or understanding of texts sometimes as much as the identifying specific words, and word-parts. Susan was
entitled to a scribe by state law, but I felt she would increase her sense of
academic self-esteem if she could spell on her own instead of dictating to
someone else or having someone proofread for her. This is, in fact, an
intention of the charts, to foster student autonomy and provide opportunity for the student to exercise it (S. Gattegno, 2008). She did indeed
know the charts well—she had accrued so much time on them she could
recall sections from memory. From the charts, Susan did learn to read
spelling variants as they were written—visually, the large, multi-colored
words on black backgrounds are generally more accessible than black
typeface on white paper. But she couldn't reproduce those spellings. The
charts were not enough—by themselves. Her previous tutors may not
have fully exercised the spirit of exploration and discovery the developer
of the charts, Caleb Gattegno, anticipated as part of the "subordination of
teaching to learning" process (C. Gattegno, 1970), including closely
observing the individual learner.

I first needed her eyes to be able to actually see what letters were on the
page. I needed to train Susan's eyes to be able to focus on increasingly
smaller spaces. I knew this would take time. Words would be broken down
into familiar parts (*groundhog*, for example, has *grr* and *round* and *hog*; this
might precede, for familiarity's sake, identifying the eight separate
sounds in *groundhog*). There couldn't be a simple rule, because of the
dancing of the letters. For the writer with dyslexia, writing the same word
several times might be spelled in several different ways—so, *beep* might be
written *peed, bead, peep, baab, bep*, and so forth. Susan's variants, more typi-

cally, were within the word. If the "problems of adult reading" are the "problems of access," as David Bartholomae points out (Bartholomae, 1990, p. 37), then access needs to be to the letters of the words themselves as well as texts of interest to the reader.

Sally Shaywitz notes the earlier the learner is diagnosed and receives the help they need (p. 127), the more secure their self-esteem; Susan's dyslexia wasn't diagnosed until she was 35. Yet, Shaywitz affirms, the "plasticity of the human brain and its ability to reshape itself in mature adults" (p. 288) allows the adult learner to change the way they perceive—to more accurately note and make meaning of what they see. "Keep in mind," Shaywitz cautions, "that the goal is to match the instruction as closely as possible with the adult's needs. Teachers (and adult students, too) tend to overestimate an adult's reading ability and are often shocked to see the results of the testing" (p. 289).

> Susan: Gail made rectangular windows in index cards to help me see one part of a word at a time. She would write words I could recognize that had the same sound. I like black for contrast, and make notes using a thick marker, writing in large letters. Gail did this when she wrote words for me to sound out. It was slow. She would choose a word from a poem I was working on, with the editing saved for last.

I knew Susan would be more involved if the work were in context, and more involved if the context were something of interest to her. Choosing from a line of her poetry, after we'd worked on the imagery, held her interest. What's particularly tricky is that all of us are more apt to remember something new to enact or apply it again when we can actually see it. Perception is even more immediate in this than internalizing (Taatgen et al., 2008). With Susan, what she was seeing wasn't constant. Seeing things in the places they were in—not just words, but objects and parts of paintings—even though she was and is a painter—was a physiological effort for her. I was trying to increase her perception.

> Susan: Gail worked with me in independent study projects in English, so I could spend time with my poems. By the summer of 1988, I had a collection of 48 poems, 12 of them each at least two pages long. By then we also had worked on punctuation. It was still tedious, but generally less so. On the cover of the envelope I wrote, SPRING/SUMMER '88 POEMS (PUNCU-ATED) (sic).

I was amazed how quickly Susan came up with an idea. Part of my scheme in building her perception was to also coerce her to visualize more. When she would tell me what she was thinking of writing about in a future poem, I would suggest an image-based theme. It seemed like she had the entire concept of the poem before I finished my sentence. In retrospect, I wonder if this untitled collection sometimes reflected her state of mind. In "Lullaby Unorthodox," for example, is the quoted refrain, "'Child of Wonder—close your eyes!'" In this poem, she refers to a bay's independent, varying colors—each with its time and accompanying environment (such as, "Bay of azure: you are the morning.../The fisherman with pole in hand"). The refrain may be the imagining of images we were working on developing, the step toward defining perception. I could conjecture the unorthodoxy in the title applying to ways we were trying to rein in—to halt—the natural dancing of the letters. In Susan's "Naked in the Sun Am I," the poem concludes with the title repeated, followed by "to grow again in Spring...." I like the inferred hopefulness of growth. She was incredibly patient, and brave, to work, and to work so continuously, on the deciphering we were doing. It wasn't just poetry we worked on. At other times, it might be a report for her art class, or, the most challenging, terminology in biology lab reports. It was only the laborious spelling that held Susan back.

Not atypically, the learner with dyslexia may be talented, even gifted. In Shaywitz's study of adults with dyslexia, she notes "clues" to "signs of strengths." This list includes a "high learning capacity, ... noticeable improvement when given additional time on multiple-choice examinations,"—indeed, many bright people with dyslexia, in reading aloud, will occasionally substitute synonyms for actual words: their brains are very quick to add up the sum of what is known and fill in the blanks of what is not consciously recognizable. Such a reader is apt to be successful with multiple-choice tests, even understanding well what they are reading. Susan aced the college entry reading exam with a perfect score of 45 out of 45. Writing, particularly when spelling is a judged element, is another matter. This, too, Shaywitz noted, the gift of "(e)xcellence in writing if content and not spelling is important," as well as a "noticeable articulateness in the expression of ideas and feelings, ... talent for high-level conceptualization and the ability to come up with original insights." (Shaywitz 2003, pp. 126-127). All of these traits were consistently apparent in Susan's responses to different learning situations.

Susan: By 1991, I was fairly comfortable writing and editing my lab reports by myself. I would still need to write out terms in large letters, in different ways, and break them down to determine how I should spell them. I think it was about two years before I could do this on my own. When I could, I didn't trust myself. Gail let me sit beside her desk while I worked. She was doing her office paperwork. After a semester, I sat on the other side of the green divider in her room. It's not easy to place your trust in yourself. Once a week, she worked with me for an hour. I could come as often as I wanted to sit there while I worked by myself. I needed the reassurance.

I would have liked to earn a doctorate in bio-chemistry and become a research scientist, but I can't because of my dyslexia. I told Gail when she was working on her doctorate (in English education) that it was also for me.

Susan's confidence and self-trust increased, but I was still concerned with reinforcing that we were doing. Here is an example of Susan editing, in 1994, "October's Sun" with me. We are still working on creating and utilizing images, reinforcing the process toward increasing perception. I draw attention to specific words she's written and urge her to find imagistic substitutions. She comes to see more clearly, I think, the impact this has on the reader.

Gail: How can *cold* be shown?

Susan: I don't know—but I'll think on it. (After pause) Snow-laced wind.

Gail: How can *tranquil* be shown?

Susan: (No pause) In a windless sky?

Gail: What can you take out to make what you want to say clearer? To make your pictures clearer?

Susan: (After choosing lines to delete) But they'll have to think more. It'll be less like a greeting card.

The focus of her independent studies with me through the years built up to her becoming more self-sufficient as a writer. For Spring 1995, the title of the project was "Preparing Poetry for Publication." I wanted her to pursue sources on her own more rigorously. I wanted to reinsure her self-confidence.

Susan: By 2001, one of my poems was featured in *All Ways a Woman*, a little journal for and about women, again. I had headaches from the eyestrain—not the print, just the image on the computer.

We continue to meet weekly. Susan flourishes with steady encouragement. She produced volume upon volume of poetry, now more focused and unified in themes. She occasionally illustrates her work in simple, graphic designs. Her church has begun to publish some of her work in their publication. In Spring 2002, her poem "Straw Eternal" is featured. It begins with "A sprig of green rises/ From still straw/ As sun climbs higher." I certainly felt her own sun was more firmly in place.

When she gave me a copy of the published poem, she accompanied it with a note, "to suggest to me/ Sparce but true/ So i might take in to ponder/ Making uniquely mine/ your ideas,/ My gentle mentor,/ for you this note with love." And, *uniquely* was not spelled uniquely.

She has long since graduated with her bachelor's degree, but takes occasional independent studies with other mentors. In Fall 2002, I left for a teaching position with another college. Susan and I stay in contact, through mail. She sends me copies of additional collections of poetry.

Susan: When I don't feel an absolute command of what I'm saying—you know, I get devastated. This applies to speaking as well as to writing.... I taped "Autumn's Journey into Winter" (2004). This is a gift for Gail! ... I have done the <u>best</u> I can at taping. Sadly, I have <u>no</u> formal training as an orator but only as a poet and writer.

It is summer of 2008. I am taking an independent study in art, only one credit. I'm working, but it gets to be frustrating. I work harder to see than most people. I'm so nearsighted.... I contend my slowness is a function of dyslexic tendency. I am going in for tutoring, to work on the computer on a collection of poems "Sense of Nonsense." Someone is helping me—due to my computer illiteracy, it is difficult. We're going to put the poems online as charity for my church. It takes me so long to type in the poems, but I'm doing it.

CLOISTER BENEATH SNOW

Drifts devoid of sound.

Drifts white devoid of scent.

The faith to smell fragrant mud, of spring

As time eternal tolls.

—*Susan Makinen, from "February Twilight," 2007.*

REFERENCES

Bartholomae, D. (1990). Producing adult readers. In Lunsford, Moglen, & Slevin (Eds.), *The right to literacy* (pp. 13-28). New York: The Modern Language Association of America.

Gattegno, C. (1977). *Words in color* (2nd ed.). (American English). New York: Educational Solutions.

Gattegno, C. (1970). *What we owe children: The subordination of teaching to learning.* New York: Outerbridge & Dienstfrey.

Gattegno, S. (2008, October 15). Personal communication. New York, NY.

Hehir, T. (2005). *New directions in special education: Eliminating ableism in policy and practice.* Cambridge, MA: Harvard Education Press.

Mellard, D., Patterson, M. B., & Prewett, S. (2007). Reading practices among adult education participants. *Reading Research Quarterly 42*(2), 188-213.

Shaywitz, S. (2003). *Overcoming dyslexia: A new and science-based program for reading problems at any level.* New York: Alfred A. Knopf.

Taatgen, N. A., Huss, D., Dickison, D., & Anderson, J.R. (2008). The acquisition of robust and flexible cognitive skills. *Journal of Experimental Psychology: General 127*(3), 548-565.

CHAPTER 24

THE "POWER" OF MUTUAL MENTORING AND COACHING

Walking Alongside One Another on the Learning Journey

Kathleen P. King

INTRODUCTION

This chapter illustrates a Mentor-Coach model that expands upon the traditional approaches to encompass co-learning. Cameos of several compelling mentor-student relationships demonstrate the concepts, while also providing different contexts and strategies.

**Adult educators have passion to help
people change their lives.
Many times, this passion grows from
their own experience of transformation.**

Empowering Women Through Literacy: Views From Experience, pp. 147–155
Copyright © 2009 by Information Age Publishing
All rights of reproduction in any form reserved.

Learning Journey Cameo: Phoebe

I first met Phoebe in person when she came to my office to talk about the graduate program in adult education. In asking about her undergraduate work, I learned that her family had escaped Romania when she was 3 years old and moved to Argentina for many years. When the USA finally opened its doors to more immigrants, she ran away to the USA because she was uneducated and feared her family would be ashamed.

More to the point of our discussion, hers had been a life of "an unwilling immigrant": forced mobility, hardship, and rejection. Throughout her years of academic studies, she struggled and endured great difficulty and frustration.

In her 50's, she entered GED classes and discovered she had an undiagnosed learning disability, ADD. She then embarked upon a new journey, this time of her own choosing. She pursued learning coping strategies and finding tutors to assist her in the process. She quickly passed her GED, then her associates from NYU at 57, bachelor's degree at 59, her first masters, and now studies another master's degree.

Her desire is simple and passionate. She says, "To help other adults like me gain success and change their lives. Nobody should have to suffer like I did and for so long."

She is now a teacher in the metropolitan NYC area working with very poor students. She says they are also mostly from immigrant families, people of color, with little hope, opportunity, or vision. In speaking with Phoebe, one hears the passion and vision of the dedicated educator, *and* adult educator. Whether working with K-12 students, GED or adult literacy students, she dares to teach in the trenches of a complicated, oppressed world. She walks alongside those who do not dream of assistance, and hopes to make a difference.

Now in her 60s, she believes she might never be hired full time. Nonetheless, she wants to learn everything she can to help those she works with even as a part-time instructor.

MUTUAL MENTORING AND COACHING— HOW WE ALL LEARN IN THE PROCESS

The adult educators whom I admire most are those who daily "walk" along side their learners and guide them through small and great experiences. These educators invest in a service model of teaching and learning, because they believe that time spent cultivating vision, opportunities, and lifelong learning happens in ways not beyond classroom lessons, activities, or tasks. Instead, they believe in the power of dynamic learning experiences to open the minds and hearts of learners to create their futures. Therefore, their teaching style usually includes such varied approaches as those above, but also learning conversations, journaling, reflection, dialogue, and collaborative learning.

Educators who experience the life changing possibilities of education may seek to replicate the opportunity by incorporating reflection upon the *experience* and *results* of learning in their instruction. Even though course content may be literacy, language learning, and standardized exams, adult educators who see lives changed incorporate ways to cultivate empowerment, voice, self-confidence, and new visions of adult learners' futures.

**Teachers and learners like Phoebe enrich our lives
when we walk alongside their journey.**

Several years my senior, Phoebe's life experience is nonetheless light years beyond mine. Even though I have experienced discrimination and oppression, issues of power, persecution, and neglect dominate the history of her family, their choices, and her life.

Phoebe is a vibrant example of how I understand the dynamic of "mentoring," or coaching adult learners, and how these adult learners teach valuable life and pedagogical lessons to educators as well. I learn much from the adult learners with whom I am privileged to walk alongside whether in traditional classes, or our distance learning program. Whether I am their professor, dissertation mentor, academic, or program advisor, or they are in our professional development and mentoring initiatives, there are many different opportunities and ways to support adult learners through their transformative journeys of learning (Illeris, 2007; King, 2005; Mezirow, 1997).

MENTORING AND COACHING DEFINED

Traditionally defined, mentoring is a relationship of an experienced adult, guiding a younger person into a profession or life experience (Daloz, 1998). Formally, the term and basic concept originates in mythology and the history of Spartan and Greek older men "mentoring" young boys (Colley, 2002; Daloz, 1998). And even though in recent centuries academia has formalized the role in different ways, nonetheless the original model and relationship was overridden with sexual power and privilege (Coffin, Stacey, & Lerner, 2005).

Given my own conviction, especially within our context of empowering women, it is obvious that one needs to develop a more fully aligned definition (Colley, 2002). Therefore, I have reviewed additional sources, which are more supportive and consistent with our values and beliefs thus providing a fuller conceptualization of the "Mentor-Coach."

Indeed, not only in academia, but now also in professional settings, the image of the "Coach" has emerged as powerful construct and role (Daloz, 1986, 1998; Levinson, 1978; Sheehy, 1976). The concept of the coach, rather than the mentor, communicates more active support, encouragement, and involvement in the training and direction of learners. Indeed, using a typical sports context, I easily envision the coach on the playing field, along side the players while they are in action. Another scene in this coach-player scenario is that of the discouraged learner with the coach providing encouragement and identifying what could be done differently.

Today, the sports coaching venue is not the only popular one for the coaching model. Business organizations and individuals have been hiring professional coaches for years to assist in professional development. Although initiated circa 1939, since circa 1990 the industry of professional coaching has matured, accelerated formalization, and experienced a development of professional literature (Grant & Cavanagh, 2004).

Images of the Mentor-Coach

Together, the Mentor and Coach images are powerful in developing clarity of the potential relationship among adult educators and adult learners. The combined concepts encapsulate encouragement, support, guidance, and empowerment. A Mentor-Coach term includes active, formative guidance, and academic authoritative leadership of the learned and experienced individual.

The Mentor-Coach then becomes a working model of the vibrant relationship of educator and learner, walking along the journey of learning together. They pause to speak about fears, concerns and needs while also envisioning the possibilities, charting a game plan for action, and then picking up the pieces, when a plan does not achieve expectations.

However, the *mutual* aspect of the model is equally important and yet one which is not discussed frequently enough in professional education. It is almost as if educators are fearful of revealing that we learn from our students! However, when we do lower our guard, entrust our learners and colleagues and become co-learners in the mentoring-coaching process, there are rich results waiting for all involved.

Learning Journey Cameo: Caresse

Caresse was from Yucatan and had been working as an HR professional in New York City for some time. She was about my age, but our life experiences were not nearly parallel. Coming originally from a village with dirt roads and little value for female education, she was building upon her mother's lifelong commitment to empower women. I learned many memorable lessons from knowing and mentoring Caresse, such as confidence, critical insight into organizational issues, perseverance, and humor.

Caresse continues to consider me her professional mentor; that is, as one who guides her in her academic/professional career. Our journey as mutual learners has involved publishing together while she was a student and now many years later as colleagues. She is now an administrator in a prominent university in Latin America and founded an educational center for women in her hometown

Personally, I would never have accomplished these specific great feats. I have realized that whenever my graduates go beyond my individual reach, *we* fulfill a portion of my mission as an adult educator. Co-learners and colleagues, both relationships provide a generative dimension that gives back to many more people than myself.

Mentoring Journey Cameo: Anita

Readers might wonder where my vision of mentoring-coaching/personal investment in education started. Indeed, we know most of us did not have this experience. I was fortunate in that not only did I have long experience using a mentor/discipleship model through my work as a religious educator for 16 years, but also because of unique professors in my doctoral studies.

I was fortunate to have as one of my major professors someone not afraid to be available to her learners. Her primary focus in mentoring students, proceeding from a counseling background, was one of facilitation. Her approach was to focus on listening and provide suggestions for resources.

In my case, not only did this professor walk through my dissertation and entry into a tenure position in a tier one university, but also through my divorce, and coming out. Her approach was consistent and emphasized the whole person, but was always professional. Indeed her modeling of not being afraid to care about people and get involved, even within the often too-sterile hallowed halls of academia, broke the mold for me.

Immediately upon moving to my first major university position, I knew my orientation to student service and mentoring was different from my colleagues'. However, it has not been until many years later that I realized that this move was a pivotal turning point for my continued growth in understanding and service.

The point is an important one: mentoring-coaching does not have full-blown immediate rewards. Instead, when we invest in the lives of learners in this fashion, we facilitate change, which may grow for a lifetime. I know that for me, just like the theme of this volume, nothing is more exciting than to hear of my learners' successes—evidence of their lasting empowerment. Sharing my life journey with others enables that to happen.

MUTUAL MENTORING AND COACHING— THE POWER AND MEANS

Since 1997, my academic research has centered about the rich exploration of transformative learning, radical life changes, and the prompts and facilitators in peoples' lives (King, 2005). It has been a most rewarding journey for me, and true to this model's premise, the "student of transformation," has been transformed (King, Bennett, Perera, & Matewa, 2003; Perera, Bennett, King, & Matewa, 2003).

One of the most valuable vehicles for supporting students as they navigate the process of personal change is that of the Mentor-Coach. As stated above to walk the walk of dialoguing with, guiding, supporting, and encouraging our students fills the education process with opportunities. Serving as a resource, facilitating discussions of reflection, and introducing opportunities for professional growth beyond the school setting are more examples of simple ways to serve our learners in ways they can benefit from as individuals personally and professionally.

Reflection

Consider the people who served this role in your life. Even if they only had a small part, did they not stand out among the other educators? Were not those learning opportunities more rich, memorable, and valuable than rote learning and daily lessons? Learners certainly need both, but if educators do not step up to the plate and offer the mutual Mentor-Coach learning experience to our learners, they may never experience a vibrant learning relationship.

Indeed, whatever our cultural or religious identity, many include this same value and perspective of unselfish giving to others. Consider these brief quotes:

"For it is in giving that we receive."

—St. Francis of Assisi (1181-1226)

"I have found that among its other benefits, giving liberates the soul of the giver."

—Maya Angelou

"They who give have all things; they who withhold have nothing"

—Hindu Proverb

"Real generosity toward the future lies in giving all to the present."

—Albert Camus (1913-1960)

Rather than just engaging our learners in an always "taking" role, articulate how you learn from them, individually and collectively. Take the time to identify how they can support you in teaching a new, simple skill, or explaining a different life experience. When adults see that they provide some thing of value, they more easily receive, feel less at risk, and it "evens the playing field." Finally, everyone involved becomes richer in experience and appreciation for it.

Spanning Worlds

The reality of the Mentoring-Coaching experience is that it will incorporate fundamental principles, some of which we have seen above and many others. These issues may span the range of understanding stages of adult development, to coping with race, and many dimensions of diversity; from family issues, to academic studies, economic problems to medical concerns, counseling needs, to professional placement, organizational structures and politics, from continuing academic studies, to academic probation, motivation, or legal issues. (Daloz, 1986, 1998; King, 2008; King, Tillman, & Davis, 2007; Levinson, 1978; Sheehy, 1976; Wlodkowski & Ginsberg, 1995).

The relevance of Mentoring-Coaching to the adult learning context is that it is the ultimate situated learning opportunity (Argyris & Schon, 1974). Adult learners learn best when the lesson relates to the context of where they will apply it. Therefore, when we teach, learn, work and walk alongside them and demonstrate how critical thinking, problem solving, and coping skills can be used in their every day, personal, and professional world, they not only understand the content and skills, but their motivation to learn increases for many reasons.

Moreover, building upon a solid basis of how to communicate and value diversity understanding across cultural, language, national, sexual orientation, religious, and other dimensions is vital in successfully navigating Mentor-Coach relationships (Hudson, 2008). However, the preparation and effort is definitely worth it immediately in many aspects of our teaching of adults. Specifically in the Mentor-Coach dynamic, lessons of appreciating cultural celebrations, collective history, trauma, and fundamentally understanding the perspective of "the other" are frequently realized. The personal/professional space of Mentor-Coach learning opportunities can be empowering and transformative for both people.

The Mentor-Coach model has much to offer our learners, if we will appropriate the privilege of engaging in it, and allow ourselves to co-learn with them. I believe it misses the mark when it is a one-way transaction. Instead, the rich Mentor-Coach dynamic is one of giving and receiving, teaching, and guiding one another; it is an opportunity for lifelong empowerment for all.

INVITATION

I look forward to hearing from you if you have had similar experiences and if you decide to use some of these approaches and ideas in your own practice. I desire to see this model become more dominant in our field of adult and literacy learning.

ACKNOWLEDGEMENT

I would like to acknowledge Shemeka Peters, with whom I have had some terrific conversations about coaching and mentoring. In ways, I serve as your coach, in others you are mine—the power of co-learning. Thank you, Shemeka.

REFERENCES

Argyris, C., & Schon, D. A. (1974). *Theory in practice*. San Francisco: Jossey-Bass.

Colley, H. (2002). A 'rough guide' to the history of mentoring from a Marxist feminist perspective. *Journal of Education for Teaching, 28*(3), 257-273.

Coffin, J., Stacey, R., & Lerner, R. (2005). *Western civilization, Volume 1* (15th ed). New York: W. W. Norton & Company.

Daloz, L. (1986). *Effective teaching and mentoring*. San Francisco: Jossey- Bass.

Daloz, L. (1998). Mentoring. In M. Galbraith. (Ed.). *Adult learning methods* (2nd ed). (pp. 353-372). Malabar, FL: Krieger.

Grant, A. M., & Cavanagh, M. J. (2004). Toward a profession of coaching: Sixty-five years of progress an challenges for the future. *International Journal of Evidence Based Coaching and Mentoring, 2*(1), 7-21.

Hudson, J. H. (2008). Bridging across cultures: Dealing with cultural differences in the coaching relationship. *Choice: The Magazine of Professional Coaching, 6*(20), 27-29.

Illeris, K. (2007). *How to learn*. New York: Routledge.

King, K. P. (2005). *Bringing transformative learning to life*. Malabar, FL: Krieger.

King, K. P. (2008). Slamming the closet door and taking control: Analysis of personal transformation and social change as LGBTQ podcasting blazes a trail of democratization of the media. In T. Bettinger & J. Gedro (Eds.), *Proceedings 2008 Adult Education Research Conference, Lesbian, Gay, Bisexual, Transgender, Queer & Allies (LGBTQ&A) Pre-Conference*. St Louis MO: University of MO.

King, K. P., Bennett, J., Perera, G., & Matewa, M. (2003). An international interpretation from Ground Zero: Understanding adult learners amidst societal crisis. In D. Flowers, M. Lee, A. Schelstrate, & V. Sheared (eds.), *Proceedings of the 44th Annual Adult Education Research Conference* (pp. 223-228). San Francisco: San Francisco State University.

King, K. P., Tillman, L., & Davis, G. (2007). When empowerment spills over: Transforming the workplace through empowered learners. *Perspectives: The New York Journal of Adult Learning, 5*(2), 28-34.

Levinson, D. (1978). *Season's of a man's life*. New York: Knopf.

Perera, G., Bennett, J., Matewa, M., & King, K. P. (2003). Societal tragedy and transformative learning: A view from international-multicultural perspectives. *The*

Fifth Annual International Transformative Learning Conference. New York: Teachers College, Columbia University.

Sheehey, G. (1976). *Passages: Predictable crises of adult life*. New York: E. P. Dutton.

Wlodkowski, R., & Ginsberg, M. (1995). *Diversity and motivation: Culturally responsive teaching*. San Francisco: Jossey Bass.

CHAPTER 25

FANCY FOOTWORK

Australian Women Write From Experience and Reflection

Delia Bradshaw and Lynne Matheson

In April 2005, Delia Bradshaw invited a group of women to embark on a collective journey for the explicit purpose of sharing histories and reflections on the world and work of adult education. The Women of Spirit group, comprised of Jacinta Agostinelli, Clara Brack, Delia Bradshaw, Beverley Campbell, Helena Spyrou, Jules de Cinque, Lynne Matheson and Liz Suda, met every six or eight weeks throughout 2005 and for most of 2006. From the beginning, we shared a common belief in the value of writing.

The focus of the group was adult education in general, with each member, either currently or in the past, working as adult literacy teachers in a range of community, vocational and university settings. There was a sense of transition as members of the group were variously realigning their roles

Co-written by Delia Bradshaw and Lynne Matheson, this article includes extracts from *Fancy Footwork: Adult Educators Thinking on their Feet*, with permission of the writers, August 2008. [Order Online: http://www.valbec.org.au/05/fancyfoot.htm]

and commitments in education more broadly. Allie Clemans, a contributor of ideas from the beginning who also participated in editing and writing the introduction, was responsible for securing funding support from the Professional Learning Research Group in the Faculty of Education, Monash University. This made publication of the book, *Fancy Footwork: Adult educators thinking on their feet,* possible. Helena Spyrou, an active participant in the group discussions, proved invaluable as the designer and desktop publisher of the book. The Victorian Adult Literacy Basic Education Council (VALBEC) supported the book launch in May 2007 and provides ongoing distribution through its website.

Women of Spirit was a name chosen for the group to embrace aspects of women's spiritedness—courage, passion, compassion, contemplation and inspiring leadership. Early on, Beverley wrote:

> Drawn together initially by a shared passion for adult education, after nine months of meeting, we have become a group. Now we are bound together by shared values about what adult education might be, and a commitment to making these values explicit...we not only meet to talk about what we value in adult education but we...write a piece for each meeting as well.

Clara continues the story:

> Early on, we decided to write responses to a common question arising from discussions in the meeting. The writing would provide continuity and focus for discussion at the next meeting. We decided not to read other's writing before writing our own piece, so as not to be influenced. We would keep discussion for the meeting.

At the outset, there was the idea of a publication and, whilst there was no deadline or publisher in mind, the importance of documenting some of the rich traditions of adult education in Victoria was central to the group. As teacher educators, the group was acutely aware of the scarcity of publications available that featured Australian women's voices and perspectives on adult education. To give a taste of the diversity of views and tones of voice in *Fancy Footwork*, the quotes that follow illustrate the educational threads that weave themselves in and out of the writing.

The role of the teacher was discussed vigorously and appears often as a topic in the book. Here is what Jacinta has to say:

> I do not overestimate my power as a teacher. Change is ever only small. It is incremental and comes from many sources. If I look at my own life, it is the confluence of many people and events and my perceptions of these that have influenced change within me. What I teach and what students learn together create change, but not of an earth shattering kind. Change comes in shades, and on a day-to-day scale it is imperceptible. We adapt to change

and may not even notice it happening. The person I see when I look in the mirror is the same person I saw twenty years ago; the only difference is that I have realised the potential that was waiting in the future. For the students I teach, my teaching is just a component of their self realisation.

A range of views represented the purposes and content of adult education. Liz puts it this way:

I guess I tend to veer towards the political because I am concerned that a content neutral approach to adult literacy means that we are not educating for life as active citizens - informed consumers and voters. I wonder if we share the same political perspectives even in our small group of 'spirited' women who seek to educate. Freire argued that all education is political. Is that a negotiable concept?

As evident from above, closely related to the what and why of education are the when and where of learning spaces. Jules evokes this intimate connection when she writes:

Spirituality is about connecting with time and place. That is, our land, and the living things upon it, past, present and future. This interconnectedness creates passion for social justice, peace and harmony. And from spirituality is born art, as a means of expressing and experiencing spirituality.

When I work with young people I strive to impart more than content. In fact the content is merely the vehicle for accreditation and accreditation is just the means of negotiation through the system. There are more important aspects to education.

Many of the young people I work with are sad and in pain. I often think of them as difficult, hormonal teenagers with the life experience of an 80 year old and the emotional needs of an infant. As their teacher, I want to begin the healing process. I try to facilitate a constructive connection with others. I try to create a safe learning environment where they can be calm in the present, learn from the past and be hopeful about the future.

Beverley expands on this with her metaphor of "small heart gardens":

The adult educators I know put their heart and soul into their work. They create small heart gardens. If we step back from what actually happens in the learning spaces, from the practical realities of what is taught and how, I think that the ethos of adult education is informed by a belief and a hope in creating a better world. Through their teaching they hope that the learners they encounter might develop a love of, a respect for, a positive regard for, themselves, the other, the community, the world's resources. The hope is that learners might 'have a heart' for some of the world's concerns. Of course these hopes are never achieved without struggle and that is the challenge of teaching.

Questions about the purposes of education inevitably lead to questions of professional identity. This relationship is named explicitly by the editors, Allie, Beverley and Delia in their collective introduction:

> The writing in this collection points to the need to reframe notions of professionalism which are traditionally associated with what is public. Too often, the private and personal stay in the shadows unacknowledged and undervalued. The professional identities and actions of adult educators, these women say, rely on the dissolution of private and public spaces. Here, readers will find that educational professionalism depends, in fact, on insights, reflections, influences and values drawn from life. There are no rigid boundaries between the public and private, personal, political and professional. The spaces do, and must, blend productively to become the inspiration for professional judgment and robust professional action.

Beverley goes on to say:

> Teachers embody unarticulated values and attitudes – so do learners, and these are negotiated in complex ways. Teachers 'read' learners and learners 'read' teachers all the time. A reflexive teacher is aware of some of these unarticulated processes that are an integral part of imparting the content of learning.

As demonstrated by the passage above exploring professional identity, the awareness of the interplay between formal learning and informal learning was present. As Lynne reflects on this, she concludes:

> The lived experience of a new concept or skill, as mind and body absorb and enact, are the markers of our educational journey. As we continue daily learning new things and reaching higher levels of understanding, the often random intake of information or else the enforced study to broaden our knowledge base, all contribute in one way or another to the bigger sense of individual lifelong learning.

As initiator of this group, Delia is often asked what this project, this community of practice, means and has meant to her. In her reflections published in *Fine Print* (2007), the journal of the Victorian Adult Literacy and Basic Education Council (VALBEC), she identified some of the ways in which this collective process and its fruits have enriched her life, both personally and professionally, and illustrates how this community of women may inspire others.

> On those Saturday afternoons when Women of Spirit met at Beverley's or at my place, we were conscious of the many parts of our lives that came together in our conversations. For example, we were simultaneously adult learners and adult educators, consciously living the values and ethos we

advocate for healthy and democratic adult learning environments, that is, the sharing of power and of life experiences. Each person took responsibility for the life of the group and no artificial boundaries existed between "private" and "public" lives. I loved living this "wholistic" learning.

There was such pleasure in the convivial conversations and gripping story-telling, a multi-modal fusion of narrative and reflection, dialogue and analysis, in speech and in writing. I see it as 'blended learning' with a new face. The speaking and listening, the reading and writing, the constructing and deconstructing, electronically and in person, all these strands were knitted into a complex and integrated fabric of social, cultural and political commentary on adult education. We continually came back to the same topics, knowing our multi-generic thinking was always a work in progress.

In the transformative spaces created by the group, and aided by the six-weekly cycle, change occurred slowly but surely. Each woman relished this gentle pace that often prompted a synchronicity of thoughts and experiences. Moreover, the unhurried rhythm allowed ample time to absorb new insights and to explore new ways of being. Delia continues:

> Something else I cherished, and still remains, was the positive energy generated by our group's gatherings and afterthoughts. When I think of our times together, images of laughter, compassion, wisdom, gutsiness, generosity, grace and the trust of genuine companionship come to mind. So many jokes were told. So many moral and pedagogical dilemmas aired and examined. So many courageous stories told and applauded. So many delicious cakes and biscuits savoured.

As a result or our meetings and work, we have published *Fancy Footwork: Adult educators thinking on their feet* (2007). This unique and affirming collection of women's writing grew organically from our experience and reflection. As *Fancy Footwork* makes abundantly clear, the contributors are all deeply committed to the ethical foundations of adult education. All of us see a close connection between a robust commitment to social justice and a broad and deep understanding of spirituality, a fusion that results in multi-dimensional educational practices fusing body and mind, head and heart, contemplation and activism.

REFERENCES

Bradshaw, D. (2007). Fancy footwork: What does it say to you? *Fine Print, 30*(3), 3-6.

Bradshaw, D., Campbell, B., & Clemans, A. (Eds.). (2007). *Fancy footwork: Adult educators thinking on their feet*. Melbourne, Australia: Victorian Adult Literacy and Basic Education Council (VALBEC).

CHAPTER 26

THE PUSH AND PULL OF PEERS ON WOMEN LEARNERS

Heidi Silver-Pacuilla, Edie Lantz-Leppert, and Laura Porfirio

This reflective essay represents our look back to trace the important influences of peers on our trajectories through higher education. We (Heidi, Edie, and Laura) met through our experience teaching in an adult education program and later, studying adult literacy at the university. Patty joins us as our major advisor at the university who, through our classes and projects, became more involved in adult literacy. Additionally, the experiences of women literacy learners who were participant-researchers in the adult education program reveal additional critical insights. Their experiences have greatly informed our understanding of the role of peers on persistence for women's learning.

Through reflection, we expose the sense of responsibility we feel to bring each other along on our intellectual growth, to "lift while rising" as black feminists (such as Collins, 2000) and community development workers (such as Belenky, Bond, & Weinstock, 1997) would say.

Bringing each other along as a motivation resonates with female development theory that emphasizes the relatedness of girls' development. A hallmark of girls' social behavior is cohesiveness, doing something together and keeping the relationship as priority, not the activity.

Empowering Women Through Literacy: Views From Experience, pp. 163–174

Through girlhood, adolescence, early and mature adulthood, females place a strong value on friendships and family relationships (Gilligan, 1982). Relationships figure prominently in how females describe their identity (Brown & Gilligan, 1992), their adult learning (Belenky, Clinchy, Goldberger, & Tarule, 1997; Hayes & Flannery, 2000), and emotional well-being (Chodorow, 1978; Ruddick, 1995).

This sensibility of bringing each other along is also at the heart of feminist ethics (Grasswick, 2003; Walker, 2003a and b), which insists that we are responsible for what we have learned and obligated to act on that knowledge. Feminist ethics draw on the moral imperative of caring for others and social justice and requires a high degree of reflection.

Given the relational underpinnings of female social and cognitive development, it is no wonder that through our schooling, peers are an important factor. The push and pull of peers begins early and continues all of our learning lives. We look to each other to keep us company, emotionally and intellectually. We watch, listen, and learn from others' experiences and wonder if we could do/endure/achieve to the same level. We use each other as mirrors of ourselves and our possible selves, watching cool older girls and articulate younger women and questioning mentors and we feel the push and pull on our own ambitions, persistence, doubts, fears, and hopes.

What brought us together as peer learners was a shared perspective as students of adult learning. We are good students of our students and share a deep belief in participatory education. We want to know how to teach and lead more effectively and respectfully, working toward a more equitable and just community. This shared perspective has rippled through several endeavors, including this multivocal essay. Sparked to reflection by a question, "What has happened since...?" the following sections share the roles that women peers have played in our educational journeys and the implications for us as women, learners, and educators. We recommend to others to create a dedicated, shared reflection time as a means to expose the push and pull of peers so that it can be nurtured as a resource in literacy programs.

SHARED BURDEN AND PURPOSE: *HEIDI SILVER-PACUILLA*

As I look back on what kept me going through twelve years of higher education, in addition to my economic concerns and my own natural persistence to see things through, I see women friends and classmates exerting a powerful influence on me. Classmates who were slightly ahead of me in the program especially motivated me. They seemed to possess a glow, having gotten through some class or hurdle that I was dreading. They had advice on how to position oneself, which professor was more flexible with assignments or which professor could explain statistics. They were also more "in" with the professors, having begun to work closely with a professor or two on their research.

Those savvy doctoral students were women who were not raising young children, however. One of my friends was particularly insistent on pointing this out to me when I got discouraged: "Heidi, look around," she'd say, "None of us have kids…Give yourself a break!" It is amazing that this wasn't obvious to me without being told. Now that I look back, I see that I tried to keep up with the faster-paced, less encumbered students. They pulled me along, being role models of what lay ahead, like cool older girls in my childhood.

My professors, supportive as they were of me personally, were concerned about my focus. Adult literacy still is a field without a strong research base—how would I create a research career? How would I fund research? Were there even professorships in adult literacy? Wouldn't I be better off doing my doctorate in something more mainstream? But they allowed me to shape my trajectory toward adult literacy and learn how to extrapolate research from one group to a vastly different population. They pushed, although not always in the direction I was headed.

Meanwhile, as I continued through graduate school and a career path in adult literacy, I encountered multiple opportunities that would have put my studies on hold. For years, leaders at programs or the state level asked, "Are you done yet?" holding out some position if only I would finish or better yet, *be* finished with my degree. They were not exactly encouraging of graduate studies in these conversations, being as they were, in need of someone for a current position. Such conversations always left me feeling behind the curve, if only I had started earlier, taken more classes each semester, waited to have that second child…These types of conversations were definitely a push toward finishing, challenging me to finish what I had started.

Jane Hugo was one such leader who kept an eye on me. As a woman with a Ph.D. and head of the Women in Literacy initiative in what was then Literacy Volunteers of America, she served as a role model for making a doctorate in literacy seem economically viable and interesting. She introduced herself at one of my conference presentations early on in my doctoral career and when we met again years later, she encouraged me to apply for the Women in Literacy grant program for my dissertation research. I was fortunate to have had this encouragement, because having that funding support, albeit a small amount, legitimized my proposal to conduct participatory action research with women literacy learners with disabilities.

For one year I held focus groups with women literacy learners with disabilities in the adult education program where I was working as a part-time disability specialist. We worked together as researchers, trying to articulate for all of us what it meant to be a woman with a disability in a literacy program. We used the unfolding matrix (Padilla, 1993) as our framework, to work ideas over and over as we confronted our realities and misconceptions. All of the women had stories of being "misdiagnosed, misunderstood, and mistreated" (Wren, 2000) through their school careers. The whole year was a consciousness-raising event for all of us; I was taught so much by the group about class, race, gender, poverty, disabilities, and unequal access to learning.

Framing the work in the adult education program as participatory action research conducted in conjunction with the Civics program afforded the women's words and knowledge a platform for informing the rest of the program. They presented workshops for instructors, authored program recommendations and a brochure for other women learners. The groups were co-facilitated by Laura, the leader of the Civics program. Laura's involvement gave the group legitimacy and roots into the program that my part-time status could not.

Colleagues, men and women, at the adult education program sustained me with their enthusiasm about the importance of the work the women's group was doing. They also sustained me personally as a working mom, celebrating during that year the birth of my daughter and providing a great deal of understanding, patience, and help during her first year while I carried and nursed her through meetings and events.

There is one memory that remains vividly with me from my year of focus groups. One hot afternoon we had begun a meeting of six or seven women in a room with all of our materials and refreshments spread out. Soon into our meeting we were asked to change rooms for scheduling accommodations. Inwardly I panicked at the lost time and momentum that the disruption would bring. We started packing up and moving equipment and ourselves. As I turned around with too many things in my arms, I faced a semi-circle of women with arms outstretched, ready to push, pull, hold, and catch so that our work together could continue. I saw in that moment and can still feel it now a wave of relief and a sense of shared burden and purpose.

It was years later after I had moved away to take a research position that the pull of my own trajectory into graduate school was drawn for me to see. Again, it was Jane Hugo who, this time on a plane trip to a conference asked, "What has happened in the adult education program since I left?" "Have the students persisted?" "Have my colleagues continued their studies?" I was surprised to realize that indeed, several of my former colleagues had gone on to further graduate work in literacy in the program I had graduated from. Edie and Laura's stories below reflect degrees of push and pull from my experience, the women's focus groups, and each other as they engaged with the university to shape a graduate path of study in adult literacy. Edie articulates the importance of a peer group for her engagement and persistence.

DRIVEN TO SHARE: *EDIE LANTZ-LEPPERT*

The thing I have loved about adult education throughout my career has been that there are so many things to learn. As a teacher, I've discovered that if I'm not learning myself, I stagnate as a teacher and it shows in my lessons and classes. When I'm stimulated and learning, students see that enthusiasm and catch the energy, too.

The summer before my first daughter was born, the staff development committee for the adult education program decided to take on a big project. We felt that we, as a staff, needed to revisit our roots in the participatory approach. We planned a summer institute on the theory and practice of the participatory approach.

Heidi led the group of staff developers in what was basically a short graduate seminar in the theory of participatory approach and adult learning. We read Freire and Horton, Mezirow and Brookfield—stuff I had never read before and would never have picked up on my own. Reading it at home alone, I was frustrated and completely lost. Mezirow annoyed me. Nothing he said made sense. Freire wasn't much better! He didn't seem to get anywhere. Meeting back with the group, we had the most wonderful discussions that usually started with our frustrations and confusions and led to a group process of finding meaning in these dense texts. With the goal of helping our summer institute participants explore and understand the things we were exploring and learning ourselves, our work as a group laid the foundation and served as a model for what we hoped others would be able to do.

The summer institute was a great success—for me as a staff developer particularly! As is often the case, the institute was more powerful for those of us on the facilitation team because of all the learning and planning and evaluating that we went through before and between each session. It was my introduction to graduate level texts and the academic reading.

I kept hearing about the Language, Reading, and Culture (LRC) program at the university where Heidi and another colleague were completing their Ph.D.s. I explored the program and decided to take a class to see what it was like and if I could manage coursework, a teaching job, and a new family. Somehow, if Heidi could nurse an infant through meetings and planning sessions and conferences, maybe I could take a class once a week.

My first course was a nightmare. I had a tough, well-known, well-pub-lished professor and the class seemed to be full of Ph.D. candidates and others farther along on the journey towards a master's...and me. I was mostly silent that semester and just admired the articulate younger women from a distance. One of my next courses was on Adult Basic Edu-cation and Heidi was there co-teaching along with our advising professor, Patty Anders. Without them, I probably would have spent another silent semester, listening to others expound on a field in which they had little or no experience. Having a trusted colleague pull me out into class discus-sions validated my experiences and I started to find my voice both in graduate school and at work.

I loved it. I still do. I've taken one class each semester for the last five years and am almost finished with my master's, but I doubt that I'll ever really be finished. I've become a lifelong learner. I feel like I'm just start-ing to understand literacy and teaching adult learners.

It has been the best thing I could have done for my career, too. Gradu-ate studies have opened many doors for me. I found texts that I was excited about sharing with my colleagues who are interested in reading, too. We started a study group four years ago that meets monthly to read and discuss various academic texts. We're still going strong with new members joining. I've used my learning in my own classes, teaching ESOL and ABE/GED reading. I experiment with the theories I learn and use my teaching experiences to inform my reading. I'm excited about teaching reading and I enjoy helping others explore their teaching, too.

I wouldn't be here, though, without my peers pulling me along, hold-ing a baby when I needed to attend a conference session, and engaging in conversations about reading and teaching. Heidi modeled new ways of reading and thinking and showed me that graduate-level learning is not beyond my abilities. She taught me that scholarship and motherhood are not mutually exclusive. Laura has provided encouragement and support to continue studying and teaching while parenting. She's pulled me into professional development leadership opportunities and helps me believe that I have knowledge to share with other educators. She helped me through a tough course and co-presented with me many times. Laura's story is one of finding time for herself on top of family and work responsi-bilities—something we all struggle with.

TWIN CHALLENGES: *LAURA PORFIRIO*

From the moment I started working in adult education, I never looked back. I was so engaged with real people from different cultures and back-grounds, learning every day about the world around me through the people with whom I work. But after working in adult education for about 15 years, I finally decided it was time to further my own education.

The idea that I could do such a thing started when I got involved in Heidi's participatory action research with the women's focus groups. I'd been practicing participatory approaches in my teaching and in my work with the Civics and Citizenship program—constantly encouraging students and staff to examine their issues and concerns about the community and take action toward social change. Being a part of Heidi's doctoral research on women, disabilities, and adult literacy opened my eyes to what it takes to go very deep with students and their issues – into their pasts, their families, their traumas and dreams. The other thing that impressed me was soaking up what it takes to be a working-mother researcher. I co-facilitated the focus groups, reflected with Heidi afterwards, and talked with her throughout the process about her experiences of having a baby while working and doing her dissertation.

Before I got pregnant, I had visions of myself following in her footsteps. I thought I could do what she did so artfully—read and write late at night, nurse the baby during meetings, allow my co-workers and students to dote on my baby while I continued to work in adult education, one of the passions of my life. Then I got pregnant with twins, and my illusions of mixing work with infant care were shattered. Once I got over the fact that my babies just weren't that mobile—public nursing of twins just isn't the same thing at all—I settled for the basic challenges of work and motherhood. Heidi put my mind at ease, saying that my life would never be the same, but that graduate studies would be there when I was ready. She gave me permission to loosen my expectations and prepare for the giant task of mothering two babies. It helped that someone like Heidi, a doctoral scholar, didn't put education above all else.

By the time Edie invited me to be a part of the Reading Study Group, I was very interested in the Language, Reading, and Culture program at the university. Being in the Reading Group organized by Edie opened my mind and transformed my thinking about many things: research about reading, putting research into classroom practice, the value of graduate studies, and the value of being part of a learning community. I have learned about myself as a reader and a learner.

I was still very skeptical about my possible future as a graduate student. I now had twin babies to take care of and a new position as the assistant manager at a learning center. How would I be able to do it? The more I reflected on myself as a reader, teacher, learner, the more I couldn't deny that graduate studies might be just the right thing, in a kind of twisted way, to balance out my hectic life. In the end, going back to school was just the thing I needed. I loved being a student again, despite the fears and pressures and time demands. I loved getting on my bike, getting to class early, listening to what everyone had to say. I was very lucky to have a *pro-fesora*, Patty, who is an accomplished scholar and genuinely interested in her students' ideas.

Edie encouraged me to see that while being a working mother is challenging, pursuing graduate studies is very fulfilling on many levels. We are both seasoned adult educators, with a great deal of practical wisdom about adult learning and literacy. She helped me realize that not only would I learn a lot in graduate school, but I would serve as a conduit between the academic world and the grassroots community in which our adult education programs are based. She also represented an ideal model of working mom, dedicated student, and a professional who shares what she's learning at the university with her students and colleagues.

Overall, I do feel a strong sense of responsibility as a female professional working and studying in the field of education. I am doing this for myself, for my own growth as a person who wants to continue learning, challenging myself, and thinking critically about the world so that I can make my community a better place. I am doing this for my family so that I can show them, especially my daughters, that a woman can do what she wants, when she wants to, and that the men and women in her life have a role to play in supporting her. I am doing this for my students and colleagues because I don't want my practices to stagnate or be static. I'm doing this for my community, which includes my school systems.

The stories shared by the women in the focus groups were in sharp contrast to our stories as teachers, coming from supportive families. We watched the student-researchers form bonds of friendship over the year we were together and we witnessed the influence of peers take hold in their engagement and persistence. Their stories are shared next.

LEARNING TO SPEAK UP: *WOMEN FROM THE FOCUS GROUPS*

Stories of early schooling for these women contained mainly horror plot lines. These girls were teased unmercifully for their poverty and impairments and no one—across the decades and across the geographic spread that their experiences represented—championed their rights to attend school unbullied. There were a variety of factors that conspired against these girls having strong friendships or peer connections: extreme family dysfunction, poverty, isolated classes for students with disabilities, lack of self awareness and confidence, etc. They simply endured the teasing, low expectations, and lack of attention until they couldn't take any more and then left school with painful memories, scarred identities and poorly developed skills. Many moved directly from abusive and/or neglectful birth families to abusive relationships and early motherhood. Their experiences highlight the middle-class and functional family assumptions of much of the female development theory that does not speak to such damaging early years.

The decision to return to adult education also seems to have been made without strong support. Many of the women were raising children as single mothers and recognized the economic imperative of improving their skills; some were initially motivated to improve their own skills so that they could help their children in school. Others attended the program over the protests of their partners and children. Once in the program, they struggled to overcome the reverberations of earlier traumas (Horsman, 2000) and trust a supportive environment with adults they could consider their peers and mentors. With or without support for their commitment to education from their families, they found themselves drawn to learning. The women's group gave them an even deeper opportunity to connect to education and a chance to explore the impact of impairments and disabilities on their lives, their self concepts, and dreams and hopes. Almost all of them reported that they had never—ever —had the chance to talk about their impairments and disabilities with other women with disabilities. Putting their feelings into words was a significant part of their experience.

The participants also understood the power of their stories, not only for themselves, but as a lesson to teach others. We had structured and emphasized from the beginning that the research project was a chance to create knowledge currently lacking in the literacy field: the needs of women literacy learners with disabilities. Their stories and experiences would be instructive to their teachers, instructors in other programs, and to other women entering literacy programs. We worked with the goals to produce materials and presentations that would share the knowledge we created together. Their stories and voices were how we learned.

The women took this very seriously. No matter how difficult the telling, the stories were carefully captured and discussed. Many hands helped keep the tape recorder turned to catch even the quietest voice and many eyes watched to ensure that it was recording. There was an expectation that everyone share and this push and pull of peers could sometimes be seen physically working on a woman as she leaned in to take a turn to speak, got up and walked around, moved away from the table and back as she experienced internal struggles with painful memories she was compelled to share.

The pull of the group kept everyone involved through the entire year of funding and beyond and has rippled through the group in unpredicted ways. Those of us who learned from their stories realized the misassumptions made about our students' ability to draw support and encouragement from others in their lives or even the ability to receive such support. As the year went on, the participants encouraged each other to come to the group, offered rides to each other, and called each other when someone missed a meeting. The women talked about "being missed" as a pull on them to persist with their classes and the group.

One important recommendation the women authored was to create women's groups in literacy programs so that they could learn how to receive and give support.

MAKING SPACES: *PATTY ANDERS*

Pockets of possibility exist in the academic and other literacy-oriented communities for women and others who are oppressed to find space for mutually supporting relationships. The women who shared their stories here help us see how caring women initiate, sustain, and nurture these possibilities. Reading between the lines, we see strong, smart, determined women, who doubt their own abilities and who question whether they can be women and also be successful scholars. We also see women returning to claim their rights to education and showing us how important supportive peers can be in our literacy programs.

I think we doubt ourselves for two reasons: 1) we don't have enough models to see how we can do what we are driven to do and 2) the power structure doesn't include us and we assume we don't "fit." The best lesson I ever learned as a first-generation college graduate was that I do fit into an intellectual community. I have a right to be here. As a woman professor, I take responsibility for making spaces for all students.

Edie writes about how much she loves to learn and how continuing to learn keeps her stimulated and her enthusiasm rubs off on her students. This happens to me, too—Heidi, Edie and Laura have buoyed me up and made me a better teacher and scholar. All of us, students and teachers alike, influence and stimulate each other. The ways we say things and our manner have great power (Johnston, 2000) and the women writing here are telling us that.

Laura writes about how being a student at the university helps to balance her hectic life—it provides a "room of one's own," an idea with a long feminist tradition (Woolf, 1929) and one that is key to the idea of needing spaces for possibility. Heidi describes the "push and pull" of her colleagues, her research participants, her teachers. This push and pull is normal—recognizing it and reflecting on it opens doors for enjoying its benefits and for offering it to others.

Why do we bring each other along? Why is it important? It's a matter of social inclusion and justice. As we each reflect on our paths and note who is there for us, we make space to bring others along. It is a sustaining process. We are challenged to push and pull ourselves into new spheres so that those who are excluded may join.

CONCLUSIONS

We recommend that educators, particularly women educators, dedicate time to reflect with peers about learning and teaching. Through reflective conversations, we have been able to hold up mirrors for each other so that we could see our own growth, learn from each other, and support each other. We have been able to see how the persistence and achievements of our women students are similar to ours and where there are significant differences that must be acknowledged and respected. The women literacy learner group recommended that programs give the highest priority to hosting support groups as nurturing spaces to learn to give and receive support. As graduate students and professionals, we endorse their recommendation wholeheartedly.

REFERENCES

Belenky, M. F., Clinchy, B. M., Goldberger, N. R., & Tarule, J. M. (1997). *Women's ways of knowing: The development of self, voice, and mind.* New York: Basic Books.

Belenky, M. F., Bond, L. A., & Weinstock, J. S. (1997). *A tradition that has no name: Nurturing the development of people, families, and communities.* New York: Basic Books.

Brown, L. M., & Gilligan, C. (1992). *Meeting at the crossroads: Women's psychology and girls' development.* Cambridge, MA: Harvard University Press.

Chodorow, N. (1978). *The reproduction of mothering: Psychoanalysis and the sociology of gender.* Berkeley, CA: University of CA Press.

Collins, P. H. (2000). *Black feminist thought: Knowledge, consciousness, and the politics of empowerment.* New York: Routledge.

Grasswick, H. E. (2003). In R. N. Fiore & H. L. Nelson (Eds.), *Recognition, responsibility, and rights: Feminist ethics and social theory* (pp. 89-104). Lanham, MD: Rowman & Littlefield Publishers.

Gilligan, C. (1982). *In a different voice.* Cambridge, MA: Harvard University Press.

Hayes, E., & Flannery, D. D. (Eds.). (2000). *Women as learners: The significance of gender in adult learning.* San Francisco, CA: Jossey-Bass.

Horsman, J. (2000). *Too scared to learn: Women, violence, and education.* Mahwah, NJ: Lawrence Erlbaum Associates.

Johnston, P. (2004). *Choice words.* Portland, ME: Stenhouse Publishers.

Padilla, R. V. (1993). Using dialogical research methods in group interviews. In D. Morgan (Ed.), *Successful focus groups: Advancing the state of the art* (pp. 153-166). Newbury Park, CA: Sage Publications.

Ruddick, S. (1995). *Maternal thinking: Toward a politics of peace.* Boston, MA: Beacon Press.

Walker, M. U. (2003a). Truth and voice in women's rights. In R. N. Fiore & H. L. Nelson (Eds.), *Recognition, responsibility, and rights: Feminist ethics and social theory* (pp. 169-194). Lanham, MD: Rowman & Littlefield Publishers.

Walker, M. U. (2003b). *Moral contexts.* Lanham, MD: Rowman & Littlefield Publishers.

Woolf, V. (1929). *A room of one's own.* Orlando: Harcourt.

Wren, C. (with Einhorn, J.). (2000). *Hanging by a twig: Understanding and counseling adults with learning disabilities and ADD.* New York: W. W. Norton & Co.

CHAPTER 27

WE LEARN

Working on Fertile Edges

Mev Miller

WE LEARN ON THE FERTILE EDGE

In *The Earth Path*, Starhawk (2004) asks the forest "How do systems change?" She ponders, as many activists have, whether systems can be changed from working within them or by confronting them from the outside. In the end, she takes her lead from Mary Daly who discusses working from the edges. As Starhawk puts it, "Wherever we are, we can look for those fertile edges of systems, those places where unusual niches and dynamic forces can be found, and make change there" (p. 38). WE LEARN (Women Expanding Literacy Education Action Resource Network) provides learners, teachers, tutors, researchers, librarians, feminist/womanist activists and other constituents that fertile edge and unusual niche to explore the possibilities of women's empowerment through literacy.

WE LEARN (Women Expanding Literacy Education Action Resource Network) is a community promoting women's literacy as a tool that fosters empowerment and equity for women. Through learning events (including conferences), publications, research, special projects and a Web site of

Empowering Women Through Literacy: Views From Experience, pp. 175–188
Copyright © 2009 by Information Age Publishing
All rights of reproduction in any form reserved.

175

Figure 27.1.   WE LEARN Logo:
Designed by Mev Miller.

resources, WE LEARN works to increase awareness and support of women's literacy issues, assists adult literacy educators to support women's learning, and provides opportunities and resources for literacy learners to engage with women-centered materials. A participatory organization guided by feminist/womanist principles, members of WE LEARN understand that empowering women through literacy means creating social change and transforming our world. In this way, WE LEARN addresses the barriers and impact of gender-based differences on women's literacy learning and how those differences affect women's success and ability to progress socially, economically, and politically. Women-centered education means seeking and creating teaching/learning environments supported by holistic (mind, body, emotion, spirit) possibilities.

Some Background

I am the founder and director of WE LEARN, which has occupied my creative energies and organizing work for close to 15 years (as of this writing in 2008). The network as a formalized nonprofit organization celebrated its fifth anniversary in 2008. My interest and experience in the empowerment of women through literacy evolved through my experiences as a girl, a reader, a feminist activist and through 20-plus years as a professional in the alternative and independent book industry—bookselling (wholesale, distribution, and retail), marketing, publicity and promotion, publishing, writing, collecting, and reviewing. I understood my professional work NOT as doing business but as a print *movement* to build cultural and social movements against all forms of oppression. I view reading as an access to information, power and knowledge. Functional literacy, supported by critical thinking and an array of literacy practices, empowered me. Sharing my experiences with print literacy learners informs my commitment to the vision and mission of WE LEARN.

As a young child in the early 1960s, I had an intuitive and innate sense of justice. Boys should not have more privileges than girls. Blacks should have the same rights as Whites. And everyone should be treated with respect and without cruelty. I grew up in an authoritarian setting (home, school, church, community, and government) and I intuitively distrusted what I was told about the rules and expectations of society. I rebelled against discussion (shouting) that was more about asserting criticism and suppression rather than building shared understanding or coming to higher consciousness. Being able to read meant being able to find things on my own—to access alternative viewpoints and information. It opened my world while saving my life. Reading was how I could be smart, maybe even valuable. I could escape being a stereotypical girl and compete for male privileges.

Being able to read provided me access to voices and viewpoints of women's lives and experiences unfamiliar to me and out of my cultures. It opened insights into women's issues from so many different contexts. And reading has been the way to discover my-*self* as I explore the cultures of *me* (lesbian, woman, mixed-class, fat person) hidden from and misrepresented in the malestream (a term coined by Mary O'Brien in 1981 then taken up by Dale Spender). Being able to read provided privacy to explore, in my own way at my own speed, the thoughts and feelings I did not feel safe talking about or knew were socially unacceptable. Through reading, I found my voice and courage to speak for social justice and become an activist for my own liberation. What I read offered theory to support and strengthen my actions.

Through my activism and book industry work, I discovered my experience was not unique. I have met hundreds of women with similar experiences for whom the access to women-centered (and feminist and lesbian) literature has impacted, changed, even saved their lives. They, too, sought information and support about the experiences affecting their lives: healing from sexual abuse or domestic violence; understanding health issues such as breast cancer or menopause; exploring alternative expressions of spirituality; establishing workplace equality and equitable pay; exploring non-traditional ventures in business, science, trades; understanding workplace or educational sexual harassment; searching for identities in cultural context; and organizing against oppression in all forms based on gender, race, class, age, sexuality, disability, language, ethnicity. Sometimes they simply wanted enjoyable fiction, stories, or memoirs resonating, voicing, and reflecting women's multiple experiences.

As a feminist always learning more about the realities of women's lives, I eventually became very aware of the large numbers of women who could not read very well or who were so-called illiterate. My own awareness of the issues connected to adult women's literacy emerged over a period of several years but finally took shape in one revelatory moment. While shelving books in the feminist bookstore where I worked, I began skimming through a well-known and generally respected academic book viewed as important to feminist research and activism. As I read the cover copy, glanced at chapter headings, and selectively read paragraphs, I realized it made no sense to me. I could not get the words or the gist of the paragraphs. That book seemed impossible to understand so I became annoyed, frustrated, angry—and awakened. Looking at other publications throughout the store, I realized that many writings—both popular and academic on a variety of topics—held similar challenges in accessibility for readers at various levels of reading proficiency. I realized how that for women with low or basic reading levels, the challenge of print literacy might be both overwhelming and a source of exclusion.

As I understood how my own feminist activism had presumed print-based literacy, I recognized that print resources I value and rely on for information and enrichment remain inaccessible to large numbers of women with low, pre-basic, and even average reading abilities. How could I claim to be an activist in the Women in Print movement and not have been aware of issues of basic literacy for women? What would it mean to have the rich ideas available in a feminist bookstore or women's studies classroom made accessible to women with very basic and plain language reading proficiencies? What would it mean if feminist authors were motivated to present their ideas in plain language prose for varied audiences? How might feminist thought be altered if the voices of non-reading women were heard? How might bringing the visions and analysis of adult women learners into places of feminist organizing enhance learning and critical thinking processes for academics, activists, and community members? What might develop if feminist educators *really* turned their attention to the issues and daily struggles surrounding women challenged by limited literacy/education? These and similar questions provoked my activism into the field of adult basic education and literacy (ABE).

True to my nature, I began looking for information. I found *Something in My Mind Besides the Everyday* by Jenny Horsman (1990). This book profoundly affected my thinking and direction. From it, I not only learned something about the lives of the women for whom print literacy presents challenges, but it also pushed me to consider what it means to *be* literate. Other books and articles followed to inform and broaden my thinking, and strengthen my resolve. My searching led me to understand the contexts of women's learning and the day-to-day realities of women seeking basic education. Additionally, I began to think in terms of literacy practices and to make the connections between my feminist activism and an understanding of popular education.

Given my book industry expertise, I decided a reasonable solution might be to create a publishing company to produce feminist and women-centered literacy materials. But since I wasn't involved directly in adult literacy services, I did not want to presume my solution provided an appropriate source of action. I had no idea if such materials already existed, were needed, or even desired. If they were available, were they being used, and how? My experience as a feminist activist challenged me to consider constituency-driven efforts (networks) directly involving those impacted by the project. Consciousness-raising, awareness groups, community research and participation, and collaborative grassroots solutions create meaningful social change (rather than top down, service oriented, paternalistic structures). I engaged in a multi-year process of activities and modified participatory dissertation research project to create what ultimately became WE LEARN. Readers can find the details of this process detailed in "Claiming My Place: The Journey of a Reflective Practitioner," the second chapter of my dissertation project available at http://www.litwomen.org/Dissertation/cmp.html (Miller, 2002).

"When we understand what shapes us as readers, we are better able to see our part in shaping or reproducing the instructional context" (Neilsen, 1998, p. 65). Understanding how reading has supported my own empowerment makes me such a stronger advocate for women-centered reading materials accessible across all literacy levels. My interest stems not so much for the love of reading but for the access to power/empowerment afforded through print—the strength of community we can build and the possibilities for collective action and liberation. I want the possibilities of reading for enjoyment AND function to be available for all women but especially for those who have been denied avenues to power and privilege because of the inaccessible and overwhelming aspects of print-based information and decision-making. AND I want liberatory movement building to include all women in-spite of their reading capabilities—across all literacies.

Some Challenges and Barriers

Understanding systemic change(s)—namely, the empowerment of women through literacy—created by the existence of WE LEARN often feels elusive to me. WE LEARN survives though located in an unusual niche at the fertile edge. Adult basic/literacy and developmental education as a field exist in a time of accountability to standards and the requirements to document learning gains. Social change or progressive non-profit organizations find themselves in a time of a developing non-profit industrial complex where they are expected to act and report in a corporate model. Our coalition or movement building agendas become easily co-opted. In both cases, we encounter the move towards patriarchal based descriptions of professionalism and accountability while maintaining the creative struggle and juggle to legitimize our work and rationalize our existence on our own terms.

For WE LEARN as a community-driven organization based in popular/feminist education and grassroots activism our visionary efforts exist with contradictions and conundrums. WE LEARN strives to develop a transformative and critical stance for women's empowerment and literacy issues relevant to programs, educators, and students encumbered by the challenges and restrictions of the Workforce Investment Act (WIA), the National Reporting System (NRS), and other external state-mandated educational, labor, and funding policies. WIA continues within the context of a long history of paternalistic and vindictive legislation mostly aimed at women and children in poverty. The NRS expands the debilitating effects of No Child Left Behind (NCLB) into the arena of adult basic/literacy education. Generally, these systems/policies assume deficient qualities in adult learners and insist on punitive restrictions through very specific assessment and reporting measures. And though educators and legislators may want to develop honorable practices, in fact, these measures depend on the bottom line, namely, funding.

Every educational innovation has to prove itself worthy of the funding it receives. To receive funding, programs have to show narrowly defined and measurable student learning gains within a short time frame. This creates limitations on what teachers and programs can do or are willing to risk in terms of curriculum development and lesson planning.

And these expectations directly contradict what WE LEARN members experience and observe (not quantify) about women's literacy and learning, namely, that we need broader terms of definition as some changes can only be incremental or may take awhile to observably manifest themselves. WE LEARN engages educators who are extremely committed to students, and women students who strongly desire to learn anything (everything) that will expand their life possibilities. Though many educators and students embrace WE LEARN's offerings, we also encounter statements such as, "I can't use that curriculum package or those women-centered materials" because: "we don't have time," or "there's so much specific content to cover," or "we can't use alternative assessment measures and these materials are not what the students get tested on," and (my personal favorite) "they're not appropriate because I teach in mixed gender classes." And students will ask questions like "how will this help me to get my GED?" or insist that the only way to learn English grammar is through completing numbers of worksheets.

Finding grant support in the current economic environment continues to be a difficult matter for WE LEARN. As a non-profit, it's normal to apply for grants (a time-consuming venture in itself), but the uniqueness of WE LEARN means we often don't fit foundations' criteria. For example, national women's organization funding education usually focuses on K-12 girls (especially in math and science), or (access to) higher education. Funding for women in ABE falls through these cracks. For many foundations, we don't qualify because we don't offer direct services, or serve a specific geographical location, or other similar requirements. Many foundations won't support what is the core of our work, namely, an annual conference/gathering and publications. They don't support what we need most, namely, to pay staff/workers. Even those foundations supporting alternative grassroots movement building may not recognize or value the work of WE LEARN primarily because the change we create can be viewed more as personal rather than largely systemic; incremental and slow, not immediately observable or countable. Many progressive foundations only support locally based or regionally specific efforts (not national ones such as ours). We haven't (yet) created programs to directly affect policy or to pursue specific avenues of research. Our coalition building remains small and we don't do intervention on specific causes.

The change WE LEARN creates or the successes we have may not be easily identifiable or measurable in the ways funders (and educational systems) demand. WE LEARN understands there is some value to assessment. We know that limited funding resources create a situation in which funders want to be sure they spend their limited dollars in the best or most effective ways. But for WE LEARN, the continual challenge remains, how do we assess or prove what may be more qualitative and affective rather than what can be quantifiable and cognitive? How do we remain critical and holistic when professionalism and academentia seem to contradict our vision? How do we celebrate and account for the daily, seemingly simple, accomplishments made by learners in a women-supportive environment that generally do not get recognized or counted? (Some examples: the woman who finally participates in a class discussion after being silent for months; the woman who finally leaves an abusive relationship; the woman who figures out the best way to advocate for her child; the woman who questions a doctor or develops one useful technique to alleviate stress; the woman who takes on a specific leadership responsibility, and so on.) How do we justify the emotional/spiritual support and professional development needed by educators doing this work? How do we make our vision and mission visible to feminist academics and social justice activists?

Creating Spaces for Women's Learning—The Annual (Net)Working "Un"-Conference

The active members of WE LEARN consistently reflect on what projects we do, their success and impact, and how to create them as continually richer and meaningful learning events. One such program is our annual (net)working conference—so-called because we invite all attendees to actively participate in creating the community learning environment—the *work* of WE LEARN. I would assert that this annual occasion as it has developed over the years can be understood as working a fertile edge towards the transformation of women's literacy empowerment.

Each year since 2004, this event has been developed and planned by a dedicated group of WE LEARN member volunteers. Theme ideas have been generated by stated needs of participants. We have invited keynote speakers and panelists from within our member ranks as well as outside "experts." As one attended from 2005 commented:

> One element that I think many of us might learn from and think about was the way in which learners and practitioners participated together in many of the workshops in ways that had more to do with our commonalities as women/people and far less to do with the distinctions between our roles as learners or teachers. In part, this was because facilitators geared their workshops specifically to include all, but also because the tone of the entire conference was such that we had gathered because of a wide range of shared interests and were made to feel welcome, were listened to, and had opportunities to speak in a very receptive space. (2005 conference participant and presenter from Providence, RI)

After reading the 2006 evaluations, the conference planning work group laughingly described the WE LEARN event as an *un*-conference. The committee recognized that the typical experience or definitions of academic or professional conference did not describe what we have created; our learning/sharing space felt more like an energetic celebration gathering, festival of sorts.

This event does have all the identifiable features of conference, namely, keynote address, workshops, panels and town hall, and small exhibit area. But is also prioritizes many atypical characteristics in the ways we create a women-centered learning environment. The workshop presenters include ABE students as well as teachers and researchers. The topics span from practical application, participatory to reflective, and theoretical/academic. We include a designated quiet space for reflection (healing, crying, meditating, journaling, etc.). We integrate time for attention to spirit and body through activities such as yoga, on-going art-making, walks, stretching and other physical activity. We offer food from community-based student-training venues that is nourishing, healthy and considers vegetarian needs as well as other health limitations (less sugar, more whole grains, and notations of foods with allergens such as nuts). We purposefully make a sensory environment—colorful banners, fresh flowers, and other places for beauty. We have even provided a labyrinth for meditative walking and chair massage. We include a student writer's celebration during which students read their stories published in *Women's Perspectives*, an annually WE LEARN member produced journal of writings by adult literacy learners. We include music, performance art and storytelling, and other alternative happenings.

Women breathe more freely, and they (re)discover how learning can be enjoyable, fun, and playful. One of our members who has attended all the conferences commented, "I don't know how you do it, but every year I think it can't get any better, then it does!" We continue to find ways to create a participant-centered teaching/learning environment involving the whole person—mind, body, emotion, and spirit, cognitive/affective, action/reflection, basically, an atmosphere of nurturing worthiness and wellness. We are marginalized women creating our own sources for networking and support. We create a safer village of learning for a few days. The relative smallness of the conference (no more than 200 people) contributes to the comfortable community environment.

Artwork by Sally S. Gabb.

Figure 27.2.   Threads of Experience:
2007 Conference Art.

We understand the critical importance of accessibility, not only in terms of literacy, but also in terms of logistical, cultural, and financial components. For example, the space location must be ADA accessible, near public transportation (both locally & nationally), and parking. We avoid the uninviting sterile hotel setting and opt for collaborations (though our members) at local university campuses. We try to maintain cultural accessibility as well. For example, members who noted we had primarily been using Ivy League institutions challenged us to make connections with more genuinely community-based public institutions, and so we have. We continue to seek welcoming and comfortable spaces.

Cultural accessibility also refers to the ways we embrace and reflect the many diversities of our constituents. The programming committee works to assure our speakers and presenters include learners, teachers, researchers, and administrators not only in adult basic education but also in other related activist women-centered work. Our workshops and presenters include women reflecting the broad ranges of ages, races, ethnicities, languages, sexualities, educational experience, and interests. Workshops represent a spectrum of learning styles through interaction, participation, drama, poetry, literature, movement, media, and technology.

Financial accessibility remains critical for this event. Taking into account that the accommodations and travel are costly, we have tried to keep the registration fees low. Many of our constituents are poor or low-income with limited access to funds. Cost not only affects ABE learners and graduate students but also includes the majority of literacy practitioners who often juggle several part-time, un-benefited positions in order to make ends meet. Their programs rarely have budget to support student involvement in events such as this, and the teachers receive only limited funding support for professional development. Keeping this in mind, we offer early bird discounts, discounts to presenters, and some work-exchange opportunities for part-time teachers and students. We offer registration discounts to members and have established a scholarship fund to support ABE students. WE LEARN balances the uneasy tension between using the conference as a "fundraiser" while making it affordable and meaningful to the attendees.

Though in itself, an annual conference may not appear all that radical or even movement building. However, the WE LEARN Annual (Net)Working Conference does offer a participatory teaching/learning environment in a broad sense. Elisabeth Hayes and Daniele Flannery (2000) outline a myriad of ways in which women are learners. This research suggests that we do a disservice to women by viewing education in narrowly prescribed institutional and formal parameters. They outline a broad kaleidoscope of coexisting links for women's learning through social contexts, self-esteem and identity, voice, communication, and transformation. In most cases, this learning does not always involve print-based media or tangible curriculum standards but depends on more interactive and interpersonal motivations and contexts. These contexts provide the foundations for WE LEARN's annual conferences. We encourage and celebrate the relational and communal aspects of women's learning needs. There's plenty of time built in for both formal (such as town hall) and informal caucuses, discussion, and networking. (Net)Working means not only do individuals and organizations have time to connect with each other, but also time is built in for participants to have input into and to do the work of advancing WE LEARN's mission. We can't always know the impact...but through the evaluations attendees have offered reflections that give us a glimpse of its revolutionary potential.

WE LEARN Empowering Women

Everyday I wonder if WE LEARN makes a difference. Do we empower women's literacy? Do we support teachers? Does our attention to the literacy needs of disenfranchised women impact systemic change? Do learners benefit from our projects? And then an e-mail or membership renewal arrives with a quick note about how the writer is so glad we exist, such as one that came while I was writing this article.

> You and the other WE LEARN leaders have done great organizing in 5 years of operation! I found the community organizing workshops as well as the variety of programs represented very energizing and illuminating.
> I have also been very pleased to keep contact with [a member I met at the conference] since last year and we have worked on a few initiatives with her, hoping for others in the future. I feel very fortunate to have made the connection with your organization as a result of the efforts and work of [WE LEARN member names]. (E-mail correspondence received 11.2.08)

Then I remember ... fertile edges of systems ... places of unusual niches ... dynamic forces to be found. WE LEARN grows organically. Yes, I did have a vision for what WE LEARN could become—but not a well-thought out plan on how to get there. The only real plan was that the network should grow and develop according to the needs and interests of those who participate in building it. Action-reflection-action, my role remains to facilitate and to support the efforts of our members. The network intentionally remains open for the constituents who believe in women's literacy to find and make their way—to make their voices heard—to take power through multiple literacies in their own time.

I've always understood that change takes time. WE LEARN doesn't have to get big, fast. We don't have to show quantifiable learning gains in a short period of time. But, yes, we do evaluate and reflect responsibility on the projects we pursue. Yes, we need some money to survive (and can always put more to good use) but we make do with what we have. In so many ways, our process creates our success—our empowerment as a network. Being persistent to build a coalition of learners and educators and activists committed to women's learning and holistic achievements remain at the center of our work. Members of WE LEARN are learning *how* to become a community that promotes women's literacy as a tool that fosters empowerment and equity for women.

WE LEARN thrives because we are a learning community respectful of differences in learning styles, needs, and achievements. Women on our board of directors learn new skills and what it means to be a board of directors. Volunteer members learn how to organize an annual conference or event. Women literacy students have access to holistic opportunities that support not only their academic achievement but also their larger experiences as women in the world. Accomplished women readers from a local community learn how to facilitate and to interact with women different from themselves through Women Leading through Reading Discussion Circle. Students learn how to write lesson plans and to select themes and writings for their publication, *Women's Perspectives*. We all learn how to make an annual gathering or project into a holistic learning, sharing and networking celebration that feeds our souls as well as our minds. We explore ways to build the content and interactivity of our Web site. We've begun to initiate regional WE LEARN supported organizing. And we learn how to acknowledge and revere and celebrate our differences as peers in a common mission.

One of the amazing realities about the participants connected with WE LEARN has been their commitment to feminist/womanist pedagogies and activism, their own familiarity with and connection to Freirean-based popular education, and their stances as critical knowledge-makers and co-learners. Even though my doctoral degree was in critical pedagogy, I am continually humbled by the way WE LEARN members articulate and integrate into practice the languages of resistance and their radical/critical lenses. We tend not to worry so much about deconstruction but rather to vision and build, from the grassroots, more holistic (mind, body, spirit, emotion) teaching/learning possibilities thus supporting women in the broadest educational sense.

As a membership network, WE LEARN embraces the energies, expertise, and experiences of teachers, advocates, students, and community members who have seen first hand the ways that literacy education opens a world of opportunity for women. We are all activist-scholars who continue to explore, understand, unpack, and challenge the repressive policies and curriculums that impact women learners in ABE generally marginalized or disenfranchised through institutionalized oppressions based on race, gender, class, violence, ethnicity, citizenship, learning disability, and other intersecting factors.

Yet, as we seek to transform women's lives through adult basic literacy education, we build an organization/movement in which constituents feel not only like they belong but also that they can affect the organization and its direction through active participation and input. And, by extension, they can impact the larger systems of oppression that limit women's lives and possibilities as well as those of their families and communities. The key to WE LEARN's work and vision remains that we continue to mobilize a grassroots coalition building a movement to support women's literacy empowerment through collaboration and critical consciousness. We do so with women-centered visions of shared power, empowerment, joy, enjoyment, rejuvenation, and possibility. WE LEARN and we *are* the fertile places, working on the edges to weave dynamic forces for transformation and change.

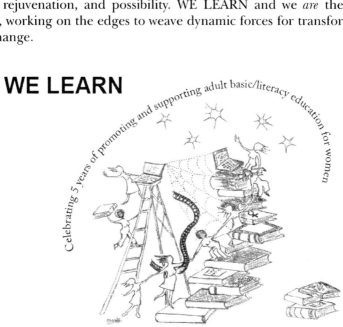

WE LEARN / Women Expanding Literacy Education Action Resource Network

Artwork by Sally S. Gabb; Design by Mev Miller.

Figure 27.3.   WE LEARN 5th Anniversary Celebration Calendar Cover.

ACKNOWLEDGEMENT

Behind every successful woman is another powerful woman. I would like everyone to know that WE LEARN's existence has depended greatly on the "behind the scenes" support of Nancy M. Howard, my partner of 20 years. These supports have included the willingness to have the garage and basement filled with WE LEARN "stuff," or the house taken over with the next bulk mailing or conference preparations, the weekends sacrificed to board meetings or my working, preparation of numbers of meals while I work to meet deadlines, the extra cup of coffee brought into the office while I write yet another grant, the carrying of the main household financial responsibilities so I don't have to get a "real" (paying) job, and numbers of other countless large and small acts of kindness. My capacity to put in the long volunteer hours to get WE LEARN up and running so smoothly has been directly due to Nancy's humor, insight, generosity, patience, and kindness of spirit. For this, I am eternally thankful.

REFERENCES

Hayes, E., & Flannery, D. D. (Eds.). (2000). *Women as learners: The significance of gender in adult learning*. San Francisco: Jossey-Bass.

Horsman, J. (1990). *Something in my mind besides the everyday: Women and literacy*. Toronto: Women's Press.

Miller, M. (2002). *Women's literacy power: Collaborative approaches to developing and distributing women's literacy resources*. Retrieved November 2008, from http://www.litwomen.org/Dissertation/dissindex.html

Neilsen, L. (1998). *Knowing her place: Research literacies and feminist occasions*. San Francisco: Caddo Gap Press.

Starhawk. (2004). *The earth path: Grounding your spirit in the rhythms of nature*. San Francisco: Harper San Francisco.

SECTION III

EXPLORATIONS OF PRACTICE

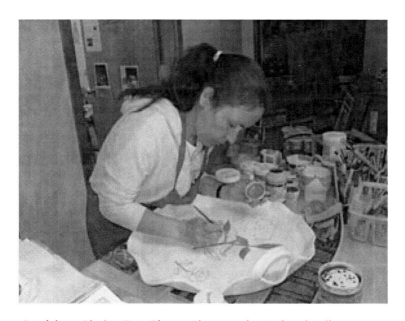

Guadelupe Glazing Rose Platter; Photographer Deborah Wilson.

CHAPTER 28

THE LANDSCAPE OF ACADEME

Lorna Rivera

Hegemonic discourses, cognitive dissonance

Are

Embedded moments of critique

Contest, resist, and disrupt the dominant paradigms

We are essentialist selves transforming space and place

Debunking aesthetics and text

Shifting the self-enacting translocalities

Conceptualizing complexity

The inconsistencies, tensions and contradictions

Are

Imagined narratives, fluid and multiple

Authentic consciousness is

Outside the boundaries of marginalization.

Empowering Women Through Literacy: Views From Experience, pp. 191–191
Copyright © 2009 by Information Age Publishing

CHAPTER 29

SCHOOL PHOBIAS

Women's Stories of Fear and
Adult Education Practices That Help

Lisa Robertson

The walls were closing in. She was suffocating. She frantically looked around for the door. Her palms were sweating so she wiped her hands on her pant legs for the umpteenth time. Her pulse was racing way too fast; she suddenly gulped for air and coughed spasmodically. She couldn't think clearly. She only knew she had to get out.

Fear of school is a painful, isolating and even debilitating emotion for thousands of women. Fear and anxiety are inherent in the learning process but when it completely hinders a person's thinking or changes their usual behaviors then it is labeled a phobia. Four common phobias associated with school and learning are fear of the school environment, fear of incompetence, fear of ridicule, and fear of the unknown.

Many women strive to cope with school phobias through one of three destructive defense mechanisms; rationalization, suppression, or denial (Smith, 1997). These three self-defeating behavior patterns protect the learner from uncomfortable self-awareness, but self-awareness is necessary

Empowering Women Through Literacy: Views From Experience, pp. 193–198
Copyright © 2009 by Information Age Publishing
All rights of reproduction in any form reserved.

in order to overcome fear. Women need to understand the source of their school phobia, accept those feelings without self-criticism and then learn coping strategies. "Emotionally, the freedom to learn is heavily dependent on emotions experienced while learning, a framework that educators have some control over" (Shuck, 2007, p. 110). As educators, when we recognize signs of fear and then manage the environment of the school in such a way that past damage and present misconceptions can be positively challenged, there is an increased likelihood of that woman continuing in school, being open to new experiences, and learning new concepts.

I have worked with many women who have learned how to cope with each type of fear, and who have adapted themselves throughout their learning process. Here are just a few of their stories in their own words, under assumed names, and the best practices that we applied to help them.

FEAR OF THE SCHOOL ENVIRONMENT: SALLY'S STORY, 50 YEARS OLD, READING STUDENT

When I went to the junior high, I was met by the teachers who had my older brothers and sisters. They made it very clear that they weren't going to take any crap from me because they remembered how my brothers and sisters had acted. On my first day of high school, I went to the office and they gave me my schedule. I looked around the hallway, it was dark, dreary; it made my skin crawl. It was too much for me.

When I first walked into the adult education office, my heart was racing; there was heaviness like somebody was just sitting on top of my chest. My face was flushed and my leg was shaking. I was nervous because I didn't know what to expect with the room, or anything. The makeup of the room was important because I didn't want to be closed in anywhere. I didn't want to be in a room full of people I didn't know, and I wanted to be able to get in and out if I had to. That feeling of needing to be able to get out of a room has been with me all my life, everywhere I go.

In our first meeting, you made me feel more comfortable by offering to leave the door open, being conscious of having a quick meeting so I could leave (that meant a lot to me); talking about my worries made me feel less worried.

Robert Marzano (2003) cites a safe and orderly environment as one of the five most important factors that positively affect learner achievement. Shuck, Albornoz, and Winberg (2007) feel even more strongly about creating a safe environment, "Adult students can feel uniquely threatened within the walls of a classroom … blocking or delaying significant pieces of the learning experience" (p. 111). Research-based strategies for alleviating fear of the school environment include:

- A brief initial intake meeting between coordinator or instructor and learner
- Review the student handbook which clearly outlines expectations and consequences for learner behavior, emergency procedures, and contact information
- Make eye contact and listen actively
- Tour the building and classroom space
- Conduct frequent "check – ins" to determine environmental comfort level

FEAR OF INCOMPETENCE: JESSICA'S STORY, 19 YEAR OLD, DIPLOMA STUDENT

I came to adult ed to finish my high school diploma. I had traveled around a lot when I was younger, bouncing between three different families in three different states. It's kind of hard to keep up in class that way; I was always coming into a semester half-way through. My last year, I thought I was finished but as it turned out I still needed half a credit of World History and one in U.S. History. That was just another thing in life I had messed up.

At my first meeting at Adult Education, we talked about the other schools some and what my goals were after finishing. I liked how the coordinator took me seriously and didn't judge me about anything. I wasn't really sure I could do the work. I mean, I could read and all, but history was never my best area. In class we did goal setting and project planning together so I would know the plan and how each project would get me closer to my goal. I have never worked so hard as I did in that class. I liked how the teacher never made me feel stupid, even when I felt like I had no idea what was going on.

It is important to understand one's own limitations, but when a woman's behavior is driven by the desire to avoid failure her learning potential is restricted. Some strategies used to assuage the fear of incompetence are:

- Provide positive successful initial learning experiences
- Set goals in class together and provide appropriately challenging learning experiences
- Refrain from negatively commenting on own mistakes, demonstrate how errors can become learning tools
- Utilize published stories of women's perseverance and courage during classes
- Get and give positive and constructive feedback
- Provide recognition of effort, not just of correct answers

FEAR OF RIDICULE: THERESA'S STORY,
45 YEAR OLD, GED STUDENT

I liked school until about Middle School, and then the kids started teasing me about my clothes and my faith. I always wore dresses and skirts and they would mock me about my dresses and ask different questions about my religion and then make fun of me for that, too. I became an inward kid. I had no friends in school. I felt like a social outcast. I gave up on relationships at school. The teachers were no help either. They didn't do anything to the kids who tormented me but worse than that they never wanted to help me with my school work. That was another slap in the face. I got busy with work and stopped going to school.

When my son got into high school, I wanted to be able to help him with his work, so I knew I needed to finish school myself. At my intake meeting, I could tell that the adult education coordinator really cared about helping people meet their goals. I also liked how the program had choices for me as far as class type. I chose small group and one-on-one tutoring. The instructors focused on building relationships, helped with resources, and knew their subject. They were always telling me, "Look how far you've come." And they're right! I feel like I can do anything!

Most women dislike being laughed at, but some have an unusually sensitive, almost paranoid, anxiety about ridicule. This stress certainly hinders learning. "Students must feel safe to interact, experiment, and explore new topics and constructs. In dichotomist fashion, they must feel safe to succeed as well as to fail" (Shuck, 2007, p. 111). Instructional practices to consider are:

- Provide safe teacher and peer interactions
- Begin with one-on-one interviews between learner and instructor before the term begins
- Liberally, but sincerely, praise for effort and right answers
- Create classroom boundaries as a group
- Reward small successes quickly
- Group according to ability

FEAR OF THE UNKNOWN: LAURA'S STORY,
65 YEAR OLD, MATHEMATICS STUDENT

I worked at an assembly line for thirty two years. This summer the company moved overseas to China. I was left without a job, and I hadn't been to school for over fifty years. It is a scary situation, deciding to go back to school at my age. A number of people I worked with had already been coming to class and they said how great it was. When you haven't been to school for fifty years, then you start to come to school you wonder if you can do it.

Things are so different now, I didn't know what school was going to be like. Technology is different, things have changed so much, and I didn't have confidence in myself. The orientation helped me feel better. Things were explained very thoroughly: The people here were very willing to answer questions. They didn't just brush you off like at some places. They took their time and listened. In class now, I know that even though I don't always understand math, I can ask questions. I look forward to coming to school now.

Transition can be difficult for anyone, but it is even more so for women who have been working the same position for many years. Going back to school seems like an impossibly daunting task. Some considerations for women in this situation include:

• Hold a group orientation on site
• Have a cohort group (same age, same situation) in the same class.
• Explain the purpose of the lesson
• Reinforce effort and provide recognition of effort as well as a job well done
• Include cooperative learning so the group can use each person's strengths

Thompkins describes what school should be:

School should be a safe place, the way home is supposed to be. A place where you belong, where you can grow and express yourself freely, where you know and care for the other people and are known and cared for by them, a place where other people come before information and ideas. (p. 127)

There will always be anxiety in learning, but by creating a safe place we can drastically decrease women's fears and put learning back in their lives.

REFERENCES

Marzano, R. J. (2003). *What works in schools: Translating research into action*. Alexandria, VA: ASCD.

Perry, B. D. (2006). Fear and learning: Trauma related factors in adult learning. *New Directions for Adult and Continuing Education, 110*, 21-27.

Shuck, B., Albornoz, C., & Winberg, M. (2007). Emotions and their effect on adult learning: A constructivist perspective. In S. M. Nielsen & M. S. Plakhotnik (Eds.), *Proceedings of the Sixth Annual College of Education Research Conference: Urban and International Education Section* (pp. 108-113). [Electronic version]. Miami: Florida International University.

Smith, B. S., & Smith, W. H. (1997). *Taking possession of math anxiety.* Retrieved on July 17, 2008, from http://www.mathacademy.com/pr/minitext/anxiety/

Thompkins, J. (1996). *A life in school: What the teacher learned.* Boston: Addison-Wesley.

CHAPTER 30

THE EXPERIENCE OF GRIEVING, TRAUMA, AND VIOLENCE

The Forgotten Adult Learner

Özlem Zabitgil

INTRODUCTION

Violence related deaths and after-effect of trauma on the learner is a topic that received barely any attention in adult literacy and education. Experience of violent death is a serious barrier for participation and learning of adults. My experience as a female grieving adult learner and educator verified having to go through bereavement complications without adequate recognition or support from the educational world. This research inquiry comes from the experience of the researcher in the aftermath of violent death of her primary family members.

Various databases and library journals hardly found any results when I typed in the key words grief, death, trauma, adult, literacy, education,

Empowering Women Through Literacy: Views From Experience, pp. 199–210
Copyright © 2009 by Information Age Publishing

adult education, and adult literacy. A similar lack of attention and avoidance of death is also observable in the U.S. culture: "...survivors often feel confused and inadequate in responding to their own feelings when someone dies or to the feeling of others with whom they share the loss" (Stephenson, 1985, p. 12). This cultural response is also prevalent in adult education where the line drawn between intellect and emotion, public and private, is a strong one. Lack of attention to this topic has serious consequences for learning of adults, and can result in drop-outs. Therefore, death and aftereffect of death, especially violent-death is a significant research topic to explore in adult education and literacy.

> **Collapse.** Death news came as a thunderstorm in my life as if a car ran over me breaking me into pieces impossible to put back.
> **Paralysis.** Life punched me on the face, broke my arms, took my eyesight and threw bullets in my heart. I am marching in the path of life as a wounded handicap.... No pleasure exists in my existence. A part of me died forever.

RESEARCHER INTEREST/IDENTITY

My research inquiry came as a result of my grieving experience during PhD studies. I experienced a a period of disability and complicated grief and learning was unachievable until serious attention was paid to my loss. the aftereffect of an unexpected death, especially of a violent death is mentally and emotionally paralyzing. When a learner is hit by a sudden death s/he is required to put this traumatic experience behind and continue with educational goals. This is a very hard task and rarely achieved by adult learners. As I went through grief, I struggled to keep up with various daily chores, let alone expectations of education. Each day had its own battle. My experience demanded expression:

Poetic Expressions: hear me out

Aftermath of Grief
After you were gone,
I was also gone.
To never return back,
To what once had been my home.

I departed everything...
Sacrificed good with the bad
Wrapped everything in a ball of wool
And threw into an abyss

A piece of me has fallen forever

I don't look back
I don't dare to
Cannot dare to see what is taken away from me
Cannot see what holds me in the threshold of past
I cannot…
Simply cannot…

Pieces of my stolen future visit me in episodes
I cry with the cry of loss, anger and misery
A vicious circle of pain pops up every often
Something screams out-loud in my weird silences

I repress tears for words
Language betrays me again
Nothing can describe this…
An invisible wound bleeds forever

An ugly game from the spirits above
For something we were not responsible
They hide and seek
Into my deserted life
Like the play of God and Devil
Except I am not a playmate and I cannot escape the game.

METHODOLOGY

Autoethnography

In the last few decades self-narratives and autobiographical research gained more acceptance in education. Postmodernist ideas along with feminist and art research inquiries encouraged experimentation of new forms of qualitative research in education (Butler-Kisber, 2005). Autoethnography is a unique research praxis and methodology. Life narratives build a bridge to others through the study of self. Autoethnograhpy is a "…research, writing, story, and method that connect the autobiographical and personal to the cultural, social, and political" (Ellis, 2004, p. xix). It is particularly useful for research inquiries compelling a first-hand depiction as opposed to being depicted by others (Reed-Danahay, 1998). When our narratives are about us, they are most personal and engaging. Though, the process of revealing the self demands becoming vulnerable by sharing what seems un-sharable. As my dear friend, Mary Lou McNichol suggested I attempt to deconstruct my meaningless tragedy into a meaningful whole by sharing and educating others through this experience. I seek to make educators and literacy workers think about a neglected topic that calls for attention.

> **Homicide.** When a tragedy visits your home, it does not knock at your door. It is there. It is sitting in your chair. You have no orientation time. Someone you love is dead. S/h is gone from your life forever. That's the end of it. You will never see them again. No explanations made. No negotiation, on timing or terms of the loss. You are left with shock, agony, and pain.
>
> This is one's response to a natural death. It is the call of nature for a life's end, as basic as birth itself. Still it shocks us at our core. What happens when your loved one did not die naturally? What if they were killed brutally in the hands of a psychopath, a maniac? There is a similar shock and disbelief, but only more agony, more shock and pain.... And a lot more, because this is not the call of nature. This is the call of a human being to end the life of another; a person who deserved to live and breathe like everyone else. Someone decided for your loved one to die...

Autoethnography provided me a space of freedom where I was able to deal with the situation of loss. Writing became a form of inquiry (Butler-Kisber, 2005), in which I explored my experience of grieving. I immersed the self, who experienced grief, obtaining the "*I witness*" position suggested by Spry (2001) looking at the self/experience from different proximities. Unlike other forms of death in which act of telling bring a resolution, narratives of violent death create a torturous replay. Thus, griever is unable to go beyond the horrific details of death (Rynearson, 2005). In an attempt to construct my complicated grief into resolution, my narrative inquiry weaved together my educational/learner and personal worlds into a disharmonious union in hopes to narrow the gap of avoidance. This process stitched different threads and colors of grief and aftereffects of violent death into a meaningful learning process.

THEORETICAL FRAMEWORK

Stage Theory of Grief

In grief research several theories have been utilized in understanding bereavement. Stage theory has been popularized by Bolwby (1980), Parkes (1972) and Kubler-Ross and Kessler (2005). This theory proposes progressive stages of bereavement in reaction to loss. (Maciejewski,

Zhang, Block, & Prigerson, 2007). Kubler-Ross and Kessler's stage theory of grief suggested a 5 stage bereavement process. These are "denial, anger, bargaining, depression and acceptance" (2005, p. 7). There is a general acceptance in the grief research that there are "certain stages and tasks to be completed" (Zinner, 1985, p. 2) in the aftermath of a loss. Kubler-Ross and Kessler (2005) warns that these stages are not neat compartments to follow consecutively. Each grief is as unique as each individual so is the order and duration. The longevity and the nature of grief depends on various factors such as the closeness of the person lost, the nature of death, and whether it is expected or unexpected, natural or violent death. According to this theory expression is essential for completing the grief work. The inability of expression or the repression of feelings due to various reasons, can lead to exploding and abnormal reactions.

It is necessary to create a knowledge base in order to help learners who experience losses: "…with these stages come the knowledge of grief's terrain, making us better equipped to cope with life and loss" (Kubler-Ross & Kessler, 2005, p. 7). It is necessary to prepare as learning communities to meet the needs of the grieving students/learners (Stephen, 1985, p. 6). The murder of a loved one is probably the most disastrous loss when "even 'ordinary' death leaves us on the brink of silence and speech" (Behar, 1996, p. 84). I lost two primary family members. Contrary to the expectations of those around me, I went into a complete silence when I heard the bad news. I froze. I was unable to cry or express any emotions. My initial shock gave way to denial of reality for months.

> **Unaware.** Two days of flights from the U.S.A. with long waits … back in the homeland. Sleep deprivation, constant crying and no energy. Going with anxious steps fearing what if I couldn't make it on time.

> **Terrible new.** My passport was seized in the airport. Police took me aside. "What is going on?" I thought. "Your mother died" told someone. I was about to cry. I asked "where is my grandma?" searching for her helplessly. "She is dead, too." My tears stopped when he said "They are murdered."

> **Resistance.** The rest is a silent movie: Moving characters mimicking ugly stories. I heard only silent words. People kept moving. Funeral. Prayers. Rituals. Nothing seemed real.

Kubler-Ross and Kessler (2005) indicates that rejecting loss allows a time for the person to adapt to the painful reality. "When we are in denial, we may respond at first by being paralyzed with shock or blanketed with numbness" (Kubler-Ross & Kessler, 2005, p. 8). I rejected the news, because I was unable to bear "what the tragedy meant" for me. My family was all I had. How could I be if all I had was taken away from me?

> **Numb**. My mind refused to register the bad news. It went numb. My body responded instead. I think my blood sugar had fallen. I was constantly thirsty…. My tongue was sticking, stickier each moment. No water was able to save me from the burning thirst. I was in a desert and all the water in my body had evaporated.
>
> **Funeral.** I refused to be close to the scene of burial. I looked at people with empty eyes. They kept moving around saying some things. I wanted to be alone. I couldn't wait it to be over with. I was watching my life on screen with horror.
>
> **Guilt**. Feelings of guilt surfaced in me again. I couldn't dare to share with anyone. "Why was I away from home … for my education. Hell with my education. How could I have left my family alone. They were murdered. All because of me. It was all because of me"
>
> **Lonesome.** Prayers went on each night. I sat numb and quiet. My mouth was sticky again. My friend brought me water. I must be drinking gallons of water. Still thirsty and waterless…. Thank God she came from her village to be with me. With her presence I was less of a stranger in the extended family's house. Without mom I left like a leftover in a wrong household. The little adopted girl in me came back so as the hurt of never being fully accepted in the rest of the family.
>
> **Prayers.** Nothing felt real. Scary movie went on. No turn off button. Everything is wrong. How could it be true? I couldn't wait for prayers to finish so I can go away and be alone. A moment broke my posture. The moment the praying lady pronounced the names of my mom and grandma, would I notice reality. When she uttered mom's name, I fell into a cliff; a harsh hammer cracked into the bubble of denial I surrounded myself.

With disbelief there comes shock. As the days followed, I was shocked over and over again, as if I heard the news the first time. "They were dead." "How could this be real?" Every day I woke up into this reality again. Insomnia had a grip of me. I was not interested in sleeping either, since sleeping always followed by waking up into the terrible reality.

As denial slowly fades away, we feel the reality of loss more and more. Denial slowly gives way to expressions of anger and pain for the griever (Kubler-Ross & Kessler, 2005). When I was no longer able to fantasize an unreal wish where things turned around and my family had been saved, I had to accept the harsh reality of loss. I was in a strange state, looking around seeing and hearing people, watching them go about their business, unable to follow casual conversations. The words and images passed through me. I was unable to listen during my classes. I was incapable of understanding what I read. It was impossible to pay bills and do daily errands. Life was too overwhelming to keep up with.

Anger is strength and it can be anchor, giving temporary structure to the nothingness of loss. At first it feels like being lost at sea: no connection to anything. Then you get angry at someone, maybe a person who didn't attend the funeral, maybe a person who isn't around, maybe a person who is different now that your loved one[s] has died. Suddenly you have a structure—your anger toward them. The anger becomes the bridge over the open sea, a connection from you to them. It is something to hold on to, and a connection made from strength of anger feels better than nothing. (Kubler-Ross & Kessler, 2005, p. 16)

> Anger came in waves of different magnitudes. I was back in U.S. again decided to go on with my educational goals as mom would have wanted. My grief started to surface. I could not suppress anymore. I prayed to God a few times for my mom's sake, because she wanted me to continue to believe in God. But I could not. I mostly shouted at God for not doing his job to save my family. I was angry he let my family suffer violence: I wondered "Where is God in this? Where is his love? His powerfulness? His compassion? Is this really God's will?" (Kubler-Ross & Kessler, 2005, p. 13)

> **God.** I am angry with you because you had to take away maliciously. I am angry with those bloody murderers because they killed you (plural). You never did anything wrong. You were the best woman, best mom this earth could know? Shame on this earth for witnessing such brutality without God's interference…. I no longer trust God.

My anger was dispersing in all directions. It had different targets each time. I was the most attacked victim of my anger: "…you may also be angry with yourself that you couldn't stop it from happening" (Kubler-Ross & Kessler, 2005, p. 12). I was full of anger for not foreseeing this and preventing it (even though there was no way I could know). I was angry for being away from my homeland.

> **Failure.** Maybe I was successful in the educational world, but I was a failure in the real world. I failed to see what was to come. I failed in protecting what was most dear to me. I couldn't distinguish between good and evil until evil destroyed the good. Guilt filled my whole being. Why wasn't I there to protect them, where I supposed to be!

Why the hell was I at a foreign country? How selfish! I was angry at my family (for dying) for not being careful and for being too good and innocent: why were they so helpless? "But I can't get angry with you mama." I know both of you struggled till the end of your human power.

Layers of pain released in unexpected magnitudes. "Underneath anger is pain, your pain" (Kubler-Ross & Kessler, 2005, p. 15). Be willing to feel your anger, even though it may seem endless. The more you truly feel it, the more it will begin to dissipate and the more you heal" (12). It was enormous and unending. Guilt follows many survivors, but it is a harsh follower of unnatural death. With murder and suicide incidents, survivors feel guilt for not being able to foresee, avoid or prevent it.

Layers of pain and guilt. I wasn't ready to peel off the skin of my wound, but it was necessary because I couldn't put a bandage over it and let the worm inside eat me.

I felt responsible for their deaths. I had to do something no matter what. It did not matter what I had done, but I had to prevent it some-how. I had to know it better. I had to protect my family. I should not have left them alone. I visualized my family frequently in my head after they died, they appeared more helpless and more in need of pro-tection than before. It broke my heart to think of them in pain. I felt that I betrayed them by being so far away. I made it easy for the enemy to kill them when I left them without protection.

Unwanted Flashbacks. The day time was full of unwanted flashbacks. Sleeping was even harder. The bloody dreams were a usual follower. I was running. We were running. We were hiding. Some nights I was able to save mom or grandma, or both of them. On other nights, I lost them both. When I woke up in the morning, the exhausting reality befell on me. Every wake up was a new shock.

Helpless. What hurts me most is that they hurt you mom? God, it kills me to think of you and your last moments. You know, images come in front of my eyes. I cannot tolerate. It takes life out of my soul. I don't know what to do. No consolation. I am unable to accept that you and grandma had to suffer. Why? Is that the reward of being good? Is that how God punishes good people?

Marching to school Another day to live through…. How hard it is to wash my face and brush my teeth. I don't know how many days has it been since I washed myself. How hard it is to feed myself and go to school. I sat on the couch I don't know how many hours. So much pain.... I had to rush out. My night class, I will be late again. People are laughing and kissing in the street. I feel so helpless.

Two different worlds existed side by side. I could not stand life's energy. It drowned me. Now I am in class. I stare with empty eyes. I am ashamed. I did not read. I don't care about reading. Last time I tried to read, I understood nothing. Sitting in a vegetation state, I heard the professor speak in class. Students participated. I didn't hear the words except sounds of gibberish. I sheepishly wrote another e-mail for an extension. I felt incompetent. I felt less bad when my professor understood me. When they did not understand, I felt very bad.

Days followed weeks, weeks followed months. Life went on. "I have to go on". I marched with a limp, a path that leads only to pain. I fell. I got up. I fell again. Life is an enemy who punches me continuously. "Oh, people are approaching. I must smile again. How hard it is to talk to people. They don't know. They don't understand. I just want to go home and be alone. I can't take all this"

On lonely days I swam in despair. It was nice when someone would check on me or take me out, but it was overwhelming to see the normal world outside. I could not stand happy people all over the campus.

Education World

The death is a taboo subject in education, and violent death is unspeakable. People are not comfortable when learners bring too much of their own pain into the educational setting. We are expected to leave our pain outside of the learning environment. After all, we are here to learn. However, death of a close one persists as a barrier in the learning of adults who find themselves caught in various types of death related losses. This demands attention in adult education/literacy praxis and research.

Educational Monologues

In the world of the education, deadlines continue to come. Responsibilities are expected to be met no matter what. Few people understood the deadline extensions I requested and my lower performance after the tragedy. Next year I was not offered an assistantship, because I was no longer as productive as before. This brought new problems of survival as I struggled to continue with my educational goals. I had to work multiple jobs as I tried to pay tuition and survive. I was embarrassed of my low performance. I was upset and angry. I did not think people understood what I was going through. Oftentimes, people in adult education and learning settings are not prepared for situations of death, let alone violent death and its aftereffects, even if they want to help.

Poetic expressions: a plea

Downfall

I am here today because of yesterday.
I am here today despite the bygones.
If I limp with hurtful scars,
It means I bury feelings.
Look deeply in my way with compassion and love
It is not as it seems
Try to see beyond the surface.

If I carry a bag [full of hurtful moments]
And stolen dreams on my humpback
If I stumble through what doesn't seem thorny
If you stare as I go about my way
Wait a moment, before you conclude
Don't fill the gaps
Spare a moment before you make
"intellectual discriminations"

You have no clue
Before you lose something more valuable than life itself

Pursuit of continuing education was a savior and hindrance simultaneously. I could immerse myself in education to create an escape from my pain, and yet, I was unable to do so because my pain interrupted my learning. I came at the verge of giving up on education many times. Continuing was not an easy path. Education and learning contexts are not prepared to deal with grieving adults. There isn't any personal attention, special programs or services to provide support for learners surviving grief.

> My pain interfered with my participation.... I was unable to follow class discussions, or understand what I was reading. I was late with deadlines. Some people understood. Some did not. I felt lazy. I felt shame. But I went on. One step at a time....

IMPLICATIONS

This autoethnographic inquiry provided a space of freedom to deal with the situation of violent loss and its trauma effects as an adult learner/

student. This research inquiry implies various challenges for the grieving learner in the process of reintegrating back to learning/education, life and society. The auto-narratives implied lack of support services in my experience. All learning milieu, especially ABE (Adult Basic Education) begs for program planning and implementation in order to help grieving adults with their integration to learning goals. Preparations at the individual and program levels will provide adequate support systems for learners and prevent drop-outs as a result of overwhelming aftereffects of a loss.

REFERENCES

Bochner, A. P. (2001). Narrative's virtues. *Qualitative Inquiry, 7,* 131-157.

Bruner, J. (2003). *Making stories: Law, literature, life.* Cambridge, MA: Harvard University Press.

Butler-Kisber, L. (2005).Inquiry through poetry: the genesis of self-study. In C. Mitchell, S. Weber, & K. O'Reilly-Scanlon (Eds.), *Just who do we think we are?: Methodologies for autobiography and self-study in teaching* (pp. 95-110). New York: Routledge Falmer.

Bowlby, J. (1980). *Attachment and loss.* New York: Basic Books.

Behar, R. (1996). *The vulnerable observer: Anthropology that breaks your heart.* Boston: Beacon Press.

Clandinin, D. J., & Connelly, F. M. (2004). *Narrative inquiry: Experience and story in qualitative research.* San Francisco: Jossey-Bass.

Currer, C. (2001). *Responding to grief: Dying, bereavement and social care.* New York: Palgrave.

Kubler-Ross E. (1969). *On death and dying.* New York: Macmillan.

Kubler-Ross, E., & Kessler, D. (2005). *On grief and grieving.* New York: Scribner.

Ellis, C., & Bochner, A. (1996). *Composing ethnography: Alternative forms of qualitative writing.* Thousand Oaks, CA: Sage Publications.

Ellis, C. (June, 2000). Creating criteria: An ethnographic short story. *Qualitative Inquiry, 6,* 273-277.

Ellis, C. (2004). *The ethnographic I: A methodological novel about autoethnography.* Walnut Creek, CA: Alta Mira Press.

Horsman, J. (1999). *Too scared to learn: Women, violence and education.* Canada: McGillian Books.

Lewis, C.S. (1998). *Grief.* Knoxville: Thomas Nelson.

Maciejewski, P. K., Zhang, B., Block, S. D., & Prigerson, H. G. (2007). An empirical examination of the stage theory of grief. *The Journal of the American Medical Association, 297,* 716-723.

Parkes, C. (1972). *Bereavement: Studies in grief in adult life.* London: Tavistock.

Reed-Danahay, D. (1997). *Autoethnography: Rewriting the self and the social.* New York: Berg Publishers.

Rynearson, E. K. (2005). The narrative labyrinth of violent dying. *Death Studies, 29,* 351-360.

Spry, T. (2001). Performing autoethnography: An embodied methodological praxis. *Qualitative Inquiry*, 7, 706-731.

Stephenson, J. S. (1985). Death and the campus community: Organizational realities and personal tragedies. In E. S. Zinner (Ed.), *Coping with death on campus* (pp. 5-15). San Francisco: Jossey-Bass.

Zinner, E. S. (1985). Group survivorship: A model with death on campus. In E. S. Zinner (Ed.), *Coping with death on campus* (pp. 1-3). San Francisco: Jossey-Bass.

CHAPTER 31

A DIFFERENCE OF DEGREE

A Case Study of Iresa Stubblefield-Jones

Carrie J. Boden

It was up to me to take a stand to change the discourse of my life that was branded on me when I was a child, that label that was put on me when I was in school.

—Iresa Stubblefield-Jones

Even when harried from arriving a bit late for the interview, Iresa-Stubblefield Jones has a quiet confidence about her. Her tall and slender frame is accentuated by a designer knit top, skinny jeans, and stylish shoes. Iresa's features are beautiful: smooth, mocha skin, a warm and inviting smile, and intelligent eyes. A woman in her 30s, she has a compelling but quiet demeanor suggesting potential, confidence, and attentiveness. As the conversation begins, Iresa opens up immediately and carefully tells the story of her empowerment through literacy.

The story of Iresa is deeply entwined with her experiences at the University of Arkansas at Little Rock (UALR). In a recent promotional campaign, UALR features a series of billboards depicting a falling drop of water at the moment it impacts a pool. A slogan at the bottom of the frame reads: "A Difference of Degree." In this visual image, the ripple

Empowering Women Through Literacy: Views From Experience, pp. 211–219
Copyright © 2009 by Information Age Publishing

effect is to be seen to reach out beyond the frame of the advertisement, suggesting that a college education will have a spreading impact throughout an individual's life—and the lives of others—in ways that are immediate and lasting, individual and societal. The image suggests that the boundaries of one's place in the world will expand almost infinitely if given the right opportunities. Rarely is there such truth in advertising as the case of Iresa Stubblefield-Jones.

Iresa's description of her educational journey starts before she entered school when she was diagnosed as Attention Deficit Hyperactivity Disorder (ADHD) and placed on Ritalin. Iresa describes her elementary school years as being plagued with doubt and struggles. Iresa was placed in resource classes for all of elementary school. She was labeled as "slow," a brand that her family also recognized as fitting. By junior high school, Iresa was in a combination of mainstream and resource classes, and at many points she was told that she was incapable of learning. For example, in a recent interview Iresa shared that in one resource class her teacher told her to "just go outside and play because you're trying to learn something that's impossible." (All quotations from Iresa Stubblefield-Jones are from a personal interview, October 14, 2008.)

Up to this point in her schooling, Iresa had received much negative feedback about herself as a learner. She came to believe that she could not learn. This fits with Belenky et al.'s (1986) observation "that others can have such power in defining how people see themselves" and this "undoubtedly helps to account for the fact that people born with all their senses intact and with a reasonable share of gray matter can be discouraged so completely from recognizing, utilizing, and developing their intellectual powers" (p. 49).

During high school, this pattern continued. Iresa was mainstreamed in a non college-bound track. Iresa recounts that in a math class, one of her classmates was tutoring her during class time. The teacher recognized this as being to the detriment of the other student and told Iresa, "You don't have to worry about doing this. Just sit here. I'll give you a 'C.' I know you can't do it." Likewise, during parent-teacher conferences, Iresa's parents were told that they would need to watch over her because she is "slow and could easily end up in the Welfare System with a house full of babies."

Because of the negative feedback that Iresa was getting about herself as a learner at home and at school, art courses became a welcome oasis. Contrary to what had been the case in her previous studies, Iresa was told that she was a gifted art student and that she had the ability to succeed in this area. This was a transformative experience; Iresa alludes to it as the beginnings of her confidence in herself. According to Clark (1993), "transformational learning *shapes* people; they are different afterward, in ways both they and others can recognize" (as cited in Merriam & Brockett,

1997, p. 142, emphasis in the original). Iresa was certainly different after she participated in an art contest supported by the local literacy council. The theme was "Literacy: the Key to Unlock Minds." Iresa submitted an abstract ink drawing that she describes as a "a person, the mind, the brain, and the inner being … lines all through it … an empty shell" waiting to be filled with literacy. Ireas's drawing won second place in the contest, and this, along with Iresa's other projects, awards, and showings, was enough for her to receive an art scholarship to the Art Institute of Dallas. Unfortunately, Iresa's family could not afford to send her to art school, so she was unable to take advantage of the opportunity. Instead, she began working several of what she describes as "dead end jobs" in the years immediately after she completed high school.

During this time in Iresa's life, her identity was largely contingent on external authority, or the views that others had of her. As she illustrates, "I wanted to be looked at in a positive light … as more than just a person who could draw and paint. You know, I liked to be looked as someone who could do more." This desire was the beginning of a transformative process for Iresa; she describes converting the negative voices about her learning into a powerful motivation:

> So all those negative things that were said about me, I wanted to show them. I wanted to show them that you cannot put a label on someone and stick it on them and expect for them to breathe it and eat it and live it. Because that person can change. So I was on a mission when I was older to change how people viewed me in school and even how my parents and teachers got in their mind that I was a dumb daughter. I let them know that I have a voice.

While Iresa had confidence in her abilities as an artist and was beginning to develop her own inner-voice, she still lacked confidence in her academic prowess. After several years of working without being able to make a living, Iresa began investigating educational opportunities. She attended General Educational Development (GED) courses at the Adult Education Center on Scott Street. "I was the only one in there with a high school diploma," Iresa said, "I've never been a good test taker [and] I would have never achieved a [college] degree, so my thing was [to attend Scott Street] as just a refresher." Iresa attended GED courses for three nights a week for about a year before she had the confidence to enroll in college. She says, "I was a D student … and they told me I had to take remedial courses in order to go to school, … so that's what I did."

Iresa's first college experiences in the 1990s were at Philander Smith College, a private, historically black college in Little Rock, Arkansas. During her first semester, Iresa initially enrolled in one course and then dropped out. Semesters later, she again went back and enrolled in Developmental Reading and English courses. Although she completed approximately 50 credits over six years, she did not feel that she received the help she needed. "I didn't get a lot of the help I needed until I attended UALR.... Things [at Philander Smith] weren't properly organized ... I couldn't ever get a scholarship ... and the teachers were just not very helpful," Iresa said. During the time that Iresa was attending Philander Smith College, her mother was attending UALR. Iresa recounts that in order to bring her family together, "I made a deal with my husband. If he would transfer to UALR, so would I."

The transfer to UALR in 1999 marked a turning point for Iresa; this change was the beginning of a clear, positive progression in her beliefs about herself as a learner. While at UALR, she had several positive encounters with faculty and staff, and she received the guidance she needed in developing her reading, math, and writing skills. In one incident, Iresa enrolled in and dropped the same developmental math class several times before completing it. During this time, she worked with the same math tutor, Yvonne Delnis, over several semesters. Iresa recalls,

> She [Yvonne] never looked down on me if I didn't know an answer ... or something basic, and she just helped me and showed me ways to look at things. She was the one I looked up to ... if it weren't for her, I don't know how I would've gotten through math. She was such a positive influence on me.

Iresa successfully completed her developmental coursework. Her math skills had improved so much that by the time she took her statistics course, she no longer needed tutoring. "I was able to apply the things that she [Yvonne] helped me with and I learned, and I applied it and did all right," Iresa said. As a transfer student, Iresa had not taken the reading placement test; however, she self-diagnosed that she needed reading help. Because of her positive experiences with the math tutoring, Iresa had the confidence to ask for help in other areas, too. She developed a relationship with Lynn Strong, the Reading Lab Coordinator, and over time Lynn worked with Iresa on her reading skills.

In addition to help with math and reading skills, Iresa received help on her writing skills from Huey Crisp, the Director of Composition. At the time Iresa attended UALR, all students were required to pass a writing examination in order to graduate from the university. Iresa took the examination during her junior year and did not pass. She recalls, "I talked to the professor and found out why I didn't pass. Dr. Crisp sat me down and went through things with me, and I decided to minor in writing. I figured that would help me become a better writer." Another professor in the English department, Dr. Zabelle Stodola, also had a positive effect on Iresa's development. Iresa shares,

She started working with me before class. We would meet sometimes after class, and she would go over my papers and tell me what I was doing wrong and what I needed to do; she had me reading extra things to get a better understanding ... she went the extra mile to work with me.

With her newfound confidence in her academic abilities, for the first time, Iresa began to consider herself "an insider" in the academic world. She arrived what Kasworm (1999) would call the "inclusion knowledge-voice." According to Kasworm, there are five categories of student knowledge voices: entry voice, outside voice, critical voice, straddling voice, and inclusion voice. Inclusion voice learners actively seek out academic knowledge and the academic world. This group of learners integrates academic meaning and application of knowledge into their everyday lives. Iresa says, "The more I learned, the more people that I have met, like Yvonne [Delnis] ... Dr. Stodola, Huey Crisp ... just people like that—educators and academics have changed me." Iresa came to see the culture of the university as "her culture," and she was a Chancellor's List student and a McNair Scholar. Among her several accolades as a student, as part of the McNair Scholars Program she presented her research on academic dishonesty to the UALR community.

Perhaps the most valuable skill that Iresa gained during this time was writing. Iresa began to find her own voice and shift to a subjective way of knowing. Belenky et al. (1986) describe the shift to subjectivism as "the move away from silence and an externally oriented perspective on knowledge and truth [to] a new conception of truth as personal, private, and subjectively known or intuited" (p. 54). Belenky et al. (1986) point out that this is

> a particularly significant shift for women when and if it occurs ... as a woman becomes more aware of the existence of inner resources for knowing and valuing, as she begins to listen to the "still small voice" within her, she finds an inner source of strength ... [and] become[s] [her] own authorit[y]. (Belenky et al., 1986, p. 54)

When Iresa needs to find her "still small voice," she uses writing. Iresa says, "When I hurt, when I'm sad, I write. When I'm angry at work, I write. When I'm angry, it helps me calm down." Further, Iresa shares, "When I want to put something behind me, I write it and tear it up. Burn it. Throw it in the trash can. It is over. It is out."

When Iresa graduated from UALR in 2003, she earned a Bachelor of Arts in Psychology and a minor in Rhetoric and Writing. Iresa went on to complete a Master of Arts in Rhetoric and Writing with a Fiction/Non-Fiction emphasis in 2006. During her graduate studies, Iresa worked with the *Little Rock Writing Project* and completed her Master's thesis, *Daughters of Arch Street*, which was later published as a double-memoir in 2007. Iresa's motivation to write this memoir initially came from her desire to improve the neighborhood of her childhood, Arch Street. Iresa's memories of the neighborhood as it was in her childhood and as it is today stands as a stark contrast to her mother's idyllic memories of Arch Street in the 1960s. Iresa recalls,

> I wanted to change the neighborhood as far as physically rebuilding the old condemned houses, get some funding in there, fix up old homes and sell them, and try to get new and different people with some kind of morals to move into those houses, which would help the neighborhood.

Iresa soon realized, though, that the physical changes might be the easier ones to make. She points out, "If you rebuild the neighborhood but the minds of the people that lived there haven't changed, then has the neighborhood really changed?" This idea sparked another stream of thought for Iresa. She explains, "So then I started thinking, maybe we need to change the way people think first. If we can change the way people think, then we can work on the physical part."

Through the writing process, Iresa again found that "inner change" is perhaps more difficult to enact than "physical" change. She had transformative moments while writing her memoir; however, the change that occurred was not the change she was expecting. As she describes how her memoir unfolds, the project became less about repairing a neighborhood and more about restoring her relationship with her mother. Iresa shares,

> I had a chance to listen to my mom and write what she had to say in her words and then write how I felt.... I had a chance to actually feel not just what I felt in what I was writing, but to actually feel some of the things that my mom was telling me and show how she felt about the neighborhood.... Even though I might not agree with some of the things that she said, ... I had a chance to be more open ... to her side.

Through the act of writing, Iresa was able to change her perspective, understandings, and, ultimately, her reality.

A theme that came up over and over again during the interview with Iresa is the role that writing has played in her life. "Writing has changed me," Iresa said. She also commented on the roles reading has taken on in her life. Iresa points out, "You can't write if you don't read." In one instance, Iresa attributes finding her voice through reading *I Know Why the Caged Bird Sings* (Angelou, 1970). For Iresa, this book speaks to overcoming struggles, "being an individual, and being able to find a way to do that without having that support group or support person," Iresa said. Iresa equates Maya Angelou's childhood silence with her own "voiceless" years as a youngster. "You know even though I had my family," Iresa said, "in some ways I didn't…. When the system told me that I was one way, they accepted that, and that's how they looked at me. They considered me … slow and my brother the smart one." Iresa recounts that "because of how teachers looked at me [and] … how my parents looked at me, you could say I didn't have a voice."

Iresa makes a clear distinction between her childhood voice and her voice now. She terms these the "negative" and "positive" voices. Even though the positive voice is dominant in her adulthood, according to Iresa,

> It seems that there are two voices. Let me tell you why … even though I've accomplished the things I've accomplished, I still have an inferiority complex that was ingrained in me and engraved on me and branded since I was a child … I catch myself even now [with that] feeling. It's a scary, sad, stupid feeling. "You can't do this."

Because of Iresa's fear of "being looked at as a dumb, stupid, slow girl," she employs strategies in order to make sure that her work is correct. Iresa says, "I have my electronic spell checker. I have my reference manuals. I'm online to look up stuff to make sure … I'm constantly second-guessing myself." Iresa recognizes that "you can draw power from negative things, from negative words … the positive voice supersedes the negative voice because I draw energy from the negative voice which turns into a positive." As an adult, Iresa has learned to use a negative voice as a source of motivation to achieve positive outcomes.

In terms of a support system, Hall and Donaldson (1997) point out that for women as learners, the social and the psychological interact. In their study, "lack of a support system" was a significant factor in women not receiving an education. Another factor was termed "lack of voice." According to Hall and Donaldson (1997),

> at the heart of non participation lies a "deterrent" so deeply embedded in some women that no theory can fully capture its meaning. The way a woman feels about herself, her self-esteem and self confidence, and the way she can express herself are significant elements in her decision about whether to participate in adult education. (as cited in Merriam & Caffarella, 1999, p. 58)

Iresa has come to the conclusion that it is very important for women learners to become their own support systems. Iresa contends, "even if you don't have the support, you can be your own support." It was this ability to serve as her own support system that enabled Iresa to have the confidence to enroll in college and to persevere. This confidence gave

Iresa the agency to take responsibility for her own learning. Of her own experience, she explains, "it was up to me to take a stand to change the discourse of my life that was branded on me when I was a child, that label that was put on me when I was in school."

Iresa has, indeed, changed the discourse of her life, and UALR, in serving out its mission as a metropolitan university, has been an integral part of this journey. Through taking advantage of the developmental classes, tutoring programs in the Academic Success Center, mentoring programs, such as the McNair Scholars Program, and other resources available at UALR, Iresa has metamorphosed an inner voice that says "I can't" into one that says "I can." Her deep and ongoing relationships with faculty and staff at UALR have improved this inner-dialogue and have made additional dreams, such as eventually attending law school or earning a doctorate, possible. Through example and action, Iresa encourages others to pursue a college education. She says,

> I was always told that I wasn't college material. Well, I'm here to tell you that anyone is college material if they want to be. It may take some extra time and some extra work, but you can do it. Anyone can.

Much can be learned from Iresa's case—for potential students and teachers alike. Iresa's educational journey, like the drop of water in the UALR advertisement, has had a dramatic impact on her inner and outer lives. She is currently working as an Extended Service Representative for Maverick Transportation and is managing her own business, Professional Writing Services. Iresa is also involved in UALR's public service campaign

Figure 31.1.   Iresa Stubblefield-Jones.

for encouraging participation in higher and technical education. As she is exploring the next stages in her endeavors, the ripples are pushing out to the community and beyond with a positive voice that says it is, indeed, possible for ordinary people to achieve exceptional goals.

ACKNOWLEDGEMENTS

Iresa Stubblefield-Jones would like to thank her husband, Christopher, son, Christopher, Jr., and her mother and father, Dwinna and Billy, for their unwavering support.

REFERENCES

Angelou, M. (1970). *I know why the caged bird sings.* New York: Random House.

Belenky, M. F., Clinchy, B. M., Goldberger, N. R., & Tarule, J. M. (1986). *Women's ways of knowing: The development of self, voice, and mind.* New York: Basic Books, Inc.

Kasworm, C. E. (1999). Adult meaning making in the undergraduate classroom. In A. Rose (Ed.). *The 40th Annual Adult Education Research Conference* (pp. 449-454). DeKalb, IL: Northern Illinois University. Retrieved August 3, 2008, from: http://www.edst.educ.ubc.ca/aerc/1999/ab1999.htm

Merriam, S. B., & Brockett, R. G. (1997). *The profession and practice of adult education: An introduction.* San Francisco: Jossey-Bass.

Merriam, S. B., & Caffarella, R. S. (1999). *Learning in adulthood: A comprehensive guide* (2nd ed.). San Francisco: Jossey-Bass.

Stubblefield-Jones, I. E. (2007). *Daughters of Arch Street: A double memoir.* Bloomington: Author House.

CHAPTER 32

MAKING A BEACH

Women, Community, and Democracy at The Open Book

Dianne Ramdeholl, Stacie Evans, and John Gordon

I remember when I began the classes we had this tiny place in the basement and in between these lockers they had these little, tiny chairs so it was uncomfortable ... I remember talking to the students before I first started. I said, you know that I have struggled too and I have struggled with reading and with studying. I know how difficult this is. I said, you just ask me if you want any help. You know like I can't give too much but I can give a little grain of sand; you know a few grains here, a few grains there, we make a beach. So that's what we're going to do here; we're going to start with a little grain of sand. (Cecilia, The Open Book's first counselor)

COMMUNITY

What community means to me: to be there for others and to try to lift each other up when we're down.... We're from different places and also different cultures, but we are still one in this school. You can't believe what this school means to me. (Maria, former student at the Open Book)

Empowering Women Through Literacy: Views From Experience, pp. 221–232

Adult education students often speak of the strong feelings of community they find in their programs–so much so that Maria's comment will strike many practitioners as familiar. Teachers and researchers cite student feelings of connectedness and belonging as a critical element in successful adult literacy programs (Auerbach, 1992; Cook 1989; Martin, 2001; Purcell-Gates, 2000). But while many in the literacy world have spoken of the importance of building a sense of community, stories that might illuminate the process have often gone unheard and the resultant changes in the ways students see themselves and their place in the world have been given short shrift in the outcome driven world of government and foundation funding. Since 1998, when the passing of the Workforce Investment Act and the establishment of the National Reporting System enshrined higher test scores as the mainmeasure—of program quality, community has all but dropped off the radar in adult education.

Why do students so often point to the significance of community? Are students, in fact, articulating a theory of learning? Is this attention to community particularly common to women? What are the implications for those of us (teachers and students) engaged in the practice of adult education?

Maria discusses the level of comfort and unity she has found at the school. She identifies mutual support and commitment to other students as key features of community. She speaks as well of overcoming divisions and barriers. Perhaps most importantly, she indicates that the sense of community she has helped to create is more than a secondary feature supporting the learning process; it is a central aspect of her experience at the school.

This chapter tells some of the story of the Open Book, a small community based literacy program in Brooklyn, New York. We explore the intersections between the development of the program as a women's space, conscious efforts to build community within the school, and our attempts to implement authentic and participatory democratic practices. We hope to show that rather than being passive beneficiaries of these developments, students—particularly women—were a driving force behind them. It is our hope as well that the Open Book experience will offer some possible directions for others interested in developing liberatory adult literacy models.

Founded in 1985 by Good Shepherd Services, a local agency providing programs for children and families, The Open Book offered basic literacy and pre-GED classes in South Brooklyn for 16 years, until it closed its doors in 2002–a victim of underfunding and the national shift to adult literacy as workforce development. Though the Open Book was open to anyone over 16 years old, the student body was primarily women. In the early years, a large percentage of students were single mothers, many of them on public assistance. The school was racially and ethnically diverse; many students came from the working class communities immediately surrounding the school. As time went on and gentrification drove those students out of the neighborhood, the student body broadened to include students from all over Brooklyn.

The theme of community emerged as students, particularly women, consistently spoke of their feelings about the school's environment, even comparing it to family.

> A lot of students feel like this is their second home. Some feel like it's their first home. It makes a difference because you feel people really love you here and they support you here. They support you all the way. (Basemah, former student at the Open Book)

> Most of us in our class give a damn about each other. They sort of look out for each other. If someone comes in and says they're upset about something, people around you understand that. They see it. They allow for it, and they don't bust your bubble. The teacher allows for it, too. Everybody seems to care for each other. (Julia, former student at the Open Book)

> We build each other up. We build each other's self-confidence up. We really do…. In the three hours when the teacher is here, she can't do it all, so we come earlier to grab more of what we can. We'll do the dictionary or we'll type. We'll read. We'll help each other. If she don't know something—she's a very good reader—she'll help me with my reading and comprehension, and if she don't know her math, I'm going to help her. That's what brings us together. We try to help each other get to where we want to be. (Rochelle, former student at the Open Book)

The teachers embraced these notions, but it was students who through their actions made it a reality. Students created community by painting the space when we first moved there in 1985, by taking responsibility to make coffee every day, by holding parties and throwing baby showers. They built community by calling each other between classes or when someone had been absent for a while, by comforting each other when they were down, and by building informal networks with each other. They challenged each other to be more focused in class, to keep the space clean, to participate more. They shared their stories, taking risks and exposing their heartaches, their pain, and their struggles.

It was through the practice of storytelling—through writing, oral histories, and in-class discussion—that women played a particularly powerful role in building community. Women used the classroom as a place to talk about what was going on in their lives. They talked about their children and their families; they told stories and shared their medical diagnoses. In her first week of class, Rose Marie shocked us when she told the class she had breast cancer. Maria, who had been in the class a while, said she also had breast cancer—something no one knew. A deep connection formed between them. The exchange brought the class together but it wouldn't have happened if people didn't feel able to use the classroom to share what was going on in their lives. That day in our first year became a formative moment in the Open Book's history, a touchstone for much of what came later.

The next year, Stephanie, one of the teachers, taped several oral histories with her students. She typed them up and brought them back into the class as texts. The storytellers, two men and two women, focused mainly on their experiences with learning, in school and out, their struggles with the stigma of not being able to read, and their efforts to overcome that. We turned those stories into a self-published 92-page book titled *Four Stories: Oral Histories from The Open Book,* which became a text for many of the classes and provoked an outpouring of storytelling. In the next couple of years, we taped six more oral histories and published two more books entitled *It Should Be Told* and *I See a Part of Myself.* These stories, all told by women, focused almost exclusively on issues of domestic violence and abuse.

Were women, in fact, consciously seeking community at the school? Or was the open and collaborative approach they brought rooted in their own cultural practices of mutual support and sharing? As time went on they became more confident and sure of themselves within the school, and earlier notions of the school as community and family evolved into a theory of learning.

Cecilia came to the Open Book as an administrative assistant one month after we opened our doors and just weeks after she had gotten her GED. She eventually became our first counselor. Born in Venezuela, she had only gone to the third grade but had read widely and was not afraid to challenge the ideas of the teachers. In positing her notion of "making a beach," Cecilia recognizes the central place of collaboration and mutual help in a slow and difficult process. In offering a humble view of her role and by implication that of the rest of the staff, she articulated a non-hierarchical perspective shaping the view Open Books's learning process. Her view reverses the notion of teacher as expert and envisions a process of co-teaching and co-learning where everyone (teachers included) contribute her/his grains of sand.

A WOMEN-CENTERED SPACE

I see a part of myself inside each woman the first time I meet them ... I dream of us working together and helping each other. I want us to stand up together. I want all women to be able to stand up for themselves the way I did. (Basemah, former student and Assistant Teacher at The Open Book)

Because the student body was overwhelmingly female, there were many opportunities for women to shape the culture. Women's concerns and perspectives tended to dominate classroom discussions, and they were likely to be involved in any activities that took place. While their sheer numbers assured that they would play a strong role at the Open Book, women embraced the program and made the space their own—bringing in plants, building relationships, and telling their stories. They brought their personal lives into the classroom and made them part of the ongoing dialogue; in the process, they asserted their values and placed certain practices at the center of the school's culture. This process proved both organic, growing out of how they were with each other, and conscious, as they articulated and developed a philosophy of education.

> They need talking. When I see someone just back to school, they are nervous. They get scared like when they were a kid. They need a lot of confidence. Call them. Talk to them at school. There are a lot of people who are in the closet because they can't read. (Dee, former student at the Open Book)

> It is important to talk to the students about the personal problems they may be having and that may be getting in the way of learning. I think many students come to school to escape from personal problems.... When people feel comfortable to share, they feel comfortable to ask questions. They write and then they come and share their ideas. You feel you're not the only one having problems.... The Open Book is stronger now. Each person has a voice and has a lot to say. (Basemah, former student and counselor at the Open Book)

Literacy programs are spaces filled with possibility. Students arrive, brimming with hopes and dreams and goals and promises to themselves. Part of a school's job is to speak to those dreams, to provide space and time for people to find and redefine themselves—on their own terms. For women, this can be an especially powerful experience. Stacie (former instructor) says, "For women there was a feeling when you walked into the Open Book, even for the first time, that you could exhale, that you could be yourself." Maddie (former student) adds, "Here you don't have to be afraid to say anything. I forget my problems when I'm here. When I leave here ... when I step out the door, I'm thinking about my problems."

Stacie's evening class had a core group of strong women who possessed an enormous amount of dignity, common sense, street wisdom, caring and generosity. One student, Chantal, was active and clear thinking in class, comfortable in her skin, funny. She asked a lot of questions, had strong opinions, and was sensitive to the social dynamics in the classroom. She got along with other students and seemed to have a lot of self-confidence. She got frustrated with the pace of her progress from time to time, but seemed very 'together' for the most part.

One night when her boyfriend came to pick her up after class, Chantal offered Stacie a ride home. As they drove, Chantal's boyfriend tossed her a newspaper and told her to read it to him, something that was extremely difficult, given Chantal's beginning reading level. Chantal said she couldn't read it and the man berated her: wasn't she learning anything in school, how long did she think she was going to have to study before she could read one word, what would happen to her if he left her when she couldn't even read a little newspaper … Stacie spoke up for Chantal, but Chantal told her not to worry about it, said everything was fine.

This happened each time Stacie accepted a ride from Chantal. The boyfriend would ask Chantal to read or spell something, ask if she had her GED already and then he'd tell her how useless and helpless she was and how much she needed to depend on him because she obviously couldn't do for herself. Stacie would intervene, Chantal would tell her not to worry about it. Stacie stopped accepting rides because she couldn't stand to see Chantal treated badly, couldn't stand to see that Chantal felt she had to accept that treatment.

Why was Chantal such a different person in the classroom? Clearly, in the classroom she felt comfortable enough, safe enough to be a more complete version of herself, not the quiet, head-down, nodding-at-every-insult woman Stacie saw after class. And, of course, Chantal's boyfriend wasn't in the classroom. The difference probably owed much more to the friendship Chantal had classmates who were kind of mother-sisters with her. They encouraged her to ask questions and say what she was thinking, to share with the group. Her connection with them provided powerful grounding allowing her to 'switch on' her more dynamic, strong persona in class.

But the Open Book was more than a place where women could be who they wanted to be; it was also a space where it was safe to engage with new ideas, explore differences, re-think old assumptions, take on new identities. One of the things Stacie liked best about the dynamic in the program was how much room was made for difference, including for *her* and the differences she represented. Although she looked like many of her students, she wasn't very much like them—not just in terms of education and background, but in terms of length of time living in New York, familiarity with the city, and—most importantly—experiences and realities as a person of color. A lot of things separated them, or could have. And that kind of separation was evident in often comical ways, such as when she walked into class one night with a vegetarian dinner and Maxine, an older

African American student, gave the dish a skeptical once-over and declared: "Stacie, you eat white people food." There were ways that the differences could have created barriers between Stacie and her students. But the students accepted her wit all her perceived oddness and she's-not-one-of-us-ness. What could have become divisive became an "of course." That willingness to make room for difference helped create the ease students felt at the Open Book.

Shirley, a tall, strong, opinionated woman, sometimes expressed anger about her life in New York and about the narrow work options her limited education afforded her. On the subject of homosexuality, she declared she was "all Jamaican," which was her way of saying she was utterly homophobic. She told the class that, if one of her children was gay, she would kill him. Other Jamaican students in the class insisted not all Jamaicans felt that way, but Shirley persisted, saying that no "real" Jamaican could stand to be near a gay person.

Soon afterwards, a new student, Edith, introduced herself to the class as Puerto Rican lesbian, beating her addiction with Narcotics Anonymous. She said she had been a member of the Guardian Angels and a runaway. The class was more than a little taken aback by her forthright entrance, but no one seemed too concerned: except, of course, for Shirley. Shirley wouldn't acknowledge anything Edith said and made a point of always sitting far from Edith. For a while it seemed that she might be upset enough by Edith's presence that she would drop the class.

One night Edith collapsed in an epileptic seizure in class. For a second, everyone froze, unsure what to do, but Shirley, who had worked as a home health aide in Jamaica, took over. In control, she calmed everyone, held and consoled Edith so she could ride out the seizure as gently as possible.

After the seizure, Shirley's behavior with Edith changed completely. She sat beside her every night, worked with her on reading and math; sometimes even put her arm around her to give her a shake when she got frustrated or angry with something. She became Edith's closest friend in the class, and a kind of 'protector.' Shirley's ideas about homosexuality didn't change, but she began to see gay people as *people*. Her friendship with Edith made it possible for her to listen when the subject of homosexuality came up in class lessons or conversations, something she had never been able to do before.

Students' commitment to bring their life issues into the classroom and teachers openness to creating space essentially created an environment that honored women's pluralistic narratives and polyrhythmic realities. Sheared (1990) explains polyrhythmic realities as women's multiple ways of knowing and understanding their realities but also of experiencing intersecting realities simultaneously, poly-rhythmically. Women centeredness honors one's everyday lived experiences grounded in race, class, and gender (Sheared, 2001). In The Open Book's teaching and learning space students defined themselves on their own terms in their own realities as they explored and co-constructed alternative ways of being and living with each other in the world.

STUDENT PARTICIPATION/DEMOCRATIC EFFORTS

> Each person has a voice and a lot to say. You get to know people in their deep insides and then you're not afraid to share. More people need to be involved. We need students as leaders...I would like to see students think of it as their place. (Basemah, former student and counselor at The Open Book)

Student participation at the Open Book began with conversations about curricula in the classrooms but made its way into all essential aspects of program planning. There were multiple spaces/places for students to practice participation in democratic decision-making processes. By attempting to foster a culture that unequivocally placed students at its center, students and instructors co-created space for students' stories and struggles. One day, for example, Basemah approached John and informed him a group of women wanted to start a group to discuss issues they were experiencing as women. The group used the library and met over the next 7 months.

> I needed this bad. Your mind can't get set on school when you have so many problems in your own house. The group helped to relieve the anger, the tears, and the frustration in my life. I wished it lasted but some students just weren't taking it seriously. (Rose Marie, a former Open Book student at the Open Book)

> When we had the first student support group, half of the group was really strong, half wasn't. We fought. Then we started again. We talked. Now we're not going to hide anything. We are going to make it work this time. When people feel comfortable, they share, they feel comfortable to ask questions. You feel you're not the only one having problems. (Basemah, a former Open Book student and assistant teacher at the Open Book)

John adds, "Several of the women had already been in groups before that were run by social workers. Here they were looking for a place where they could give each other support as women."

In 1987, a group of students and teachers went to a literacy conference at Lehman College and attended a presentation by students from Bronx Educational Services who worked as assistant teachers in their classes. Inspired, we began talking about whether we could do that. We got a small grant to hire one student who attended the advanced class three days a week and worked as an assistant teacher in the beginning class two days a week. That became the Assistant Teacher model.

Cunningham (2001) asks to what degree we are willing to democratize our practice; are we challenging the marginalization of certain groups while remaining silent about others? Hiring students as assistant teachers was one of a number of initiatives that attempted to institutionalize students' knowledge while simultaneously re-constructing landscapes of power. By subverting paradigms of teacher as expert, we open up spaces to sow seeds of democracy. "Tutoring has been a great experience not only because I've been helpful to students but they have been great tutors for me too. You could say our relationship is like the saying, "hands wash hands, but they both wash the face" (Cecilia, former counselor at the Open Book). Yolanda adds, "We all learned from each other … not only from the teachers but from other students. We all contributed a little something to people's lives and I think that's what made it special."

From early on, the Open Book included students in the hiring process. Whenever a teaching position opened up, we would form a hiring committee consisting of approximately two staff members and 8 students. The committee would meet to study resumes, interview the top candidates, and collectively decide who might be the best fit for the school's community.

> I thought that was one very important part of the program. Students felt such importance to be able to participate like that. They felt it showed a respect for them because they got to choose their teachers. It wasn't imposed on them like in other programs. (Cecilia, a former counselor at the Open Book)

There was also space for town hall meetings (where different classes got together and discussed aspects of the program they felt ought to look different), full day and weekend retreats (where students spent part of their time caucusing on their own without staff present), the counseling group (a space where students could discuss issues they were struggling with outside the program), and the student-teacher council (where a smaller group of students and teachers met to discuss issues impacting the future of the school).

What is the purpose of democratic practice/student leadership? In whose interests is this conceived? Who benefits? How exactly can students begin to envision spaces/places as their own? Adult literacy students are primarily poor people of color, a group who today are for the most part confined to the margins. (Macedo, 1994). What might the implications be of re-writing dominant narratives where marginalized groups have the possibility of authoring words and worlds instead of being confined solely to the role of consumers? To what extent can students subvert master narratives that are insidiously embedded in mainstream society's collective historical memory and explode dominant and de-humanizing notions of power into de-centralized fragments, each fragment rooted in agency and possibility?

When thinking about issues at the heart of furthering democracy, space must be made and sustained to unpack power dynamics/structures in the classroom, in programs, and in society. Democratic practice and power are closely intertwined in complex ways filled with inherent contradictions and dilemmas. Space for multiple voices/interests/agendas to be listened to and taken seriously must be co-created. We believe it is important to acknowledge that a monolithic view of democracy, privileging equal participation of all, is unrealistic. Structures must be in place for quieter voices to access these conversations as well as alternative ways to grapple with how students can re-direct dominant notions of power. Democratic practice takes us beyond cultural provincialism by attacking legacies of imperialism and colonization with a deep commitment to support a teaching/learning environment that provides opportunities to articulate and analyze multiple experiences. (Heaney & Colin, 2001). Students must be cognizant of the possibilities/ways they can co-create, shape, and influence the culture of the program. Shor (1996) refers to this as democratic disturbances to teacher-centeredness.

> When we have important decisions to make, we bring them to the students. It's not always easier that way; sometimes it would be a lot quicker to have the teachers make the decisions or for me to make a decision by myself. But we believe that in the long run decisions we make will be better if we make them as a community. (John, teacher-coordinator at the Open Book)

> What usually happens in other programs is when one person has more power, it usually means the other person has less but I didn't think that happened at the Open Book. It just seemed like when people got more power, it was good because it meant it was shared. (Nancy, former instructor at the Open Book)

At the heart of democratic practice are attempts to re-distribute power in more equitable ways. Through unpacking cultures of school—who produces knowledge, whose ideas are privileged, whose interests prevail in decision-making, who teaches, who learns—the Open Book posed an alternative to dominant narratives. Here everyone co-constructed knowledge. Currently, structures of power privilege a few. The goal is to transform oppressive structures into something more liberatory that explicitly states everyone has a basic right to be treated with dignity and humanity. The Open Book strove to enact some undergirding assumptions towards this reality. Was sustainable agency actually fostered in the Open Book's culture? We would like to believe yes. Was this true for everyone? Definitely not. Even in seemingly equitable landscapes, we need to be mindful of to what extent power dynamics are being truly re-routed or the old order of competitions/rewards of dominant schooling inadvertently being re-created? Is the space dominated by students with the most clearly shaped ideas? Do we (as administrators) unconsciously signal approval to those whose thinking reflects our own? Are internalized dominant notions of power ever fully ejected from any of our consciousness?

To what extent did all of this occur and get unpacked at The Open Book? Did people sometimes feel silenced, choose not to engage, retreat? How can we learn to co-create equitable landscapes that shift power without being destroyed by invisible landmines? Freire (1970) reminds us that education can never be neutral. Unpacking power issues can move us closer to clearer understandings of (and fuller participation in) democracy. Only then can we begin to unshackle oppressive chains of history that have left us all as oppressors, oppressed, and often both. While practicing principles of democracy can seem daunting and elusive, it is only by attempting this that we are able to live out the contradictions, grapple with the dilemmas, and finally be part of dismantling legacies of colonization, in order to truly transform the world.

WEAVING TAPESTRIES WHILE REFLECTING CRITICALLY

We believe there is an urgent need for stories in the field that recognize alternative sets of possibilities in literacy. The public collective historical memory of literacy as involving more than workforce development is fast receding. The history of adult literacy in social justice struggles is mentioned less and less. As a field, we can no longer afford to continue working in varying degrees of historical amnesia. In order for adult education to be consistent with fostering democracy, students' voices must be heard at every level of program planning, decision-making and policy. Adult literacy programs need to engage in emancipatory models of education if the field is to be true to its historical roots and become a site for practicing more humane and loving visions of society.

REFERENCES

Auerbach, E. (1992). *Making meaning making change.* Washington, DC: Center for AppliedLinguistics.

Colin, S., & Heaney, T. (2001) Negotiating the democratic classroom. In C. Hansman and P. Sissel (Eds.), *Understanding and negotiating the political landscape of adult education*. New Directions for Adult and Continuing Education, no. 91. San Francisco: Jossey Bass.

Cook, J. (1989). *Indicators of program quality*. New York: NYC Office of Adult Literacy.

Cunningham, P. (2000). A sociology of adult education. In A. I. Wilson & E. R. Hayes (Ed.), *Handbook of adult and continuing education*. (pp. 573-588). San Francisco: Jossey-Bass.

Dueno, A., Santiago, A., & De Simone, R. (1993). *It should be told: Oral histories from the open book*. Brooklyn, NY: Self Published.

Freire, P. (1970). *Pedagogy of the oppressed*. New York: Seabury.

Macedo, D. (1994). *Literacies of power*. Boulder, CO: Westview.

Martin, R. (2001). *Listening up*. Portsmouth, NH: Heinemann.

Purcell, G., V., & Waterman, R. (2000). *Now we read, we see, we speak*. Mahwah, NJ: Lawrence Erlbaum.

Roa, E., Jaber, B., & Ramirez, I. (1994). *I see a part of myself*. Brooklyn, NY: Self Published.

Ruiz, A., Torres, C., Smeraglino, S., & Gonzalez, C. (1990). *Four stories: Oral histories from the open book*. Brooklyn, NY: Self Published.

Sheared, V. (1999). Giving voice: Inclusion of African American students' polyrhythmic realities in adult basic education. *New Directions for Adult and Continuing Education*, no. 82. San Francisco: Jossey-Bass.

Shor, I. (1996). *When students have power: Negotiating authority in a critical pedagogy*. Chicago: Chicago University Press.

Students and Staff of The Open Book (1991). *We're all in this together: Leadership and community at the open book*. Brooklyn, NY: Self published.

CHAPTER 33

PARALLELS IN THE MARGINALIZATION OF ABE WOMEN EDUCATORS AND WOMEN LITERACY LEARNERS

Sandra D. Bridwell

Over thirty years ago, I began my education career in adult basic education (ABE). I was fortunate to have a salary with benefits. I worked under very favorable and supportive conditions and I genuinely loved what I did. The lessons I learned from my students and colleagues grounded my commitment to the promise of education. This writing shares some of those lessons. Perhaps the most important lesson is my observation that ABE educators, the majority of whom are women, are committed to empowerment goals for women in literacy programs but often feel the effects of marginalization in ways that make them the most vulnerable in the educational field as women in literacy programs are the most vulnerable ABE consumers.

Most people who enter the adult basic education field are already committed or soon experience a strong identity with goals of social justice and empowerment. ABE proudly traces its evolution to defining empowerment milestones in our country's history such as goals to educate

Empowering Women Through Literacy: Views From Experience, pp. 233–242

Americans for full participation in a democratic society after the revolutionary war, the establishment of schools for freed slaves after the civil war, the education of immigrants during the country's great industrial age, and the establishment of freedom schools during the civil rights movement.

ABE has always been in the forefront of defending injustices and facilitating the advancement of marginalized populations. However, it has been my experience as an adult educator and researcher that too often ABE practitioners experience marginalization in ways that threaten their capacity to fully address empowerment goals of the students they serve. Circumstances like unfavorable working conditions and part-time employment with no benefits take their toll in ways that are personally and professionally demoralizing.

An *English for Speakers of Other Languages* (ESOL) literacy teacher perfectly captured the essence of the dilemma when she said "As a teacher we are always looking toward making sure learners' needs are met. I can't do that if my needs are not met.... If I'm going to teach students to voice their opinions and to make changes, I need to do it also" (Smith, Hofer, & Gillespie, 2001, p. 15). The formulation of solutions should begin at this place of clarity. I will begin by sharing how easy it is to allow the appeal of the work to overshadow the profession's obligation for providing optimal conditions for practice and by suggesting why it is important to understanding the problem from a broader historical, social and cultural context. I will present examples of how research findings of marginalization among adult literacy instructors are actually experienced by a practitioner. From these understandings of societal and professional barriers to empowerment, I will offer some strategies for policy and practice.

Those new to the profession quickly learn that ours is more than just a job. Many for the first time experience the joy that educational theorists and philosophers tell us education is supposed to be about. We fondly remember the honor of observing the results of our work when we see an adult's awe at having read a first book, or newspaper article, or first sentence. We take pride in supporting our students' great courage in exposing vulnerabilities like their inability to read. Often such vulnerabilities are eclipsed by the greater fear of risking not being able to support their children's educational goals. As such, adult educators are routinely privileged to witness that magical spark of recognition, that moment of clarity when our students make a connection between real life experience and the written word, when they are emboldened toward the next challenge and adventure that is learning.

In the midst of supporting our students' accomplishments that make us so love what we do and rank our work among human endeavors that make the world a better place, it is easy to lose sight of the fact that we perform our roles in a larger social context. In addition to the personal gratification that is a natural outgrowth of our work, practitioners must remember that gender disparities exist in the world and still reveal themselves in unspeakable violence against women.

Obviously, being able to experience gratification in one's work, especially when that work serves a higher purpose, is ideal. However, there is a danger in carrying out daily routines without adequate reflection on the larger historical and societal context of violence and discrimination against women. It is imperative that unfavorable working conditions experienced by women adult literacy educators are recognized as part of a global pattern of devaluing women. For example, at this very moment in the 21st century, the brutalization of women in war is a recognized tactic for decimating societies and cultures. We hear of it in places like Afghanistan, Congo and Darfur. In our culture, disparities that are part of this larger pattern in the world are revealed in everyday occurrences such as women receiving less pay for the same work as men. I offer this example as a caution against failing to see the marginalization of women adult literacy educators and women literacy learners as part of a larger global struggle that should encourage a sense of urgency for taking action.

It is important not to blame the victim, in this case ABE learners and teachers, because marginalization impacts the quality of professional lives for women in many professional fields. However, it is particularly evident in the field of education and perhaps felt most keenly by ABE practitioners. I am reminded of a 1990 committee that examined the status of women faculty in science at The Massachusetts Institute of Technology (MIT), one of the nation's most prestigious higher education institutions and found a disturbing pattern of marginalization that repeated itself with new generations of women faculty. The committee found marginalization of women in salaries, space, awards and resources. The findings further revealed differences in positions of power and administrative responsibility and an overall toll on professional and personal lives. Such disparities for adult literacy educators continue almost 20 years later.

About the time I began my career as an ABE teacher in the late 1970s, Park (1977) concluded that women employed in ABE were victims of discrimination. She surveyed adult basic education program directors in five states and found that most teachers were women who worked part-time without benefits while most administrators were men who were employed full-time. It seems that little has changed and future projections are not optimistic. A 14% increase in the number of adult literacy and remedial instructor jobs is projected by 2016 (U. S. Department of Labor, 2008). This growth is faster than the average of all occupations and is based in part on the projection of high turnover in part-time hourly wage workers and volunteers who disproportionately comprise this education sector.

One can speculate that such instability in the adult literacy sector contributes to less than optimal conditions for women educators to form alliances to improve working conditions and insufficient time in the field to reach optimal professional capacity in the provision of best instructional practices for women students.

Part-time workers heavily populate ABE. Young, Fleishman, Fitzgerald, and Morgan (1995) reported that of more than 2,600 local programs, 39% of adult education programs did not have full time teaching or administrative staff; 59% had one full time staff member and the ratio of part-time to full-time teachers was 4 to 1. Compared to full time workers, part-time employees most often have less job security, suffer unfavorable working conditions, receive hourly wages without benefits, and have less influence in decision-making that impacts their practice. Adult literacy educators, unlike educators in other sectors, generally do not have opportunities to form collegial relationships and often perform their responsibilities in isolation.

Consider the circumstances of part-time teachers in relation to the women literacy learners they serve. A correlation between level of educational attainment of the targeted adult education population by poverty level and the number who received high school diplomas showed there were more women than men in the target population (Lasater & Elliot, 2005). Likewise, the U.S. Department of Education (2001) confirmed that adult basic education largely serves the economically disadvantaged working poor, unemployed, welfare recipients and the homeless. D'Amico (2004) showed that people of color, immigrants and women disproportionately represented these learners. The impact of unfavorable working conditions on the morale of women literacy teachers who serve the most vulnerable literacy learners simply makes waiting for the 2016 projections to play out absolutely intolerable.

In a professional development study of 95 literacy teachers, Smith, Hofer and Gillespie (2001) found five categories of factors that influenced the ability of ABE teachers to do their job well. These included; access to colleagues and program directors to get feedback on their practice; access to decision making to improve the quality of services learners receive; and access to a "real job" including a sufficient number of hours to do preparation, teach and attend to program related tasks. Inadequate access to resources including classroom and program facilities, materials and technology was illustrated by 39% not having their own classroom space to teach or post materials, 29% not having their own desk or place to leave materials, 20% having no access to computers, and 65% having no teachers' room in their program where they could meet informally with colleagues. The final category of factors was access to professional development and information to better understand their classrooms, their programs, and their field. Of those surveyed, 23% received no paid professional development time and 32% received only one to 12 hours a year of paid professional development time. Of 104 in the original study, 12.5% had left the field one year later. About half cited working conditions including job stability and benefits as reasons for leaving. It should be noted that these findings were *before* budget cuts during the Bush Administration! However, I find this study's findings most valuable as a place to locate actionable directions for change directly from the voices of practitioners in the field.

To gain a more current and personal perspective, I consulted one of the most capable and dedicated adult educators I know who teaches in a women's literacy program. Her eloquent depiction of the challenges she faces in her practice gives a human face to professional marginalization. It was amazing how her narrative so closely reflected research findings in her description of personal experience with part-time employment, insufficient resources and perspective on welfare policy for women learners. In a personal communication, I asked Anna, a veteran ABE teacher in the Boston area, to tell me what she considered the three biggest challenges for adult education. I also asked if she had a magic wand, what three things would she change about her practice. She thought the lack of full time jobs for teachers, lack of resources, and the welfare system were the three biggest challenges. Regarding lack of full time jobs, Anna described her own situation as follows:

> When I got hired, I was offered part time at 30 hours. The following year, there were cuts and I was dropped to 29 hours. I was increased to 32 hours the next year. And finally, I am at 35 hours. Throughout this whole time, no matter how many hours I got paid, I still had a full teaching load. (A. Yangco, personal communication, June 8, 2005)

Anna described instances of lack of resources in her situation that included lack of funding for materials and space for teaching "We have shared space and often can't store our materials in the room we teach in." Anna also cited opportunities for trainings and time to research, find trainings and funds to attend as challenges she had encountered in her practice. Her thoughts on the third challenge pertained to the welfare system. She wrote:

> Welfare never gives students enough time to allow for the opportunity of education. I don't know about you, but it took me 12 years to do 12 grades. I am not saying that they should allow that much time, but if a student is thriving in an education program and taking advantage of school, then welfare should find a way to support that student since, in the long run, that is

what will prevent a student from going back on welfare (A. Yangco, personal communication, June 8, 2005).

Anna's commitment to empowerment and social justice came through in her response to what she would change with her magic wand:

> With that magic wand, I think I would try to make everyone see that all people have the right to education ... the right to explore the world ... to take classes and allow for personal growth such as you and I have had opportunities to do. Why does money and circumstance have to be the deciding factor in why a person can go to elementary, high school, college, and graduate school ... or continuing ed classes? We spend so much of our time trying to heal past experiences of school shame because somewhere along the way they were told that they couldn't achieve in school because of some reason or another.... It is sad when people are not allowed to grow to their greatest potential (A. Yangco, personal communication, June 8, 2005).

It is important to note that this young woman teaches women in a work environment that represents and supports best practices in classroom instruction and administrative practices. Yet, her perspective typifies the complexity of issues that must be negotiated in order to work toward encouraging empowerment goals for her students. Her circumstance illustrates all the reasons why we must improve working conditions so that she and others like her will stay in the profession and continue to share their considerable knowledge and expertise. They should not have to contend with demoralizing conditions in order to perform their duties in ways that represent the best ABE traditions for empowerment and social justice.

In a staff focus group (Bridwell, 2006) composed of this young woman and her colleagues, it was clear that all of their efforts were aimed at increasing the capacity of their students, who were all women, to expand worldviews beyond a GED. When the teachers, counselor and program director were asked to what or whom they would attribute favorable changes among the women their instruction and support programs served, they listed strong personal and professional commitments to a purposeful emphasis on self-advocacy consistent with critical theory goals. In addition to ABE classes, the staff spoke of the curriculum that stressed building self-esteem, self-awareness, self-care and leadership skills that encourage "students to dream beyond the GED... to be able to advocate and speak up for themselves" (Bridwell, 2006, pp. 5-6).

Given the complexity of issues and the urgency of need, practitioners must prioritize action for change. Places to start might include forming strategic alliances with other practitioners and administrators to impact policy because forming alliances implies first attending to the problem of isolation that is a great disadvantage for part-time workers. Many teachers in all education sectors work in isolation. That is, they are fully involved in the teaching and learning that occurs in their individual classrooms but are minimally engaged with colleagues outside the classroom. Part-time teachers are especially subject to disadvantages of isolation whereby there is little opportunity for reflection on practice or to participate in decision-making that impacts classroom practice.

Education sectors in K-12 have begun to emphasize new paradigms that encourage environments for personal reflection and collegial engagement for active participation in shared decision-making. Listening to the voices of adult literacy practitioners and incorporating those perspectives into professional development are prerequisites for initiating change. Two paradigms implemented in K-12 sectors that hold particular promise for ABE as they are grounded in organizational and adult development theory are professional learning communities and a new model of learning-oriented school leadership.

The first is professional learning communities (PLCs). Dufour and Eaker (1998) characterized (PLCs) as environments that foster mutual cooperation, emotional support, personal growth, and a synergy of efforts. This is a strong model for staff development that approaches collegial reflection and decision making from an organizational development framework. This model offers a systematic approach that ABE administrators might bring to an alliance with practitioners for their inclusion in decision making. I mention it here because it directly addresses the isolation that is the first obstacle for part-time employees.

Professional learning communities are specifically designed to bring administrators and practitioners together united in the common purpose of strategizing teaching and learning environments where practitioner voices are heard and learner needs are more effectively met in fulfilling the organization's mission. The very act of designating time to come together for communicating ideas and addressing common needs directly addresses the problem of isolation. Therefore, PLCs hold special promise for addressing adverse working conditions of part-time adult literacy educators. PLCs encourage reflection on one's own practice and examination of alternative perspectives. Both of these outcomes are more difficult to achieve by part-time workers who have little opportunity to communicate with professional colleagues.

Another exciting strategy is a new model of learning-oriented school leadership (Drago-Severson, 2004). This professional development model was based on work with school principals; however, it was grounded in principles of adult learning and has been described as resting on four pillars: teaming, providing leadership roles, engaging in collegial inquiry and mentoring. Combined, these components provide a powerful framework for professional development that directly addresses the issue of isolation that disadvantages part-time adult literacy teachers.

The exciting thing about the learning-oriented school leadership model is that it opens the possibility for more effectively designing professional development opportunities that uniquely match the individual developmental perspective of the adults and could be adapted for ABE professional development. For example, the first pillar, teaming or partnering with colleagues, includes encouragement of individual and group reflection on the organization's mission, shared decision making and exploration of different perspectives on practice. The second pillar, providing leadership roles, stresses the importance of encouraging the provision of appropriate challenges and supports for undertaking leadership roles that is different from the simple distribution of duties. The third pillar, engaging in collegial inquiry as explained by Drago-Severson (2004) is part of a larger developmental concept whereby individuals are engaged in shared dialogues of individual reflections on "...assumptions, convictions and values as part of the learning process" (p. 18). It is this aspect that I find most promising in potential for such dialogues to awaken exploration of critical thought for challenging power dynamics that work against interests of less advantaged populations. This potential is most associated with critical theory that is based on ideology critique. Through engaging in collegial inquiry, women adult literacy practitioners would have a forum for understanding the significance of their work in a larger perspective and thus conceptualizing strategies for achieving more favorable working conditions to better achieve student empowerment goals. The fourth pillar of the model, mentoring, essentially creates an opportunity for individuals to explore their own development through pairing with a more experienced practitioner. This strategy not only addresses the problem of isolation, but at the same time encourages personal and professional growth from the experience.

Both PLCs and the model for learning-oriented school leadership hold great promise for cultivating women adult literacy practitioner leaders. It is from these new leaders that a united voice for change will occur. Strong alliances and leadership from within their own ranks will make benefits such as paid release time for participation in professional development standard operating procedures as practiced in other professions.

I have attempted to share my observations about the marginalization of women in ABE from a 30 year career in education and to offer strategies that I believe would hasten the time when favorable working conditions for women adult literacy educators are similar to conditions in other professions. Until there is a united voice for change from a new generation of practitioner leaders, women adult literacy educators will continue to suffer marginalization in ways that parallel their most vulnerable women literacy learners.

REFERENCES

Bridwell, S. (2006, April) *Understanding how black women ABE learners make sense of their lives: Using developmental theories to enhance the possibilities for growth*. Paper presented at 2006 Annual Conference of The American Educational Research Association, San Francisco, CA.

D'Amico, D. (2004). Race, class, gender and sexual orientation in adult literacy: Power, pedagogy, and programs. In J. Comings, B. Garner, & C. Smith (Eds.), *Review of adult learning and literacy: Connecting research, policy, and practice* (pp. 17-69). Hillsdale, NJ: Erlbaum.

Drago-Severson, E. (2004). *Helping teachers learn: Principal leadership for adult growth and development*. Thousand Oaks, CA: Corwin Press.

DuFour, R., & Eaker, R. (1998). *Professional learning communities at work: Best practices for enhancing student achievement*. Bloomington, IN: National Educational Service.

Lasater, B., & Elliot, B. (2005). *Profiles of the adult target population: Information from the 2000 Census*. Washington, DC: U.S. Department of Education, Office of Vocational and Adult Education, Division of Adult Education and Literacy. Retrieved August 25, 2008 from http://www.ed.gov/about/offices/list/ovae/pi/AdultEd/census1.pdf

Massachusetts Institute of Technology. (1999). A study on the status of women faculty in science at MIT: How a committee on women faculty came to be established by the dean of the school of science, what the committee and the dean learned and accomplished, and recommendations for the future. *The MIT Faculty Newsletter, 11*(4). Retrieved August 5, 2008, from http://web.mit.edu/fnl/women/women.html

Park, R. J. (1977). Women in adult basic education. *Lifelong Learning: The Adult Years, December*, 1,4,12-13, 21. [Abstract] Retrieved August 5, 2008 from http://eric.ed.gov/ERICWebPortal/custom/portlets/recordDetails/detailmini.jsp?_nfpb=true&_&ERICExtSearch_SearchValue_0=EJ173048&ERICExtSearch_SearchType_0=no&accno=EJ173048

Smith, C., Hofer, J., & Gillespie, M. (2001). The working conditions of adult literacy teachers: Preliminary findings from the NCSALL staff development study. *Focus on Basics: Connecting Research and Practice, 4*(D). Retrieved August 28, 2008, from http://www.ncsall.net/?id=291

Young, M., Fleishman, H., Fitzgerald, N., & Morgan, M. (1995). *National evaluation of adult programs* (Executive Summary) (Contract No. LC 90065001). Arlington, VA: Development Associates. In Smith, C., Hofer, J., Gillespie, M. Solomon, M., & Rowe, K. (2003, Nov.). How teachers change: A study of professional development in adult education. *NCSALL Reports #25*, Boston: National Center for the Study of Adult Learning and Literacy.

U.S. Department of Education, Office of Vocational and Adult Education, Division of Adult Education and Literacy (2001). Retrieved August 6, 2008, from http://www.ed.gov/offices/OVAE/datahome.htm

U.S. Department of Labor, Bureau of Labor Statistics. (n.d.) Teachers—adult literacy and remedial education. *Occupational Outlook Handbook, 2008-09 Edition* Retrieved August 5, 2008, from http://www.bls.gov/oco/ocos289.htm

CHAPTER 34

EMPOWERING WOMEN THROUGH VOICE

Low-Income Mothers Speak of Work, [Non]Education, Poverty, and Welfare Reform

Mary V. Alfred

Sweeping changes to the national welfare system prioritized "work-first" policies and decreased educational opportunities for mothers on welfare. In 1996, the Personal Responsibility and Work Opportunity Reconciliation Act (PRWORA) was signed into law. The Act fundamentally changed the federal welfare program by replacing the Aid to Families with Dependent Children (AFDC) program with state-administered block grants through the Temporary Assistance to Needy Families (TANF) program. TANF imposed strict limits on educational programs (limited primarily to adult basic education and soft skills training) as well as time limits for recipients to separate themselves from the welfare system and become economically independent. Work, then, was seen as the vehicle for economic independence and education became secondary to work.

Empowering Women Through Literacy: Views From Experience, pp. 243–258
Copyright © 2009 by Information Age Publishing
All rights of reproduction in any form reserved.

In 2003, I held conversations with 15 African American mothers who were working welfare recipients to get their perspectives on welfare reform and to understand their lives within the new culture of welfare. Three questions guided our conversations: (a) What is your understanding of welfare reform? (b) What barriers do you encounter as you attempt to transition from welfare? (c) What suggestions do you have for minimizing the barriers?

Table 34.1.   Profile of the Women in Dialogue

Name (Pseudo)	Age	No. of Children	Marital Status	Highest Level of Education	Occupation	Years on Public Assistance	Current Benefits
Kim	29	3	Single	3 yrs.* college	Bank Clerk	10 off & on	Child care Medical
Vikki	23	3	Married	College* Senior	Retail Sales Supervisor	4	Child care Medical
Tasha	26	1	Single	3 yrs. college	Admin. Assistant	6 months	Child care Medical Food stamp
Marie	43	4	Single	Grade 12	Food Service	20	Medical Food stamp
Jean	28	2	Single	2 yrs. college	Staff Training Assistant	9 yrs.	Child care
Rebecca	40	3	Single	Associate Degree	Community Resource Specialist	10 off & on	Child care Medical
Jackie	35	13 (3 sets of twins)	Single	1 yr. college	Food Service	12	Child care Medical Food stamp
Ann	28	5	Single	Grade 12	Day Care Teacher	10	Child care Medical Food stamp
Sharon	31	3	Single	2 yrs. college	Retail Sales	9	Child care medical
Marcia	26	2	Single	Grade 12	Customer Service	8	Child care Medical
Sally	22	1	Single	3 yrs. college	Retail Sales Supervisor	2	Child care Medical
Sandra	25	3	Single	1 yr. college	Retail Sales	5	Child care Medical
Kayla	21	1	Single	Grade 12	Food Service	2	Child care Medical
Vanessa	29	4	Single	Grade 12	Day Care Teacher	11	Child care Medical Food stamp
Nikki	34	3	Single	Grade 12	Customer Service	5 off & on	Child care Medical

*Attending college at the time of the conversation.

As we can see from Table 34.1 (opposite page), all participants self-identified as high school graduates or equivalent, and nine noted to have some post-secondary education. At the time of the interview, three of the women were currently working toward a Bachelor's degree. They all worked in service-related occupations, such as clerical, retail, customer service, child care, and food service. Ten worked fewer than 40 hours a week, with wages ranging from $6.25 to $12.25 an hour. The profile of these women suggests that while they were working, their wages alone would not move them to a position of economic self-sufficiency. It is worth noting that none of the participants received assistance for postsecondary education and training under TANF. Those who attended college did so with other forms of financial assistance.

BARRIERS TO SELF-SUFFICIENCY

The women were asked to describe their experiences with their state's version of welfare reform and to identify barriers to their transition to self-sufficiency. The barriers fell into three broad categories as displayed in Table 34.2: (a) Welfare reform philosophy and local agency practices (b) workplace barriers, and (c) personal barriers.

Work-First Approach to Welfare Reform

The objective of the Personal Responsibility and Work Opportunity Reconciliation Act (PRWORA) of 1996 was to change the culture of wel-

Table 34.2. Barriers and Challenges

Welfare Reform Philosophy and Agency Practices	Workplace Barriers	Personal Barriers
The philosophy of the work-first approach	Low-wage labor market	Fear of failure and fear of change
Lack of opportunities for post-secondary education and training	Lack of employer support and understanding	Unfamiliarity with workplace cultures
	Inadequate training, mentoring, and coaching	Lack of social support
Unrealistic demands of working mothers	Discrimination and the stigma of welfare	Lack of financial resources
		Substance abuse
Policy implementation at the local level	Limited opportunities for promotion or advancement	Domestic violence
Interpersonal relationships with case managers	Lack of critical fringe benefits	Physical and mental illness

fare from a system of dependency to one of personal responsibility and self-sufficiency. As a result, when Wisconsin instituted its W-2 initiative (the state's version of welfare reform), the mandate to caseworkers was to move recipients to the workforce as quickly as possible so as to decrease their dependency on cash assistance. The women shared their challenges and frustrations with the work-first philosophy.

> The goal of W-2 is to get people off of welfare. First of all, they want all these people to get jobs and to keep working. It is not that easy. Some don't even know how to orientate themselves to go out. Some people don't even know how to read and write. They made it through high school, and they don't even know how to fill out a job application. They need to have these classes to help them, but not make them so demeaning. Some of these classes that they have for W-2 transition are so demeaning. (Rebecca)

> Working for a living is a good idea, and I believe in work; but the way they went about W-2 was unfair. I know people who cannot keep a job because they don't know how to think about work and how to think about tomorrow. Some people quit a job after the first or second paycheck. Some of them think I have this check so I don't have to work any more; that check should last me. (Sharon)

> The government is supposed to know what is best, but I don't think W-2 was planned very well. They want people to be self-sufficient, and they think you can be self-sufficient with a six-dollar-an-hour job. Many of these people had never worked before and have no education or job skills. They should provide programs for people to build their skills and let them complete the program before they make them quit for a minimum-wage job. (Jean)

> I believe in what the government is trying to do, but it is not right how they are doing it. How can you take someone who has never worked, has no education, and want them to be self-sufficient without job skills? People need education and training for them to stop depending on the government. (Kayla)

The participants felt that they were not adequately prepared to become self-sufficient and were not provided with adequate training to meet employer expectations. As their stories revealed, a significant barrier to economic independence was the lack of opportunities available for higher education and skills training under the plan. Human capital theory suggests that increasing human capital is directly related to education and training (Cote & Levin, 2001). Therefore, in order for individuals to increase their competitive advantage in the workplace, they must engage in opportunities that will increase their education and their preparation for sustainable work. Frustratingly, the women talked about a system that did not promote education as a vehicle for economic self-sufficiency among low-income adults.

Everybody wants to make a lot of money, but in order for you to make a lot of money, you have to have education. And by you not having the education, you aren't going to go nowhere, and if you don't have anybody to help you get that education, then you are really stuck. I want to go back to school and finish the two years, but I can't go back to school, work, and then pay for childcare while being single. If I was married and had someone to support me, it would be much easier; but me being by myself, it is real hard. I see where a lot of females are going through the same thing I am going through, especially those that do not have their mother to extend support. (Sharon)

I know I have to go back to school if I am ever going to make it on my own. I don't have anyone in my family to show me the way and I do not have anyone to help with the kids. Before, it was easy to stay home and take care of the kids; I did not have to worry about making it on my own. Now it is tough. I want to go to school, but the system will not help me to go to school during the day to learn some kind of skills. They prefer for us to work minimum-wage jobs. (Jackie)

When W-2 was first implemented, individuals who were in school full time and received support under the old system had to give up school for the work place in order to meet expectations of the new welfare system. They spoke of a desire to return to school, but with full-time work and family obligations, many found it impossible to fulfill their dreams of earning a college degree. Here is one of their comments:

If they had helped me with childcare to go to school when I had my daughter, I would have been out of school and graduated and I wouldn't have been still needing assistance. I was going to school for nursing and had one more year to go, but I had to drop out to qualify for daycare for my daughter. They could only pay for her to go to daycare if I was working, and they wouldn't pay while I was in school. I didn't understand that. I wanted to go to school full-time and work part-time so I could finish my clinicals. That way, I would have done finish and I would not be needing their help. (Tasha)

The women I spoke with realized that education was the key to their economic well being and all were willing to go to school; however they were trapped in working minimum wage jobs at the expense of gaining long-term self-sufficiency through education and training.

Policy Administration at the Local Level

Several of the women discussed the humiliation they experienced at the hands of case workers and the unrealistic demands and expectations that they had to meet as working mothers.

The case workers are supposed to help you, but they don't bend and meet you half way. I know they are trying to get people to help themselves, but people sometimes need a little help to get there. Sometimes I go down there and they say you have to bring back this and that, I don't have a paycheck yet, I just got started. Well, no, we have to have this. I am like, can't you be a little more understanding; I can't keep taking off work to come here. They want you to keep coming back and forth and keep a job at the same time. They need to be a little more flexible. (Jean)

These caseworkers can be nasty to you. They make you feel like you are nothing. Some people don't come back, but that does not mean that people are working. That is how you become homeless; that is how your children go hungry because if I feel that if I go back down there tomorrow, she is going to be mean to me and put me down; I don't even want to go back. Some people don't go back and just drop off the system. (Marie)

They tell us that we must work and they will pay for day care, but we must work with our case worker to file the paper work. I tried for three weeks and my case worker would not return my call. I could not take off work to go down to the office as I just got that job and did not want to take off. The daycare told me that I would have to pay $166 a week until I file the papers and have W-2 to pay for it. I only made $9 an hour. If it wasn't for my parents, I would have had to quit work and take care of my son. There was no way that I could afford to pay for his day care on my own. (Sally)

W-2 needs more professionals and people who are understanding with us clients and say, I understand, instead of treating people like they are not worthy because you are getting aid from the state. Just because you are getting aid does not mean you are not a good person; that does not mean that you are not trying to do something for your self. (Vicki)

While some interactions with agency personnel were pleasant, most left the women with a shattered sense of self. As a result, participants spoke of friends and acquaintances that left the system because of the effects of these encounters. There was also the revelation that some of those who left turned to illegal underground economies to support their families.

The system is painting a rosy picture that it is getting people in jobs, but that is not all that it is doing. The welfare system is not what they are saying it is. They are not saying that we have people out there who are killing themselves, that are homeless, or haven't eaten; W-2 has forced women into prostitution, drug trafficking, and drug abuse. Women are stripping in clubs, selling stolen goods. They are not talking about the horrors of the system. They are only talking about how many people they got off welfare. They are not talking about where these people are. Where are those people who are off welfare? Before they can talk about how successful the program is, they need to go out and find these people who are no longer in the system, and they will know about the destruction they have caused in the lives of women and their children.... We are not opposed to working; we want to work, it's just the way it was done; that is not right. (Ann)

While the literature speaks to the realities of women caught in the culture of welfare reform, there is another group who are most affected, but often neglected in such discussions, and that is the children of families in transition. The participants' stories revealed the grim economic world within which they and their children live, despite their participation in the world of work. Jackie, who worked at one of the school cafeterias, shared her observations.

There are so many other variables that they don't take into account. I see children who are getting hurt every day. I see children who haven't eaten. I can tell you that they don't have money. I see the assistant principal paying for lunches, buying food. I do sometimes, even though I don't have it like that. The mothers don't have it. I saw one little boy that was being sent home because of discipline. He did not want to go home and he later told me "if I go home now, I won't have anything to eat all day." These are the realities. This is the reality of it. Our children suffer while we are out working and still cannot provide for our kids. (Jackie)

Implementing the welfare reform legislation has disempowered women with far more negative consequences than the program planners had anticipated. From the women's narratives, it appears the primary roadblock to women's economic empowerment lies within the system itself, primarily with its work-first philosophical approach, the limited opportunities for postsecondary education, and agency practices that leave women questioning their self-worth. While they believed in the philosophy of work, they disagreed with its practical implementation, particularly when other structural barriers, especially those associated with work, are ignored.

WORKPLACE PRACTICES AS BARRIERS TO WOMEN'S EMPOWERMENT

Workplace barriers represent those policies, practices, and behaviors that create obstacles to women's employment access, retention, and advancement. The path to self-sufficiency rests with women's ability to maintain long-term employment with wages that will push them above the poverty level. Compounded with women's participation in the low-wage labor market, participants revealed several other workplace barriers as identified in Table 34.2.

The Low-Wage Labor Market

As most studies of welfare reform have pointed out, having just a job is not enough to move recipients to self-sufficiency. Results from these studies clearly indicate that the emphasis on the "work first" approach to economic self-sufficiency is more of a myth than a reality when dealing with low-income families who are concentrated in the secondary labor market, and the recipients shared that sentiment.

> Even before W-2 came about, I have worked in many jobs; they were all dead end jobs. I first worked at a restaurant, I have worked as a bar tender, I worked at Target; I worked at Toys R Us, I worked in fast food places, but they pay you nothing in those jobs. Now I work here, and the pay is not any better, but I really love taking care of the children.... I would like to get a better paying job, but I cannot get anything above minimum wage unless I go back to school. (Vanessa)

> I work for $7.85 an hour, but I only work about 35-38 hours a week. The company offers medical benefits, but it is so expensive that I could not afford to get it for me and my son. I could not afford the daycare on what I make. The daycare alone is $156 a week, so I get daycare and medical from W-2. I have been on this job for two and a half years. I have gone from $7 to $7.85 an hour, and I don't think that I can go much further unless I go back to school. (Kayla)

In addition to the low-wage market, the women strongly agreed that employer understanding and support were crucial in keeping low-income working mothers in the workplace. They expressed the desire to be treated as an equal employee and not as a W-2 recipient, to have an employer understand their situation, and to be flexible with their scheduling when family emergencies occur. They also thrived better in a work environment that promotes a sense of family and community.

> I have had many jobs where the employer did not care about you as a person. Now I work for a daycare center and I have a good supervisor. She owns the daycare and she treats us like family. She is very understanding and tries to work with us when the kids are sick or we have a problem that we need to take care of. She is very easy to talk to.... This does not pay much, but I really like it because of the family atmosphere. (Vanessa)

The employers must realize that sometimes, especially when you are a single parent, there are times when you can't come to work when your child is sick, and you can't send a sick child to daycare. Sometimes as a single parent, your child definitely has to come before certain things, and some supervisors cannot understand that. (Kim)

Employers must understand that we truly want to work, but sometimes things get tough. Many of us are single mothers with no support. Sometimes I have to decide between staying home and taking care of my son because the daycare will not take him if he is sick and coming to work. It is not a hard decision; I will take care of my son, knowing that I may lose the job. We need supervisors who understand of our situation. (Sharon)

From the women's narratives, it became apparent that a sense of community, trust, and respect promote a sense of worth and empowerment among low-income women in the workplace. In addition to the need for understanding, the women highlighted the need for more training, coaching, and mentoring to promote their learning in the world of work.

They should have orientation and let people know what it means to be professional. What is professional to me may not be professional to you. Some women have people who will tell them how to be professional, but many of them don't know anyone in the business. It's just that some women don't know because their mother didn't know, their mother's mother didn't know, and it just goes back. People need to know what it means to be professional, and the employers should provide the training and provide them with something like a mentor or someone to help you out. (Jean)

Sometimes they would put you in a job and they would not give you good training. I had this computer class with W-2 and they put me in this temporary job at the court house. There were times when I didn't know how to do the work, and I was afraid to tell them that I did not know. Sometimes, I would cry because I did not know what to do. Now you are in the workplace, you are supposed to know, and I didn't know. Because I had the class, they thought I knew everything. (Ann)

Research on coaching and mentoring support the women's assertion that such workplace activities promote employee development, promote retention and advancement, and empower women for greater success in their careers.

PERSONAL BARRIERS

Throughout our conversation, the participants were frank in highlighting the personal barriers that kept women in a state of dependency. Of the barriers identified, the ones cited most frequently were fear of change, a lack of financial and social capital resources, substance abuse, domestic violence, and lack of knowledge about workplace etiquette.

> One of my greatest challenges was fear. Yes, fear was number one. The biggest fear, I can speak for 80% of us making the transition, is failure. What happens if we fail? If this does not work out, they will say, you don't want to do nothing anyway ... I met a lot of women of W-2, who were coming from drug an alcohol, and they are telling them that now you have to have a job, you have to learn basic skills; you have to learn job skills. My biggest thing is that you have a lot of women that probably went to school to the 8th grade and all of a sudden, 15 years later, you are telling me I have to go back to school and now you are telling me I gotta learn. We were paralyzed with fear. (Rebecca)

> They say W-2 participants are lazy; not all participants are lazy. There are some that want to get a job, and it is hard for them to get a job because they are probably scared from the transition. Many of them have never worked before, and they are scared. You are asking them to change their lives, and that can be a big change for them. (Tasha)

> I was 40, and they telling me that I had to work to get assistance. I was scared to death of going to work knowing that I have to be serious or I would lose my benefits. That is scary for up to this day, although I have been working for three years now. (Marie)

Several issues compounded the fear that dominated the women's lives. There was the fear of being an alien or an imposter in the workplace, the fear of not holding a job, and the fear of running out of time limits. In addition to the fear, substance abuse compounded the obstacles to women's empowerment and their transition to self-sufficiency.

> One of the biggest problems that affected many of the women was drug and alcohol abuse, and W-2 did not address the problem. How can you expect people to function in a job if they are hooked on drugs and alcohol? If you have been on drugs for 15 years of your life and now you are telling me that I have to quit, it is not going to happen. And now you have that added burden of school, daycare, no transportation, all that. What is simple to some of us is not simple to these other women. W-2 failed us. Leave it up to me; I would put them in the best rehab before I demand that they go to work. (Tasha)

> Drugs and alcohol abuse is a big problem for us in the inner city. If you get to the core of that, I think, you would bring out a better person, a more motivated person, a person who would be a good worker. The FEP's [Financial and Employment Planner or case worker] attitude is "girl, that ain't my

problem, get over it." Sometimes that may be a caller's way of letting a FEP know they are going through this, going through pain, depression. The FEP should have that empathetic ear and say, what can I do for you. Are you getting help for your depression? This is what you should do or this is where you should go. (Rebecca)

In a survey of employers and W-2 staff personnel in Wisconsin, Martin and Alfred (2001) found substance abuse to be one of the highest personal issues facing former welfare recipients. About 80 percent of the W-2 staff indicated substance abuse to very problematic. However, these same personnel reported that their agencies were less likely to offer services to address this handicapping condition.

Another problem the women identified was the lack of social and financial capital resources. While all of them were struggling financially, many did not have the social support of family and community. An analysis of their narrative and demographic data reveal that the ones who had advanced in their jobs and were enrolled in post-secondary education had families that provided support to them through these activities.

I'm a single parent and I am trying to raise my three girls by myself. It is hard, but I have worked it out. I have a lot of help from my mother.... My mother was never on AFDC. My mother has been married since she was 18; my father had a good job and my mother always kept a job, so my mother was never on it. My father died when I was 14, but she did not go in the system. I am the only one in the family who has been on public assistance. (Kim)

I have a mother and father, and fortunately, I have a good mother and father. My brother is there for me. I really have a great family, and they are very understanding, especially my mother when I got pregnant with my daughter. I could not have done it without them. They keep my daughter at nights for me to go to school. (Tasha)

I don't have a support system, and that is my biggest problem. Before, it was easier for me to stay home and raise my kids. Now I have no support, no one to help me. If I run into a problem with W-2, I don't know what to do or where to turn. This whole support thing is tough. (Ann)

Some people think that those of us on assistance are lazy and we don't want to work, but they just don't understand. Two months ago, my old car broke down and I had no money to fix it. I could not get my kids to day care and I could not get to work. I lost the job because I had no transportation. People don't understand that you just don't have the money; you just don't have no way to turn. (Sandra)

The obstacles that the women shared form an interconnecting web, with each greatly exacerbating the other. Recognizing the obstacles, I asked the women to suggest solutions to the challenges they identified. Not surprisingly, they had much to share.

MINIMIZING THE BARRIERS TO ECONOMIC SELF-SUFFICIENCY: RECOMMENDATIONS FROM THE BOTTOM

My question to the participants was, "What suggestions would you make to policy makers and agency staff, employers, and to women like you who have to make the transition from welfare?" Because of space limitations, I have extracted some brief comments from our conversation and organized their recommendations into three categories: (a) changes in the reform legislation and in local agency practices; (b) what employers can do to support women in transition; (c) and what the participants can do to take more responsibility for their economic and personal development.

Recommendations for Legislative Reform and Agency Practices

- Make higher education and training available to those who qualify
- Be more humane in dealings with participants
- Be more in touch with individual needs and not treat everyone the same
- For those who work, schedule appointments outside of work time
- Get more qualified and professional people working in those agencies
- Provide on-going training for agency staff members
- Provide training to welfare recipients before putting them in jobs
- Provide retention services during employment
- Provide child care for those who want to go to college
- Count time in school towards work hours
- Make sure that recipients get all the information on programs and services that are available
- Partner with community agencies in providing additional services (e.g., substance abuse treatment)
- Educate employers of the incentives and money available for skills training
- Create partnerships with employers
- Train employers to be aware of the challenges of working mothers

What Employers Can Do

- Provide on-the-job training
- Be aware of the challenges of working single parents
- Provide mandatory training for managers on low-income workers
- Be aware that parents in poverty have special needs
- Be flexible with the work schedule when possible
- Create a workplace mentoring or a buddy system to support cultural learning
- Provide on-going coaching
- Schedule education and training during the day
- Partner with W-2 agencies to provide education and training programs
- Make the environment more friendly for single parents with children, by assisting with childcare, transportation, and flexible schedules in emergency situations
- Provide instant feedback on work performance
- Provide equal pay to men and women for the same work
- Do not buy into the stereotypes about welfare recipients
- Eliminate discrimination and racial profiling
- Diversify the management staff; bring in people from a diverse background

What Recipients Can Do

- Find a way to get some education and training
- Have a support system—relatives coworkers, or neighbors, but get that support
- Have a back-up plan for childcare emergencies
- Do your research about W-2 programs and services and mention them to your caseworker
- Know your rights as far as W-2 is concerned
- Learn your job as well as your coworkers' job
- Be assertive and be professional when dealing with W-2 staff, employers, and coworkers
- Dress appropriately for appointments and for work
- Don't look at work as something W-2 is making you do, but something that is good for your family

- Have a schedule; that will help with the demands of work and family.
- Go to work on time, go to work every day; follow the rules and regulations on the job. Be the best at your job and show that you can do the job.
- If you need help with substance abuse, get help for yourself; call a help line; talk to someone, but you must first get help to kick the habit

It is apparent that the solutions they prescribe call for an integrative approach to teaching and learning among low-income women with family responsibilities. Their solutions call for an investment in education and training or human capital, social capital resources, and identity capital development. Bullock, Stallybrass, and Trombley (1988) define human capital as the ability, skills, and knowledge individuals use to produce goods and services (Cited in Balatti & Falk, 2001, p. 4). Therefore, adult education can play a major role in increasing human capital by providing skills training and other learning activities to enhance women's negotiating power in the marketplace. Moreover, human capital theory suggests that lifelong learning is inevitable in an ever changing and global economy. There is the assumption, then, that an investment in education and training enhances individual competencies and promotes individual employability (Falk, 2001).

As the women suggested, education and training alone are not enough to empower them to develop self-sufficiency; there should also be investments in social capital and identity capital. Social capital is built on trust, acceptance, and mutual obligations (Kerka, 2000), and it focuses on the "interactions between people rather than on 'skills' and 'knowledge' possessed by individual members of the communities" (Falk, 2001, p. 7). Social capital encompasses the norms of networks and relationships that can enhance one's value in the employment marketplace. As Garavan, Morley, Gunnigle, and Collins (2001) note, "The requirement to cultivate networks and gain access to other people's knowledge and resources is considered an important element of employability … and individuals with better social capital earn higher rates of return on their human capital" (p.52). Therefore, drawing from the women's stories, low-income single mothers are in dire need of social capital resources embedded within family, community, institutions, and the workplace to help them make the transition for governmental dependency to economic independency.

In addition to human and social capital resources, the women's stories also reveal their need to build a strong sense of identity to counter the personal and structural barriers that they encounter. Cote and Levine (2002) define identity capital as "investments individuals make and have in who they are" (p. 147). Accordingly, one must establish a stable sense of ego identity to negotiate life's course and maintain positive interactions in order to reap the benefits of social capital resource inherent within communities of support (Cote & Levin, 2002). Therefore, identity capital manifests itself in individual agency, self-efficacy, self-esteem, and locus of control. These constructs suggest that individuals must develop a sense of authorship over their own biography. However, because some women have been caught in a cycle of welfare dependency, marginalization, and negative stereotypes, in order to empower them as they learn, adult educators should have knowledge about who their learners are and their realities in and out of the classroom.

Overall, the lived experiences of mothers transitioning from welfare paint a portrait of their struggles to earn enough to provide for their families, their yearning for education in order to realize their vision of a better world, and the need for financial and social support to manage the challenges. By empowering women through voice, we come to know who our learners are and how we should proceed in the planning and delivery of instructions for the different population we are tasked to educate.

After all, adult education as a field endorses adult development as an integral component of its literature base. Researchers have examined adult development within the context of adult learning, but few have examined the economic development of women, particularly those who are caught in the cycle of poverty, illiteracy, and low-wage work. For example, discourses on welfare reform have been sweeping the nation since the inception of the 1996 reform legislation. Yet, we have remained silent as the debates on economic self-sufficiency among low-literate adults continue. Nesbit sees this neglect as a lack of vision in the field for the broader societal issues, and he writes, "...an overall impression is given, perhaps unwittingly, of a profession that appears detached from many macro-political and even cultural realities" (p. 75). This apparent lack of concern for the sociopolitical issues is reflective in our neglect to adequately address and interrogate the concept of welfare as it relates to women's lives.

REFERENCES

Balatti, J., & Falk, I. (2001). *Socioeconomic contributions of adult learning to community: A social capital perspective.* Paper presented at the European Society for the Research on the Education of Adults Conference, Lisbon, Portugal, September 13-16, 2001. (ERIC Document Reproduction Service, ED 463 425).

Cote, J. E., & Levine, C. G. (2002). *Identify formation, agency, and culture: A social psychological synthesis.* Mahwah, NJ: Lawrence Erlbaum Associates.

Falk, I. (2001). *Sleight of hand: Job myths, literacy and social capital.* Center for Research and Learning in Regional Australia (CRLRA) Discussion Paper. (ERIC Document Reproduction Service, ED 463 427).

Garavan, T. N., Morley, M., Gunnigle, P., & Collins, E. (2001). Human capital accumulation: The role of human resource development. *Journal of European Industrial Training, 25*(2/3/4), 48-68.

Kerka, S. (2000). Lifelong learning: Myths and realities. Columbus, OH: *ERIC Clearinghouse on Adult, Career, and Vocational Education.* (ERIC Document Reproduction Service, ED 441 180)

Martin, L., & Alfred, M. (2002). *What employers and W-2 experts think about retention and advancement barriers and services.* Madison, WI: Department of Workforce Development. Retrieved November 23, 2008, from http://dcf.wisconsin.gov/tanf/pdf/w2surveysreport.pdf.

Nesbit, T. (2005). No direction home: A book review essay. *Adult Education Quarterly, 56*(1), 71-78.

CHAPTER 35

BREAKING FREE

The Power of Experiential Learning as it Impacts the Development of Self-Efficacy in Incarcerated Female Adult Learners

Dawn E. Addy

The world is round and the place which may seem like the end may also be only the beginning.

—Ivy Baker Priest (1958).

Skillful teachers and practitioners of experiential learning believe that learning is achieved by reflection upon "education that occurs as a direct participation in the events of life" (Houle, 1980, 221). Experiential learning is a creative and practical path to knowledge-building filled with simple discoveries waiting to be revealed in the small reflective moments. Experiential learning techniques have been used by the Alternatives to Violence Project (AVP) since it was developed by the American Society of Friends in cooperation with inmates at Green Haven men's facility in 1975. Designed for use by both male and female learners, AVP is based on the simple assumption that everyone has knowledge and experience to

Empowering Women Through Literacy: Views From Experience, pp. 259–270
Copyright © 2009 by Information Age Publishing
All rights of reproduction in any form reserved.

share and can learn from the experiences of others. Over years of assessment and continuous improvement the exercises have been adjusted to meet specific learner needs of various groups across gender, race, age and status (free or incarcerated). These programs have a lasting effect that continues beyond when participants leave the training site. Through a series of fast paced educational experiential exercises participants: think through behavioral issues, build community, and develop self-efficacy. Experiential learning helps participants internalize concepts and principles and lays the foundation for other learning experiences.

For the purpose of this chapter, I chose to examine how experiential learning techniques in AVP address the special literacy and learning needs of incarcerated women. A high percentage of female prisoners have been victims of violent acts and sexual abuse prior to incarceration. In AVP workshops, women are given the opportunity to use concrete examples of violent and abusive acts: through role playing, story telling, picture sharing and a wide variety of other techniques, they test ideas and utilize group feedback with the intent to change practices and outcomes (Kolb, 1984, pp. 21-22).

WOMEN IN PRISON

The special needs of women in prison extend far beyond the obvious physical issues of women's health or maternity care. Women are far more likely to have been victims of violence, sexual abuse or ill treatment prior to entering prison. According to the Correctional Association of New York, Women in Prison Fact Sheet (2008):

- About 47% of women in state or federal prisons or local jails were White, almost 37% are African American, and just under 16% are Latina. White women, however, have significantly lower incarceration rates among their own racial group than African-American women (3.8 times the rate for White women) and Latina women (1.6 times the rate for White women).
- As of 2003, more than 70% of female inmates were incarcerated for non-violent drug, property or public order offenses.
- Nationally, more than 65% of women in state prisons and 55% of men in state prisons report being parents of children under 18. About 64% of mothers in state prisons lived with their children before prison, compared to 44% of men.
- Female inmates are more likely than male inmates to have histories of serious physical or sexual abuse.

- A 2004 study found that 73% of women in state prisons nationwide either had symptoms of a clinical diagnosis of mental illness and/or had received treatment from a mental health professional in the past year, compared to 55% of men.
- Nearly 30% were receiving public assistance before arrest, compared to 8% of men. About 37% had incomes of less than $600 per month prior to arrest compared to 28% of men.

Prior to incarceration women are often the low-income or no-income family care givers. Many come from broken homes, lack appropriate role models, have poor educations and are generally socially maladjusted (Sloane, 2003). Upon entering incarceration, these women must find other family members or friends to care for their children. At worst, those "others" may be the person(s) who abused them prior to incarceration. In a recent report (2008) by the European Parliament, it recognized this need stating: "Member States are urged to provide psychological support, especially to women prisoners who have suffered such violence, to mothers with family responsibilities and to minors" (Panayotopoulos-Cassiotou, 2008, p. 13). This report discovered that unskilled and low literacy levels upon re-entry produced poor labor-market integration. The U.K. reported only 3% of women in prison had been working prior to incarceration and over half of them had been living on state welfare benefits. Although most studies on recidivism have been fairly inconclusive most have posited that a correlation exists between increased literacy, increased job marketability, and decreased recidivism rates (Glass & Barberry, 1993; Hull, 2000; Jancic, 1998; Kelso, 2000; Nochols, 1998; O'Neill, 1990; Ryan & Desuta, 2000; Saylor & Gaes, 1995; Schumaker, 1990; Stiles & Siegel, 1994; Thorpe, 1984; Wilson, 1994;).

Also acknowledged in the EU report was the reality of budget reductions as they affect minority interests. "Due to lack of resources for prisons, women in prison are a minority whose special needs are not sufficiently taken into account in EU countries" (Panayotopoulos-Cassiotou). In the EU women account for about 5% and in the U.S., just under 10% of the total prison and jail population (however this is still over 2 million) making them a minority. In its final analysis, the EU report calls for more literacy, lifelong learning and vocational education training programs for women. Approximately 94% of the money spent on prisons is ear-marked for construction and maintenance. The remaining 6% goes to prison-based education programs (Boulard, 2005). Results from the 1995 Florida Correction Report supports these findings, noting that few women leave prison with job skills, and many with no drug abuse training. "The result of this lack of care and direction from the prison staff is that almost a quarter of the women re-offended." Most women in prison are not given proper information while in prison on how to make plans to better themselves (Morris & Wilkinson, 1995).

Issues of victimization for female offenders, the isolation and low self-esteem, become exacerbated by the prison environment.

> Prison is, to a greater or lesser degree, a concentration of debasement symptomatic of the system itself rather than the system's victims. In any system where the operational needs of the institution take priority over the needs of the users, the potential is great for direct and indirect abuse to flourish unregulated. (Hearn & Parken, 1983, p. 239)

ADULT EDUCATION IN PRISON

Advocates stress that inmates have better re-entry success when they return to society with adequate educational and vocational skills to earn a living, enough to support themselves and their families. However, as government funding has been reduced, many of these prison education programs have been eliminated. When available, prison education usually takes one of four forms: 1) basic literacy and general education programs (e.g., GED or college level courses); 2) substance abuse education; 3) vocational education or job skills training; and 4) social skills training. Most prison education programs for women (in Florida and in many other states across the U.S.) fall into the first two categories, targeting basic literacy, substance abuse and possibly some job skills training if they are lucky. These classes are typically taught by prison educators or psychological staff.

Social skills usually refers to interpersonal skills such as communication, conflict resolution, development of self-esteem, and possibly dealing with stress, managing emotions, prejudice reduction, relationships, anger management and violence reduction such as Alternatives to Violence Project (AVP). There are some social skills programs available in some of the facilities but there is an "inconsistency of practices" (Addy & Gomez, 2007, p. 3) across the institutions and these social skills programs are most frequently facilitated by *outside* volunteers who often lack any official standing. This lack of consistency and official standing may explain why there has been so little research on the effectiveness of these programs. It has been difficult to locate research on the effectiveness of social skills training, especially by volunteers, in the prisons (Sloane, 2003). The obvious lack of focus and importance on the social skills area by the prison systems (especially the State of Florida which I am most familiar with), is difficult to understand since most prisoners were incarcerated for some type of aggressive and anti-social behavior. As Frey observed children's behavior (2002), she discovered that aggressive behavior in childhood could predict high-risk behaviors later in life. It seems reasonable to assume that if new social skills can be learned in prison and there are noticeable behavioral changes while in prison, that those same skills can be transferred to effect behavior in post-release.

ALTERNATIVES TO VIOLENCE PROJECT

The Alternatives to Violence Project (AVP) is a non-sectarian, non-political, non-profit organization. The project began in 1975 and is based on the belief that there is a power in everyone that can transform hostility and destructiveness into cooperation and community. The program uses experiential learning methodology and techniques offering people the opportunity to create change. One speculation about why the Alternatives to Violence Project (AVP) is often successful in producing noticeable lasting behavioral change is attributed to the "volunteer" aspects structured within the program. Facilitators, as well as inmates, must volunteer to participate in the program. Facilitators are drawn from both the *free world* (outside prison walls) and *inside* (inmate) facilitators, who have completed rigorous facilitator and training and apprenticeship programs. However, the *inside* facilitators do not go home to the *free world* at night. Inside facilitators are often viewed as role-models, mentors, and serve as daily reminders of AVP principles.

The following participant comments about the AVP facilitation team are typical evaluation responses and are identified by the use of fictitious *adjective names*. The *adjective names* of participants were changed to insure anonymity. Part of the AVP process requires each of the facilitators and participants to select an *adjective name* at the beginning of the workshop. The adjective must represent a positive characteristic that the person believes she has or aspires to obtain. All participants use adjective names throughout the weekend workshop which reinforce the positive environment of the workshop. There have been numerous accounts of times when one AVP participant used another's adjective name to alert and support the other person during a potentially violent incident, helping them to remember the AVP principles and to "think before reacting."

> When asked how this program differed from others she had been involved with, Humorous Hana remarked, "I think it was very innovative, hands-on, interactive, very effective. It was far more interesting than just lectures. It really allows you to work on yourself from the root of the problem to the present."

Creative Cynthia seemed surprised that, "the facilitators are equal with the participants. There was a lot more openness and trust and everyone seemed to give their all instead of holding back as other groups do."

Dynamic Diane deducted, "The program works if you want it to. I liked having a safe space to open up and learn about how to deal with issues that have led to violence in my past. I learned I can still trust and care for others."

All inmate quotes were gathered from written workshop evaluation responses following two, 3 day workshops at a women's State correctional institution in Florida during July, 2008. Every AVP workshop includes these evaluation and verbal feedback sessions to gather information for the purpose of continuous improvement in future workshops. Evaluations were conducted in English and Spanish (responses were later translated into English.)

Mutual sharing by the facilitators increases the level of trust exhibited by these women, who have often experienced victimization and abuse, and tend to be particularly suspicious of others. The goal of AVP is to reduce the level of violence by introducing people to new ways of resolving conflict that reduce their need to resort to violent solutions. Learning to trust is essential to the success of this process. The experiential learning process uses life experiences of participants as a knowledge base, building on those experiences to help them reflect, and then deal constructively with the violence in themselves and in their lives. When the women were asked how AVP is different from other educational experiences they have had, Exotic Erika responded, "I like the creative ways that I was able to learn so much about myself. I will take so much away with me from this weekend. Its organization, unity, and the gentleness of the program and how it gave us positive ways to solve problems. It has helped me deal with my daily problems and with the anger and frustration." Fantastic Flor agreed, "It's so simple and childlike. It allows you to be a child, to relax and let go, be honest, shed your masks and just *be*. I have a better ability to communicate my experiences without feeling self conscious. I still need to deal with many things." Joyful Julie responded, "I liked doing the exercises. (Julie cannot read or write well and needed assistance from a facilitator to complete the evaluation) I learned a lot through everything —about meditation and to listen so that we could do the exercises. During the discussions I saw things from others points of view. Other exercises allowed me to act out situations in more ways than one. This program makes you think."

Participants learn to see value in the process of valuing others even though they may not be able to articulate that process. "It showed me that people here in prison really do care about the next one. There is always something good in someone else" (Lovable Luz) "...that each and every person I cross paths with in life- that we learn from each other. It made me see who and what we are as women" (Mellow Mary). They learn that others are not necessarily a threat, a shift which becomes operative in changing attitudes to enable the development of social skills that include communicating and community building. "People have been in my shoes. We all share a common bond. It made me really think about who the person is beside me as an inmate in this place. As a woman I could interact with other women who have been there like me" (Nice Nancy).

When asked, "How did this program meet your learning objectives as a woman?" responses were overwhelmingly positive. Outstanding Olga remarked, "I haven't been interested in becoming friends or joining groups of women (prior to participating in AVP). We learned to tolerate and how to say things in our own words, using our own examples. I have a different view now. It showed me we can all lean on each other." "It made me take a look at myself and realize the things I would like to change. Also I realized the good qualities that I want to continue to develop. I want to motivate other Hispanics to be a part of this program. It made me see who and what we are as women" (Terrific Teresa).

Many prison participants did not have good experiences with traditional K-12 educational models: learning from text books and lectures. Participants often have trouble applying the things they read to their own lives. Experiential learning allows participants to embrace lessons learned from experience; what we learn from our emotions and sometimes from what we learn by making mistakes. Concepts alone, without experience, often seem like so much dull theory or dry lecture. Experiences alone, without concepts, often appear as confusing or meaningless events. The AVP process brings concepts and experiences together with a general result of reflective insight or *Ahaah* feelings. When asked to describe ways they will change or ways they have already incorporated AVP principles into daily life, the women responded:

> There is no wrong way of answering questions, only options of learning. There is always a different way to handle things. (Awesome Angela)

> I realize anger is an issue that comes from other issues. So to deal with one you have to deal with many more. And I learned that instead of reacting to anger, I can write about it! (Respectful Regina)

A conceptual framework model for AVP (Figure 1.) was developed by Stan Sloane in 2003. It depicts how the AVP *process* begins with inmates, who come to AVP with their individual background experiences and characteristics. Most group members lack normal social development so AVP must establish a sense of dignity and self-worth among participants. As facilitators open up and express personal experiences it instills a willingness to share and motivates participants to communicate.

> (As stated by Powerful Paola,) "There is a better way to handle things and I can make the choice to do it a better way- as the facilitators (*inmate facilitators*) have done. I have the power to choose who I want to become."

> Sincere Sarah recognized, "Things in the past no longer exist so they should not control my life today. Dealing with violence and self reflection helped me to deal with my self-esteem. It made me realize what a wonderful woman I really am."

Gradually the women open up to trust each other and value what each of them has to share. This process of increasing trust levels and recognizing the value of self and others helps to modify the input factors into output factors that are closer to normally accepted social behavior. The women often express a sense of community and altruism while building skills of negotiation, conflict resolution and communication. This process creates an emotionally supportive and non-judgmental environment that offers participants the tools that provide the *how*, as well as exercises that provide them with opportunities to practice skills and concepts identified as desired outcomes.

Although AVP utilizes *here-and-now* experiential techniques, the process of facilitating and training requires a great deal of facilitator team planning and structural design prior to each workshop. Victorious Virginia has been putting these techniques to use, "With meditation I can calm down and think things through. I learned to communicate and be assertive about my feelings when a problem arises. We all worked together and found great positive solutions together." Each team of facilitators works hard to set session objectives and develop agenda that will accommodate the accomplishment of desired outcomes. Typical goals for a basic level AVP workshop include: 1) Affirmation/Self-Esteem Building; 2) Community Building; 3) Communication; 4) Cooperation; 5) Creative Conflict Resolution; 6) Trust; 7) Life Values; and 8) Closure. The workshop is not completed until all these goals have been achieved. The following comments demonstrate this goal attainment.

The AVP learning experience is a revelation to some female inmates. For many it is the first time they have been taught to communicate in a non-toxic manner, replacing socially dysfunctional paradigms with functional ones.

> Wise Wendy disclosed, "I learned to think before reacting—that others may not have control over themselves. I learned I am not alone. I wish I would have found this program before I got into trouble."

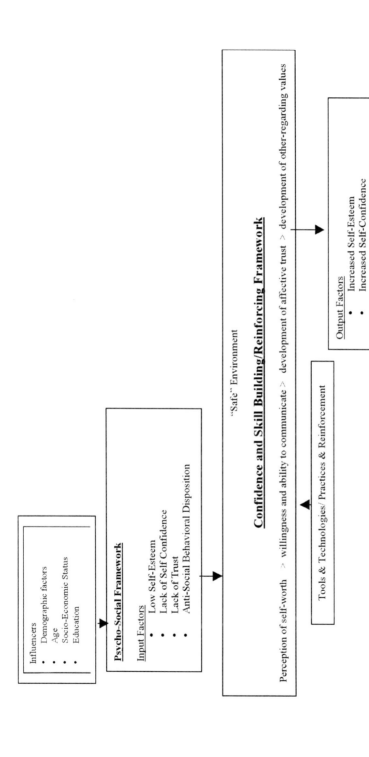

Figure 35.1. Alternatives to Violence Project Conceptual Framework (Sloane, 2003, p. 19).

Joyous Jaqui discerned, "I need to expect the best from others because that's what I want in return from others when I fall short. I realize now that I don't have to feed into others' negativity. I do have a brain and can make choices of my own."

AVP specifically attempts to build interpersonal trust, empathy, and community. Once this environment is established, pro-social behavior develops quickly with the opportunity to practice new skills while being reinforced in a *safe* and supportive environment, as expressed by Youthful Yaite, "It helped me get in touch with my inner self and thoughts. I liked being able to express myself freely. I felt comfortable sharing and with smiles and encouragement everyone was helpful."

Participants often express community building or other altruistic goals as having motivated them to attend the workshop. About 50% of the women who attend the workshops are eligible for release, but that leaves the other 50% who have very little chance of re-entry into *free* society. It is easy to understand how those who are planning to go home might want to acquire new tools and different ways to respond to conflict so that they will never return to prison. But why would those with little or no hope of ever leaving prison want to be involved in a program designed to promote change? The answer is simple. They want prison to be a better place for them to live, a new beginning for building a positive and productive life. "I want to make something of my life. This program really works for me. I've healed from everything that I've shared ... I'm free!" (Interesting Ivette.)

SUMMARY

Over the twelve years I have conducted these workshops in the prisons I have witnessed the growth of peaceful, supportive communities. Experiential learning, within the AVP format is a democratic and highly accessible form of education. For many women, it has reassured and supported them to take a risk and attempt other educational opportunities such as GED, college courses, or to attend other *inside* programs. Empowering themselves, female inmates increase self-esteem, gain some level of responsibility and a sense of control over their lives, and while in prison it also gives them a sense of direction. AVP has become a powerful tool for self-efficacy to the female participants in prison.

In closing, I want to share a true prison story from about five years ago. It began one very hot and sultry Florida night in July. The air conditioning system in the women's prison had broken down and all of the dormitory units were heating up. With many of the women in various stages of menopause, some were heating up faster than others. Tempers began to flare when, suddenly, in Dorm C several inmate facilitators began singing the silly AVP song, *Dum, Dum, Da, Da*. They sang it and taught it to everyone in their dorm. When the dorms on each side of them heard this, the AVP facilitators who resided in those dorms immediately began teaching it to their dorm-mates. It wasn't long before the entire compound was singing it and laughing. They laughed and laughed until, exhausted, all fell asleep. What most certainly would have turned into a night filled with violent incidents, became instead, a story of inspiration and power that lives on in the hearts and minds of the female AVP community. The moral of this story and of this exercise is that, *practice may not make perfect, but it makes better. Keep practicing, and you too have the power to make the changes you desire.*

REFERENCES

Addy, D. & Gomez, P. (2007). *The effects of human capital on the department of corrections and taxpayers of the state of Florida: An analysis of tangible and intangible costs.* Tampa: Florida Department of Corrections White Paper. (Unpublished).

Boulard, G. (2005). The promise of a better tomorrow: due to lack of funding, the percentage of inmates participating in education programs is declining, while the prison population continues to surge. *Black Issues in Higher Education, 22* (1), 1-35.

Correctional Service of Canada (2002). *Assessing gain and outcome.* Retrieved July 8, 2007, from http://www.csc-scc.gc.ca/text/rsrch/reports/rprts-eng.shtml

Correctional Association of New York (2008). *Women in prison fact sheet.* Retrieved June 20, 2008, from http://www.womenandprison.org/?gclid=COimh9aNjJUCFQyenAodpiSGfg

Florida Corrections Commission. (1999). *Florida Corrections Commission report.* Retrieved June 15, 2007, from http://www.fcc.state.fl.us/fcc/reports/final99/1eld.html

Frey, K. S., Hirschstein, M. K., & Guzzo, B.A. (2000). Second step: Preventing aggression by promoting social competence. *Journal of Emotional and Behavioral Disorders, 8*(2), 102-112.

Hearn, J., & Parken, P.W. (1983). Gender in organizations: A selective review and a critique of a neglected area, *Organizational Studies, 4*(3), 219-42.

Houle, C. (1980). *Continuing learning in the professions.* San Francisco: Jossey-Bass.

Hull, K., Forrester S., Brown J., Jobe D., & McCullen C. (2000). Analysis of recidivism rates for participants of the academic/vocational/transition education programs offered by the Virginia Department of Correctional Education. *Journal of Correctional Education, 51*(2), 256-261.

Jancic, M. (1998). Does correctional education have an effect on recidivism? *Journal of Correctional Education, 49*(4), 152-161.

Kelso, C. (2000). Recidivism rates for two Education programs' graduates compared to overall Washington State rates. *Journal of Correctional Education, 51*(2), 233-236.

Kolb, D. (1984). *Experiential learning*. Englewood Cliffs, NJ: Prentice Hall.

Morris, A., & Wilkinson, C. (1995). Responding to female prisoners' needs. *The Prison Journal, 75*(3), 295-305.

Panayotopoulos-Cassiotou, M. (2008, Jan. 29). *On the situation of women in prison and the impact of the imprisonment of parents on social and family life*. Retrieved May 15, 2008, from European Parliament Web site: http://www.europarl.europa.eu/meetdocs/2004_2009/documents/pr/689/689483en.pdf

Glass, B., & Barberry, M. (1993). *Recidivism study*. Land O'Lakes, FL: Pasco County District School Board.

Ryan, T., & Desuta, J. (2000). A comparison of recidivism rates for operation outward reach (OOR) participants and control groups of non-participants for the years 1990 through 1994. *Journal of Correctional Education, 51*, 316-319.

Saylor, W., & Gaes, G. (1995). *The effect of prison work experience, vocational, and apprenticeship training on the long-term recidivism of U.S. federal prisoners*. Washington, DC: U.S. Federal Bureau of Prisons.

Schumaker, R., Anderson, D., &Anderson, S. (1990). Vocational and academic indicators of parole success. *Journal of Correctional Education, 41*(1), 8-12.

Sloane, S. (2003). *A study of the effectiveness of alternatives to violence workshops in a prison System*. Plainfield, VT: AVP Distribution Services.

Stiles, D. & Siegel, G. (1994). *LEARN Program evaluations and research*. Pima County, AZ: Adult Probation Department of the Superior Court.

Thorpe, T., et al. (1984). Follow-up study of offenders who earn college degrees while incarcerated in New York State. *Journal of Correctional Education, 35*(3), 86-88.

Wilson, P. (1994). Recidivism and Vocational Education. *Journal of Correctional Education, 45*(4), 158-163.

CHAPTER 36

OUT OF THE STANDS AND ONTO THE FIELD

Participation, Engagement, and Empowerment of Women Literacy Learners Using Web 2.0 and New Media

Kathleen P. King

INTRODUCTION

The traditional model of learning may be described as a spectator sport, the teacher actively performing in front of the class while students watch. They listen, watch, and take notes, but they never step out onto the "playing field."

When teachers understand their capabilities, Web 2.0 technologies provide a convenient means to change that paradigm. Podcasting, wikis, creating and posting on private blogs, Web-based video, and social media are the creative and free power of Web 2.0, which can capture learning experiences and create new levels of active involvement (King & Gura,

Empowering Women Through Literacy: Views From Experience, pp. 271–280
Copyright © 2009 by Information Age Publishing
All rights of reproduction in any form reserved.

2009; Richardson, 2006). Suddenly formerly disenfranchised women literacy learners can gain a worldwide audience. Bohdi confirms this view of technology as empowering: "If the international community is slow to respond to women's disadvantage largely because of the exclusion of women's voices from the public world, then the Internet is helping to bring women's voices into public space." (In Goulding & Spacey, 2002, p. 7).

This chapter describes simple, free Web-based technologies, which young adults gravitate towards and use everyday and mature adults desire to know, but may have not learned. By appropriating both of these motivations and combining them with easy to learn technologies, learners can not only gain empowerment but also improve critical thinking, problem based learning, research, writing and speaking skills. Web 2.0 technologies and new media are a "slam dunk" success for catalyzing literacy and language arts learning with motivation and real world application.

NEW MEDIA FOR EMPOWERMENT

Voice

I clearly remember the face of the woman who sat silently in the back of the room for 4 long semesters. One semester we started using an online discussion board (Blackboard.com or Tappedin.org) to conduct extended class discussions.

It was about 1993 and it was the first semester I conducted a hybrid format with a class. A hybrid format means that the class is conducted using multiple delivery modes for class activities/material. In this case, we had regular face-to-face sessions, but we also had an online portion of the class. Specifically, I created a private, password protected online space and each week I would post a few follow-up questions for our class to discuss.

No one was more amazed than I at the depth of responses and support the students provided in their online postings. Indeed, the class was full of surprises, because Ellen, my previously silent student, was actively engaged in the online discussions from the first week.

Moreover, about three weeks later, I heard a different voice respond in our onsite class. For the first time she casually responded to a question. In part, I expect because she had already been part of the discussion online. This transference of academic online dialogue to in-person participation had become much easier for her.

Celebrating Empowerment

Being an educator of adults, my learners continue to surprise me. Fast forward to Spring 2008, I taught an unpopular course for the first time. I saw this situation as a great challenge, and examined the material using adult learning principles to develop immediate applications to their professions and connections to their current interests (Wlodkowski, 1998).

I designed assignments wherein students chose their own topic, conducted research, and developed essays of their own opinions and perspectives. Furthermore, rather than just sharing the results with the teacher, they would post it online for their classmates to read and for the world to use as a resource. This strategy provides both an authentic context and an audience to guide and motivate student writing.

Rather than just doing their research and developing critical essays on relevant topics and having only the professor see them, I asked the adult learners to participate in creating a global resource for teachers and students. As I explained the possibility and means of accomplishing the task, they lit up. The result was that they posted their essays on our collaborative public blog. On the third assignment, the learners had the option of creating Web-based digital audio. By the end of the semester, we had posted 38 postings of substantial research, 4 podcasts and 23 presentations all centered on our content area *in a global forum*.

Surprises

It was surprising to me that the women were the students most invested and *initiated* using technology to express their work and opinions. They took greater risks in developing creative topics and using new media for the first time. Moreover, I later learned that the women were so empowered by our digital media and global resource that they e-mailed the blog URL to their family and friends so all could read their work. Empowerment through critical thinking, research and writing- hallmarks of literacy. I was very pleased with this development because I knew that usually students do not pass their homework and essays around to friends, but through the new media projects, their confidence and self-efficacy overflowed (Dewey, 1938; Headlam-Wells, Craig, & Gosland, 2006; Matthews, 2003; Wlodkowski, 1996).

One of the benefits of this activity for the learners was that this collaborative Web-published project could be included on their resume. (The references for a few of the sites we created over the last several semesters are included in the reference list as King et al., 2008a, 2008b.) Valuable empowerment aspects for these learners included creating a collective publication (also a global resource) and becoming more active in classes. Based on these students' experiences, it was the first time they had used these resources even though they were free. These experiences and observations confirm extensive studies demonstrating the many benefits gained from using technology in different ways with women to cultivate new skills and empowerment. For instance, Headlam-Wells, Craig, and Gosland (2006), in a specifically designed and quantitative study, found that women engaged in e-mentoring demonstrated improvement in:

- key employment-related skills,
- personal development skills in identifying their personal strengths and weakness, and
- interpersonal skills as regards to networking.

Furthermore, at the end of this course, I was surprised to learn that many of the learners planned to continue to use blogging and a few to use podcasting. More fundamentally and of their own volition, these learners discussed how technology was powerful in motivating, attracting them to learn difficult topics, providing powerful opportunities for peer learning, and expressing well-grounded opinions.

In this respect, many students reported that they were not asked their opinions in other classes. These learners shared with us the surprise and empowerment of being invited to discuss their ideas and perspectives, and freely develop essays which express, support, and validate their views. They also said that the mere fact that we used a class discussion to generate the list of topics of their research and essays was another novel, powerful, and validating experience. These experiences compounded dramatically to change their concepts of what was possible for themselves in learning and classrooms.

Questions

Why do we not cultivate student opinion and voice more frequently? Why do we shy away from critical and difficult discussions of race, diversity and classism when we can cultivate a safe environment of respect and have a learning opportunity to explore such topics?

It may be that many adult educators have not experienced such forums themselves and that they might not be sure how to handle them. But if we continue to skirt the issues, if we do not get into critical topics and help students explore difficult questions, some with no answers, we may be missing vital conversations and situated learning in which to build critical thinking, analysis, higher order thinking and dialogue (Argyris & Schon, 1974; Brookfield, 1991).

For me, it is worth the effort to invite and engage with learners in meaningful dialogue and to cultivate their voice. This is especially important if we want to support women's learning (Hayes & Flannery, 2000; Headlam-Wells et al., 2006). Facilitating such discussions is not always easy, but is it fertile ground for expanding the minds and aspirations of adult learners. In this case, the technology tools afforded by new media provided an additional platform for the students to voice their opinions, share their research and validate their efforts to think critically and for themselves.

This semester of projects interwove many powerful lessons for the learners and for me. No higher compliments have been paid to me as a teacher than "she valued our opinions," "she encouraged us to share our views," and "my perspective of the possibility of the classroom is changed forever."

Rolling Back the Techno-Fog

From an educational perspective, it is important that educators understand the proliferation, popularity and variety of these new media for at least two major reasons. First, many adults are either adept at using the technology *or* interested in using it. Second, new media is rich in opportunities to collaborate, integrate original content and multiple perspectives. Additionally, it demands critical thinking, and decision making skills and cultivates voice and empowerment (Anderson, 2006; Gardner, 2006; King & Gura, 2009; Prensky, 2008).

This chapter mentions several technology terms and tools. In this section, I briefly introduce terms and resources for readers desiring to continue their learning. In addition, the WE LEARN Web site has more extensive Web 2.0 companion resources for this chapter of the book.

Web 2.0 is now a widely circulated phrase. From the start, the World Wide Web (WWW) heralded more than html pages and Web-based programs. However, from 1993-2003 the focus of the Web was on information gathering and Web page creation. (Simonson et al., 2008). Some technical skills were needed to do Web page development.

Web 2.0 technologies, known as "the next generation" of the Web, help fulfill the original promise of user-created content (like the learners in the cameos). These technologies include new media such as blogs, wikis and podcasts; social networking sites, such as Linked-In and FaceBook; and Google® applications which operate via the Internet rather than individual computers. Users can find or create content on all topics and have become a major force in the field of news, politics, business, entertainment and personal expression (Tapscott & Williams, 2006).

The power of new media is revealed when women learners create and distribute their own opinions and work to the world, and also engage more purposefully in their learning. New media moves learners from the stands to the playing field, from singing in the shower to being on a global stage.

EMPOWERING—CREATING THEIR FUTURES

Introducing adult learners to new media technologies also accomplishes something much more: 21st century lifelong learning skills. Since the wide adoption of the personal computer and the WWW, our society has experienced many rapid changes (Simonson et al., 2008). While not all the changes directly resulted from these technologies, nonetheless, they co-exist and all continue to accelerate.

Rapid changes and trends continue to dominate our world, including

- a global economy, news, and politics,
- less demand for jobs in manufacturing and agricultural,
- a highly information–based economy which demands a skilled and educated workforce, and
- assumptions that heads of household (often single mothers) adeptly access all governmental, educational, and health information via the WWW (Anderson, 2006; Enriquez, 2001; Gardner, 2006; Goulding & Spacey, 2002; Rainie, Fox, Horrigan, Lenhart, & Spooner, 2000).

New media can be an additional tool to breaking down some of these barriers. Adult educators who engage women literacy learners in active learning cultivate corresponding skills, while also building confidence, voice, empowerment, and financial independence (Gibson, 2006; Jonassen, et al., 2003; King, & Sanquist, 2009).

Women have different propensities for technology use than men. For instance women tend to use technology more for gathering information to solve their family and personal needs, news updates, as well as to communicate with a wider sector of communities (their family, business and medical relationships and transactions, etc.). Whereas men, in general, have been documented to be more inclined to use technology for business applications, sports, news and gaming. Moreover, the information technology and communication needs and patterns of families reveal differences in single parent households, which demonstrate needs for women's greater technology comfort in order to support their families in many dimensions.

Use of new media in literacy classes greatly assists with addressing the barriers which women currently experience in technology use. Just a few of these barriers include

- Women-led households are often less affluent and fewer have the widespread cell phone and Internet access of male-led households (Goulding & Spacey, 2002).
- Many more members of married-with-children households view material online together than those of single parent households (Kennedy, Smith, Wells, & Wellman, 2008).
- Women, in general, do not have a public voice in public spaces (Bohdi in Goulding & Spacey, 2002).
- Most women do not have as many professional mentoring opportunities locally available as men (Headlam-Wells et al., 2006).

One way of thinking about the educational uses of new media is to determine if they are student created, teacher created or professional development materials (teacher to teacher) (King & Gura, 2009), teacher-student dialogue, and existing content. These designations can guide educators to consider how to use new media for empowerment opportunities for women literacy learners. To learn more about how to get started using new media visit the WE LEARN Web site (www.litwomen.org/welearn) publications page for the companion resources for this chapter of the book.

CONCLUSION

New media technologies facilitate voice and empowerment and may have stimulated new ideas and opportunities for literacy educators and women learners. More than only learning technology skills, students benefit by growing as confident individuals, and discovering self-efficacy and expression. Appropriating lifelong learning skills embedded in 21st century technologies has benefits across women literacy learners' personal and academic lives as well as professional growth, job opportunities, and careers (King & Sanquist, 2009). These technologies are opportunities for silenced learners to climb out of the spectator stands and onto the playing field of learning and life.

GLOSSARY

Blogging is an easy way to create a Web site. Bloggers use ready-made site templates and can have an entire new blog site simply established in 30-60 seconds. By using templates and predesigned features, the simplified setup does not require much time. With this free and easy technology, bloggers can focus on the content and the audience. (See Blogger.com and wordpress.com.)

Podcasts are audio or video files hosted on a Web server, but strung together via a special scripting language (XML). To listen to a podcast, users can go the podcast Web site and click on each episode's link to hear it. Podcasts may be listened to on a computer or transferred to a mobile listening device such as a MP3 player; they provide portable, convenient, automated and usually free subscriptions. Educational podcasts include many genres and content areas including, oral histories, primary sources, first person perspectives, historical reenactments, and original fiction and nonfiction. (King & Gura, 2009)

Wiki. Two popular definitions of wikis are "a Web page that can be easily changed by anyone" or "a collaborative Web site" (Cunningham & Leif, 2001; Tappscott & Williams, 2006). Wikis are a Web-based interface that encourages easy collaboration. Features include the ability to create custom menus, upload files and track edits made by each person. Many teachers and students are using wikis to create class projects and Web sites with multiple pages and many contributors. (See pbwiki.com and wetpaint.com.)

Social Media. Many adults facilitate their social conversations by using technology and social media (Enriquez, 2001). From Facebook.com to DSNintendo® group play and sharing Miis on their Wiis, to texting and IMing, young adults may be engaged in conversing with from one to 1,000, people at a time. Such media enables global collaboration, and expressions of personal interests and expertise which can easily be integrated into literacy activities.

REFERENCES

Anderson, C. (2006). *The long tail.* New York: Hyperion.

Argyris, C., & Schon, D. A. (1974). *Theory in practice.* San Francisco: Jossey-Bass.

Brookfield, S. (1991). *Developing critical thinkers.* San Francisco: Jossey-Bass.

Cunningham, W., & Leuf, B. (2001). *The wiki way: Quick collaboration on the web.* Upper Saddle River, NJ: Addison-Wesley.

Dewey, J. (1938). *Experience and education.* New York: Collier.

Enriquez, J. (2001). *As the future catches you.* New York: Three Rivers Press.

Gardner, H. (2006). *Five minds for the future.* Cambridge, MA: Harvard Business School Press.

Gibson, C. C. (2006). Increasing equity: Seeking mainstream advantages for all. In K. P. King & J. K. Griggs (Eds.), *Harnessing innovative technology in higher education* (pp. 133-150). Madison, WI: Atwood.

Goulding, A. & Spacey, R. (2002). *Women and the information society: Barriers and participation.* Paper presented at 68th IFL Council and General Conference, Glasgow, Scotland August 18-22, 2002. ERIC Document Reproduction Series No. ED 472 861. Retrieved November 22, 2008, from http://eric.ed.gov/ERICWebPortal/contentdelivery/servlet/ERICServlet?accno=ED472861

Hayes, E., & Flannery, D. (2000). *Women as learners.* San Francisco: Jossey Bass.

Headlam-Wells, J., Craig, J., & Gosland, J. (2006). Encounters in social cyberspace: E-mentoring for professional women. *Women in Management Review, 21*(6), 483-499.

Jensen, E. (2006). *Teaching with the brain in mind* (2nd ed.). Alexandria, VA: ASCD.

Jonassen, D. H., Howland, J., Moore, J., & Marra, R. M. (2003). *Learning to solve problems with technology* (2nd ed.). Upper Saddle River, NJ: Merrill Prentice Hall.

Kennedy, T., Smith, A., Wells, A., & Wellman, B. (2008). *Networked families.* Pew Internet & American Life Project. Retrieved November 18, 2008, from http://www.pewinternet.org/pdfs/PIP_Networked_Family.pdf

King, K. P., & Gura, M. (2009). *Podcasting for teachers (Rev. 2nd ed). SERIES: Emerging technologies for evolving learning.* Charlotte, NC: Information Age Publishing.

King, K. P., & Sanquist, S. (2009). 21st century learning and human performance. In V. Wang & K. P. King, (Eds.), *Fundamentals of human performance and training. SERIES: Adult education special topics.* (pp. 61-88). Charlotte, NC: Information Age Publishing.

King, K. P., Barnabo Cacohalo, B., Beauford, D., Berman, C., Bowman, C., Buerkle, L, Carew, C., Cocchiaro, A., Connel, S., Cook, B., Cortez, J., Costantio, M., Daniels, J., D'Ononfrio, A., Hollwitz, K., Jeraci, E., Kanarek, L., Kaufman, L., Ljutic, M., Marrero, M., Montgomery, E., Morgenstern, S., Moritz, J., Mundy, L., Peluso, J., Pitt, J., & Warga, K. (2008a). *UEGE 5102 Spring 2008 Critical Perspectives of Foundations in American Education.* Retrieved March 28, 2008, from http://uege5102.blogspot.com

King, K. P., Bethel, T., Dery, V., Foley, J., Griffith-Hunte, C., Guerrero, M., Lasalle-Tarantin, M., Menegators, J., Meneilly, K., Patterson, S., Peters, S., Pina, A., Ritchie, D., Rudzinki, L., Sandiford, D., & Sarno, I. (2008b). *EDGE 6101 Fall 2008 Race and Multicultural Education with Dr. King.* Retrieved Nov. 1, 2008, from http://edge6101-08f.blogspot.com

Matthews, W. J. (2003). Constructivism in the classroom. *Teacher Education Quarterly, 30*(3), 51- 64.

Rainie, L., Fox, S., Horrigan, J., Lenhart, A., & Spooner, T. (2000). *Tracking online life. Pew Internet & American Life Project.* Retrieved November 18, 2008, from http://www.pewinternet.org/report_display.asp?r=11

Prensky, M. (2008, June). Young minds, fast times; The 21st century digital learner. *Edutopia*. Retrieved September 25, 2008, from http://www.edutopia.org/ikid-digital-learner-technology-2008

Simonson, M., Smaldino, S. E., Albright, M., & Zvacek, S. (2008). *Teaching and learning at a distance* (4th ed). Upper Saddle River, NJ: Prentice Hall.

Tapscott, D., & Williams, A. D. (2006). *Wikinomics*. New York: Portfolio.

Wlodkowski, R. (1998). *Enhancing adult motivation to learn* (Rev ed.), San Francisco: Jossey Bass.

CHAPTER 37

TRANSFORMATION IS THE WAY

A Study About Forum Theatre and Critical Literacy with Brazilian Immigrants in an ESOL Class in New England

Maria Tereza Schaedler

For two months, I conducted a pilot study involving Brazilian women immigrants in an ESOL classroom. The study consisted on utilizing Forum Theatre techniques as a pedagogical tool to help these students develop critical literacy skills in English. Some of the findings of this study are that this technique helps develop participants' social understanding; assists people into becoming subjects in their own lives; and helps develop language skills.

The setting of the study was an ESOL class for adults held in Everett, Massachusetts, a working class suburb of Boston. This class was an academic year-long program for local residents. The entire class was composed of 20 adult students from such countries as, Brazil, El Salvador,

Empowering Women Through Literacy: Views From Experience, pp. 281–288
Copyright © 2009 by Information Age Publishing
All rights of reproduction in any form reserved.

Vietnam, Pakistan, Yemen, and Haiti. This class was considered at an intermediate/advanced level.

Participants in this study were four Brazilian women from this ESOL class. Anita (all names have been changed to assure anonymity) had been living in the U.S. for two years. She worked as a housecleaner. Zélia, also a housecleaner, arrived in the U.S. seven and a half years ago, seven months after her husband, to reunite the family. Mirna had been in the U.S. for seven years. She worked as a housecleaner and babysitter. Karla arrived in the U.S. five years ago. She worked at a local Dunkin' Donuts. All four women had family members, children or husbands also living in the U.S. The unskilled jobs these women performed in the U.S. were not a reflection of their professional realities in Brazil.

Research was conducted over a two-month period, which included seven class sessions of two-and-a-half hours. Data were gathered and analyzed while exploring participants' reactions, through interviews, group discussions, and observations. This study had the collaboration of Marc, the official teacher of the class who also shared his interpretation of the fieldwork notes and observations.

The research intervention for this study was the application of Forum Theatre to the curriculum. Forum Theatre is a Theatre of the Oppressed (TO) technique. TO is an educational and participation tool, created by Brazilian theatre director Augusto Boal. TO utilizes drama to encourage understanding and to find solutions for individual and collective problems (Boal, 1985). The main idea is to empower the oppressed and transform thinking into active solutions. In a Forum Theatre session, spectators become "spect-actors" (Boal, 1985, p.154) and act out their conflicts and solutions through improvisation. By sharing personal stories of conflict and acting them out, participants become subjects of their own lives while rehearsing tactics for future conflicts.

For Augusto Boal (1985), theatre is political and can be used to empower people. This political empowerment comes from the simple act of telling a personal story and changing the outcome through improvisation. By doing this act, participants become aware of their oppression and possible solutions, which they have already shared with other spect-actors. In this research the essence of the word empowerment was related to increasing Brazilian women immigrants' sense of personal and collective power (Rowlands, 1997) by understanding their social, cultural and economic context and the impact of cultural and linguistic isolation (Schaedler, 2008).

The Forum Theatre process starts by creating a safe environment with warm-ups and improvisational theatre games for people to share personal stories. In the next step participants choose one of the stories (the one that usually they collectively relate more with) to improvise. The improvisation of the story follows by volunteers and spect-actors start imagining what they can do to change the story that is being performed. The spect-actor then replace the protagonist and improvises a new ending to the story, instead of just sharing verbally what the protagonist should or could do.

In this study, I found that no matter why the participants were studying English, the reasons were all rooted in becoming more self-assured while interacting in society. Data from this study indicate that the participants' experiences speaking English is often embedded in fear. They often noted that they are afraid of making mistakes and being laughed at.

Mirna expressed that "One of the biggest mistakes immigrants make when they arrive in the U.S. is to pretend they understand what the other person is telling them" (Schaedler, 2008, p. 78). Her explanation was that there is shame in admitting that one does not understand and she didn't want to be seen as stupid.

The participants of this study used metaphors to describe their experiences and emotions while learning English in the U.S. For example, Mirna said, "It's like if you were in a wheelchair" (Schaedler, 2008, p. 57). Zélia also described her experience through metaphors, stating, "I felt all red, I used to stammer, and I used to feel impotent in some situations, like if I had my hands tied up and my mouth gagged. It's awful, I felt mute even if I was able to speak" (Schaedler, 2008, p. 57).

The women in the study also placed all the responsibility of learning English on their own shoulders. Anita described the weight of this responsibility:

> Marc (the ESOL teacher) always encourages us, for him we are already fluent because we can communicate no matter how. But I want more from myself. When you are insecure with the language you are always afraid. I know I need time to learn, but English is not a hard language. English grammar is very easy, especially when you compare it to Portuguese. That's why I feel even more frustrated sometimes, if English is easier than Portuguese why can't I learn it fast? (Schaedler, 2008, p. 58-59)

Zélia also described her experience in the beginning of the English classes:

> It was hard to deal with myself. I felt that I was my own greatest enemy. My fear was my greatest enemy. I felt stupid. I was angry with myself. How can't I learn this, it can't be that hard. I felt really stupid. Learn a second language for me is hard. (Schaedler, 2008, p. 59)

Improving their language skills gave the participants confidence and self-esteem, as well as better chances of advocating for themselves. Speaking

English can give immigrant women confidence to communicate, interact in any social context and not depend on their husbands or their children. To speak English is more than a survival skill, it helps people to become "subjects" and not "objects" in the dominant culture (Freire & Macedo, 1987, p.156). Theatre of the Oppressed empowers immigrants who are learning a foreign language by giving them the opportunity to rehearse their language skills, ideas, and opinions in situations that are going to be relevant for them.

Karla stated, "English ends up being the only victory we take with us from this country. What I learned, no one will take away from me" (Schaedler, 2008, p.70). This statement shows clearly Karla's agency. During our conversations, she also expressed how strong she feels after experiencing being an immigrant in this country. "I could go anywhere now," (Schaedler, 2008, p. 71) she said, while describing how hard life here is and how empowered she feels for being able to survive. Karla's strong sense of identity makes her feel ready to advocate for herself in any situation. Learning English was just another tool she wanted to develop to reaffirm her autonomy.

Developing critical literacy—the consciousness individuals develop that allows them to actively engage in the world (Giroux, 1987)—and finding a voice in another language and in their lives had an impact on the participants' cultural identities. The women were transformed into what Freire called "conscious beings" (Freire, 2000, p. 39). The majority of immigrants in the U.S. represent what Freire (2000) would call a dependent, silent society. "Its voice is not an authentic voice, but merely an echo of the voice of the metropolis—in every way, the metropolis speaks, the dependent society listens" (p. 46). What is needed in this case is a "revolutionary project ... a process in which the people assume the role of subject in the precarious adventure of transforming and recreating the world" (p. 56). Conscious beings question their cultural identities and experiences and decide on what they should keep, what needs to be transformed, and what they want to acquire. They consistently become subjects in every context.

The process of becoming a conscious being is not easy and has some costs. I realized how much I was asking of the women in this study. I wanted them to run over their fears, take risks, and engage in improvisational theatre techniques. I asked them not only to use the new language they were learning, but their bodies as well. Forum Theatre put them in a very vulnerable position. Even so, during a particular Forum Theatre session, everybody in the class participated. One by one they were assuming the role of the protagonist and changing the outcome of the story. While some of them demonstrated a certain ease and confidence, others started timidly and were encouraged by the rest of the group. By the end they were not only more self-assured but also had a smile on their faces.

In this situation I found another connection between improving language skills and empowerment. The connection was made when the spect-actors forgot they were in an English class, eventually they even forgot they were speaking English. They were actively engaged in their roles and that was because the story was relevant to them. It is important to emphasize that these students were used to participating in Marc's classes through dialogue and other theatre exercises. The use of Forum Theatre only raised the risks of the act of participation by displaying their language skills, bodies, stories, and experiences.

Marc built a foundation in this class that was very important to the success of this pilot study. My role as the Forum Theatre facilitator was to only continue and deepened his approach. In order to do that I tried to build a space where participants could feel safe in order to be vulnerable. I created this safe space by playing and demonstrating the Forum Theatre exercises, by asserting that I was not looking for a right or wrong answer, and by giving them permission to laugh at me while I foolishly acted out some warm ups. Nonetheless, I was the immigrant with more fluency in English in the classroom and that gave me power even though I tried to not focus on this fact. In my experience, for immigrants in the United States, anybody who speaks better English always has more power.

For Zélia, American culture and English represent cultural hegemony. Zélia described her experiences:

> I don't like when someone calls my house and speaks Spanish because they know we are immigrants. My sister is very direct when people do that, she says, "Speak English with me because my language is Portuguese." I feel discriminated. Because I am an immigrant, I speak Spanish? (Schaedler, 2008, p. 73)

Zélia's statement is more than an affirmation about her cultural identity and how she represents herself. Her declaration is a resistance. That is why she used to refer to English as a "seven-headed monster," a monster that started looking a little bit friendlier in Marc's classes.

Zélia described other experiences related to the lack of power for those learning English. In my first interview with her, Zelia said, "In the beginning of the English classes I used to have migraines" (Schaedler, 2008, p. 76). Marc explained Zélia's statement:

> In English, people are afraid to make mistakes, so what happens when they make a mistake, they are laughed at. There are many stories of Brazilians who have more English laughing at Brazilians who have less. So people get disgraced, they back off and they leave. (Schaedler, 2008, p. 76)

For Anita, people learn from their mistakes; when things are going too well people's lack of skills is more likely to get accommodated. She explained, "My biggest difficulty is to speak. I feel intimidated by those who speak better than me. I feel very frustrated because I want to say something but it doesn't come to me" (Schaedler, 2008, p. 78). Because Anita did not work with Americans she did not use much English, and therefore felt that her lack of skills were accommodated. "I need to practice more," she said. Forum Theatre represented a great opportunity for her to practice her English and she was one of the most active spec-actors.

Zélia believed that what helped her cope with her fear of English classes was that in this program the instructors were friends as well as teachers. They were always encouraging the students. She declared:

> They tried to get close to us through our culture. They were warm; they asked about our families, they wanted to know that. All that helped me to feel more comfortable at school. It was not a "seven-headed monster" anymore. I felt like I was going to a friends' house to spend time with friends. So instead of running away of the "seven-headed monster" I started to look forward to the classes. I wanted to be there close to people that made me feel comfortable. (Schaedler, 2008, p. 76)

Coping with fear is a constant in the lives of the participants of this study. Mirna used to run away when someone would come to talk to her in English. She would get nervous. She expressed how in the beginning she would just say "yes" to everything. That got her into some misunderstandings. While her boss would explain to her what she had to do, even without understanding what the work was, she would always say "yes." The problem was when her boss would finish the sentence with, "Do you mind?" "I said 'yes' and she looked scared so I got scared too. I wondered what have I done? Did I do something wrong?" (Schaedler, 2008, p. 78).

I could not measure the efficacy of this technique outside the classroom. However, I noticed that in this ESOL class Forum Theatre helped people intensify an atmosphere of freedom where they could free their potentialities, and express feelings, emotions, and anxieties (Schaedler, 2008, p. 87). Learning English represents both an obstacle and an enabling tool. As new arrivals in the U.S., these women experienced total dependency on others who could speak English. This made them feel powerless. This feeling of helplessness started changing when they learned how to communicate effectively using English while reflecting on their experiences in the dominant culture.

Anita voiced her opinion about the work of acting in Forum Theatre in this class (emphasis by the writer):

I think theatre is very good because it's different. It's dynamic, it's not boring. I need to learn to **speak**, read, and write. But it's more difficult for me to **speak**. For me it's better when I do exercises to **speak**. I loved the warm ups … it is important to break the ice, to get to know each other so we can **speak** more. I don't like acting much, but I think it's important to **speak**, if the focus of theatre is in **speaking** I think it's great. (Schaedler, 2008, p. 83)

Zélia's comment was very similar to Anita's (emphasis by the writer):

I use a lot my body to **speak**. Body language is very useful, but I need to **speak** more. I need to use words, open my mouth and **speak**. I really like Forum Theatre because I could **speak**. I learn more from listening and **speaking**. (Schaedler, 2008. p. 83)

In this study I discovered how the simple action of engaging in a dialogue could be empowering. Being able to communicate, share ideas, agree or disagree is not a simple task when people do not share the same language and culture. Theatre of the Oppressed (TO) stimulates dialogue (Boal, 1996, p. 47). TO is useful to develop critical literacy in the classroom because it has reflective and transformative possibilities. TO helps develop spoken and non-verbal dialogue through a personalization of the learning process. New ideas are constructed through students' stories.

As a pedagogical strategy Forum Theatre demonstrated to be useful in developing communication skills in an ESOL environment. Participants in this course placed great value on developing their oral language skills. The fact that students became subjects and challenged the power structure in the classroom using this technique helped them develop critical literacy. Theatre of the Oppressed is not a magical tool and will not solve all problems. TO is a process that helps people become aware of the problems so they can analyze them and try to identify possible solutions.

As Berthoff (1987) stated, Freire taught us that "there is no way to transformation, transformation is the way" (p. xxiii). If what we are looking for is transformation, then we have to start transforming the world around us. For immigrant women to transform their realities they have to shift from being an object of their experiences to becoming a subject. Although I could not measure how the participants were using their skills outside the classroom I still believe that this work gave them the awareness of possibilities for action. In these experiences with Forum Theatre I discovered that people could become their own advocates. Participants learned that they could rely on themselves. In this study, some women were nervous to stand up, open their mouths and speak English in the Forum Theatre sessions. But they did it anyway. They became agents in the classroom.

During this study I realized that although Theatre of the Oppressed is an excellent tool to develop critical consciousness, TO in ESOL classes needs to recognize the goals of this setting, in this case language acquisition. In this study, by becoming conscious beings, the women were also able to learn English.

I never had the audacity to think that I could empower the women myself. I could only offer them a tool and hope that they would choose to use it. And they did. I have the opportunity now of continuing this work with the same group of people in a year-long project. Zélia, Anita, and Karla are now becoming facilitators of Forum Theatre activities in lower-level English classes in the same program. Forum Theatre helped them figure out what to do with this new voice in this new culture. It is a new identity they created, which added to the other identities they already had (Schaedler, 2008, p. 91). By disseminating this technique and helping other immigrants to develop their language skills, these women are now developing their own powers to transform and become agents of change.

REFERENCES

Berthoff, A. E. (1987). Foreword. In P. Freire & D. Macedo (Eds.), *Literacy: Reading the word and the world* (pp. xi-xxiii). Westport, CT: Bergin & Garvey.

Boal, A. (1985). *Theatre of the oppressed.* New York: Theatre Communication Group.

Boal, A. (1996). *Politics, education and change: Drama, culture and empowerment.* Brisbane, Australia: IDEA Publications.

Freire, P. (2000). *Cultural action for freedom. Harvard Educational Review. Monograph Series,* No. 1.

Freire, P., & Macedo, D. (1987). *Literacy. Reading the word and the world.* Westport, CT: Bergin & Garvey.

Giroux, H. (1987). Literacy and the pedagogy of political empowerment. In P. Freire & D. Macedo (Eds.), *Literacy: Reading the word and the world* (pp. 1-27). Westport, CT: Bergin & Garvey.

Rowlands, J. (1997). *Questioning empowerment: Working with women in Honduras.* Oxford, GB: Oxfam Publishing.

Schaedler, M. (2008). *"Transformation is the way": A study about Forum Theatre and critical literacy with Brazilian immigrants in an ESOL class in New England.* Unpublished Master's thesis, Lesley University, Cambridge, MA.

CHAPTER 38

SIMPLEMENTE MUJER

A Literacy Project By, With, and For Women

Gabriele I. E. Strohschen

INTRODUCTION

This essay chronicles a participatory action (PAR) project in which the executive director at a community-based organization in Chicago and I co-created a literacy-leadership program *by, with, and for* women of a Domestic Violence Prevention program. It describes the nine-month project, pointing practitioners toward contextualizing literacy programs for women within an art-based, liberatory education model. We boldly declare that the so-termed disfranchised and the enfranchised *alike and together* can empower themselves *only* when liberatory education is practiced in a mutually supportive learning community. Toward such an end, we, the education practitioners, must be willing to yield our positionality to make space for interdependent program design and implementation. In this essay, we share the hope for transformation: a transformation that can be reached when we are willing to arrive at self-awareness and community action *through* critical reflection and discourse. As Mezirow (2003)

Empowering Women Through Literacy: Views From Experience, pp. 289–300
Copyright © 2009 by Information Age Publishing
All rights of reproduction in any form reserved.

elaborates, the essential capabilities needed by adults to engage in critical-dialectical discourse are delineated in two models,

"One is what Robert Kegan (2000) identified as the development of our uniquely adult capacity to become critically self-reflective. The other is what King and Kitchener (1994) identified as reflective judgment, the capacity to engage in critical-dialectical discourse involving the assessment of assumptions and expectations supporting beliefs, values, and feelings" (p.60).

Essentially, we did just that. We deliberately engaged in critical self-reflection and brought together stakeholders in critical-dialectical discourse so that we would stand on common ground upon which to build this project. Holding ourselves mutually accountable, often painfully so, and facing our paradigmatic assumptions (Brookfield, 1995), we demystified our teaching practice. In the end, victims of domestic violence and community education practitioners emerged transformed, because we eventually engaged in this project as *simply women*.

We hesitated to write about this project for several years. We felt deeply that an article might have the flavor of "pimping" our experience for the sake of publication—a fame of sorts that runs counter what we stand for. We are also cognizant of the potential falsification the retelling of our experience may have become. As Newman (1999) warns, "in recalling experience we construct it. Giving it a beginning and an end, making it an experience, and episode, and so lifting it artificially out of the continuous flow of our being" (p. 10). We resolved this conflict only after we had gained some distance from the project and had reviewed the impact it has had on all of us, again, a few years later. Therefore, we decided to share our ideas and approaches—but ever mindful that we are speaking to you, the reader, as simply women, telling a simple story.

DOMESTIC VIOLENCE PREVENTION AND COMMUNITY PROGRAMS

Centro Romero is a 24-year-old community-based organization. From volunteer efforts of the Salvadoran community in the 1980s, it was created to meet the needs of the Latino/a immigrant and refugee population on Chicago's northeast side. Centro Romero provides interrelated programs in adult basic education, women's empowerment, legal assistance, and youth learning and leadership. Its mission is to assist a disfranchised community to access opportunities for social mobility. The agency builds on the concepts of Freirean (2001) community development, and on the values of Father Romero of El Salvador (Centro Romero Homepage, 2008).

The Domestic Violence Prevention program was developed in 1996 with the goal to "abate the cycle of domestic violence" (Centro Romero,

2008). Annually, the agency provides weekly support groups to 50 women, and serves over 1,000 women with legal assistance, counseling, translations at court hearing, and referrals and case management for human services. The pressing needs for women participants in the Domestic Violence Prevention program emerged quickly. Economic dependency on their abusive partners as much as legal immigration status of the family that depended on the spouse's status hindered the women from leaving an abusive situation. Eighty percent of the women had less than five years of formal schooling in their country of origin, and seventy per cent had never worked outside of the home. Therefore, language skills were essential to access educational opportunities as a means for self-determined and sustained existence. United States immigration laws offer the possibility for wives of legal immigrants and residents to attain legal status on their own. To protect immigrant women against violence, the U.S. Immigration and Naturalization Service (INS) permits certain abused spouses and children of U.A. citizens and permanent residents to self-petition for green cards. (HR 3355, 1994). However, without marketable skills to earn a living wage, the women were caught in a Catch 22 situation: they could not leave the abusive home if they could not escape long enough to learn skills needed to work. Without the belief that they could, even with the opportunity to learn, change, and become self-sufficient, the women were their own worst enemy.

The need for the women of this program to learn to read and write in Spanish and/or English went beyond the need for survival. The women had already survived life in countries torn by civil war and poverty only to find themselves victims of physical and psychological torture in the new country; captives of violent spouses in their own homes. In spite of living with the trauma of domestic violence, they were raising their children and tending to abusive partners. They were fighting. They were surviving. They did not realize these capacities and skills. These strengths, however, were valuable in building an existence and surviving, economically and psychologically, on their own. *Literacy* in the context of domestic violence prevention at Centro Romero meant that women had to learn to read their world with its opportunities as much as learning to read and write. We believed this could be achieved in a mutually supportive learning community.

BUILDING A LEARNING COMMUNITY

I was originally drawn to the work of Centro Romero because of the values, mission, and actions. The similarities between Latina immigrants and me were perplexingly great. We had experienced the impact of sexism, classism, and racism in this country. Although socio-economic and educational backgrounds in our respective countries vary greatly, as a Northern European immigrant woman my experiences matched those of my sister Latina immigrants at the center. I worked closely with the executive director, who shared my experience of coming to this country without English language skills. Basically, the origins of the *Simplemente Mujer* project can be found in the insight we gained when we shared our stories, our hopes, and our resources as women working together at the center.

Our strengths, once we understood the value of them and how skills could be transferred to other settings, we believed, could provide a way to support other women as well. Lee (2003) explicates the concept of learning community with four principles, "(i) they are integrative; (ii) solutions and future strategies are inherent in the communities themselves; (iii) they demand practical partnerships; and (iv) they are not projects with beginnings and ends, but are about an ongoing way of life" (p. 2). The participants in the Domestic Violence Prevention program constituted such a learning community. We anticipated that within a collaboratively developed project, we would be able to increase self-awareness of skills and heighten the mutual support among the women. We hoped the women would embrace a lifelong learning attitude by recognizing the skills and capacities they already possessed. *Simplemente Mujer* would create the context to do so. We were faced with challenges that our knowledge of liberatory education philosophy would not necessarily overcome; we needed to ground ourselves in practical application, and needed tools and techniques to do so. We created that within the project.

Confident that we could be partners in building a learning community as we had created mutual support with one another at the center, we identified that we were confronted with a form of internalized oppression when it came to starting the project. What the women seemed to experience resembles what Fromm (1990[1]) refers to as "internalized authority." We were aware of a generalized distrust by the women about airing family secrets. And, we anticipated concerns about a white woman and a Latina of higher status initiating the project. If we were to develop an interdependent learning community, we would have to critically examine assumptions in ways that would convince the women to give this project a chance. Our authenticity and sincerity as women had to be clear to us, examined and understood by the women and ourselves rigorously, and meticulously upheld throughout the process if we were to truly engage all women in a participatory way in building the learning community.

Krishnamurti (1966) tells about a man who seeks to change being tired of his life of struggles and commitments. He says, "look and be simple" (p. 82). We, too, wanted to look and allow beauty and love amidst the horror of domestic violence, social barriers, fear, unexamined assumptions, and hesitant expectations to guide our action—simply.

Hence, we decided to build on the everyday experiences in women's lives to provide the backdrop against which women could see that they have tremendous capacities and skills. By highlighting what we do well, we offered hope for transformation. We listed our beliefs about this project, which we shared with the participants during the first meeting.

Grounded in liberatory education, we were committed to developing and implementing the project collaboratively with staff, volunteers, and community women. In preparation to invite everyone to plan and develop the project, we crafted a statement of commitment, which was also shared during the first meeting. Both statements described basic design principles and a rationale for the project. Sharing the statement with the group was a first step toward building trust. The statement served to remind us and hold us accountable to liberatory education throughout the project. We felt that we *would* hold one another accountable to its processes and principles and entered the project with little doubt that we would come to question our praxis. Therefore, making the beliefs and commitment explicit seemed an easy promise to make. As it turned out, we had many discussions during which we aired our discomfort. When the group went into directions, which we deemed less "pedagogically" appropriate, we found it hard to let go of our educator role. Having shared our beliefs and commitments was tantamount to having a neon sign of accountability flare up from time to time. However, having made explicit these beliefs and commitments from the start, we were able to check both our actions and egos—most of the time. We admit that we gained a deeper insight into our own actions and egos because of the critical reflections toward which our mutual support nudged us. It was not really possible to pull the plug on that neon sign when someone else is watching.

Empowering Women
Literacy – Leadership Project Statement of Beliefs

We believe that:
Woman's lives can be improved with the skills and capacities gained from fighting and surviving in a domestic violence environment
Women's resilience, strength, and capacities can be seen in the daily tasks and objects while caring for a family
Women are not victims if they have survived domestic violence
Woman can help one another
Women could learn together to take a fresh, simple look at their situation
Writing our stories is a way of communicating knowledge
Writing our stories is a step toward helping self and others

Figure 38.1.   Statement of Beliefs.

Empowering Women	
Literacy-Leadership Project Statement of Commitment	
1.	We decided on integrating art into literacy instruction. Making paper from everyday objects that clutter our homes would be an activity during which we would become peer educators, share survival strategies, support a contextual acquisition of writing and speaking English/Spanish, learn about our women's ways of knowing and learning, and use the final product (paper) to write our stories.
2.	We agree that involving all women immediately in the development of the project, including the description of its goals, means integrating content (i.e., literacy and leadership skill building) while exemplifying interdependence as peer educators and co-learners.
3.	We insist that being clear all along with all women on how we think this strategy will offer opportunities to *learn while doing* is essential in breaking down perceived power and positionality about teachers and students or staff and participants.
4.	We promise to yield leadership to emerging leaders among us in the group when such leadership is evident to the group, and we promise to share our reflection when this occurs.
5.	We commit ourselves to invite and implement other than our own ideas on details of the design of the project even when it means changes to what we originally conceived.
6.	We commit to participate in the activities as equitable partners rather than as teachers only and to share our own feelings and vulnerabilities as they emerge during the project.
7.	In doing so, we commit to this learning community as strategic partners, willing to play the reciprocal roles of teacher and student.

Figure 38.2.   Statement of Commitment.

Hence, team leading or team teaching as described by Tisdell and Strohschen et al. (2002) is a key element in the early phases of creating a learning community.

HIGHLIGHTS: PLANNING AND IMPLEMENTING THE PROJECT

Planning

The project development began with three planning dialogues. It engaged the diverse group of Mexican and Salvadoran immigrants and refugee women who were participants of the Domestic Violence Prevention program; the Salvadoran executive director and staff, the North American artist, and the Northern European immigrant researcher. In all activities, the daughters of the women were included, which allowed the women to attend meetings, most often in the guise of taking their children to the center.

During the first meeting, we shared the belief and commitment statements after a brief introduction of the overall concept that had been designed with the artist's input. The group felt strongly that the teachers should lead the way. Suggestions that we could mutually teach one another were met with concerns that this would not *really* be education and that the women would not learn. It was clear that most of the group believed in the banking approach to education and that we needed to start the project in a more directed manner than we had anticipated. The moment was one of many when the group challenged our notions, concepts, and philosophy. We explained our values and assumptions about this project, trying to convince the women of the benefits. No matter how democratically we had conceived this project, we had come close to failing our philosophy. Liberatory education meant that we ought not stand in the way or short cut a process of liberation. So we waited as everyone debated our suggested learning objectives and this liberatory approach to education. Sharing our concepts began to build the relationship in our learning community that proved to be vital to the project's success. Our demystification of the teaching approach took time but bore fruit later as every single woman in the group moved in and out of the role of facilitator/teacher and was fully aware of it when she did so.

Implementing

We met weekly over a nine-month period in the artist's studio and made paper squares from dryer lint, our children's old school papers, cornhusks, and other discarded item we clean up every day. During the paper making sessions, we practiced conversational English and Spanish. The women took turns writing down key words and reviewing learning objectives. The center's staff conducted formal ESL instruction after the sessions. We had no qualms about using conventional techniques of instructions so long as the content had relevance to the women's lives and they could apply to their lives what they were learning "in class" everyday. Eventually, we wrote short poems and stories about significant experiences and transcribed those onto the paper squares. A good deal of non-structured discussion happened during the art activity, as woman discussed their challenges and issues and sough one another's input for solutions. When appropriate, staff intervened with resource information and clarification of legal or other support. In turn, women would then seek out more assistance at the center as needed. We then crafted a quilt by weaving the individual paper squares together.

We recorded important points about each session and provided feedback about both learning of language skills and the process of our mutual support activities. The director or I took turns in highlighting how this process in the studio was about learning to *read the world and learning to read the word*. The coordinator of the Domestic Violence Prevention program nurtured many conversations over *cafesito y pan dulce* to further illuminate how the very involvement in the planning and implementing of this project was "educational." These *dialogos* served as an informal mutual support group to the women in addition to the structured activities of the Domestic Violence Prevention program. Many of the women later remembered these dialogues as the turning point in their own empowerment and consequent involvement as community leaders.

As the project progressed, we realized that we had developed more than a literacy-leadership program and wanted to utilize the quilt to raise awareness about domestic violence. The unexpected next step, therefore, was to raise the teaching objective to the community level. We decided to exhibit the paper-poem-quilt with others in Chicago in an effort to encourage women to make healthy decisions for themselves and their families. Again, we turned to collaborative planning meetings during which each woman took turns to lead a discussion, record minutes, or follow up on assigned tasks. The decisions surprised us 'educators' when the women generated a concept based on leadership, creativity, and public performance, all of which we had not seen coming this quickly.

In two months, the group scripted a spoken word and song performance and struggled to master a choreographed dance that involved the audience. Designing the dance caused some temporary dissonance as none of us managed to dance to the same drummer. It was during the practices that clashes occurred as the formally schooled members of our group wanted to take over the planning of the performance. Once again, we recognized that the importance of having written statements of beliefs and commitment were important to nudge us into cohesion again. The executive director and I wanted to interfere with the staff's dominance so we could "let" the women make decisions. In checking in with one another, we decided to only voice our concern and let it be at that. The power struggle between the staff members and the women dissolved in the following way: the women skipped practices. We learned afterwards that they had met without staffers to make their own plan; when they returned to meetings they showed everyone the choreographed dance and performance, complete with costumes and props.

The result was a joyful premiere performance at a local woman-run gallery. This gala performance went smoothly and the ease with which the audience became encircled in a string the dancers wove around them without entangling them was testimony to truly communal coordination, one wherein everyone's role was essential. The paper poem quilt continued to travel to other agencies with presentations by individual women of the group for a few months. The executive director and I later crafted descriptions of the project and conducted sessions with other community organization staff who were interested in using this approach to mutual support, literacy education, and leadership development with women in domestic violence prevention programs.

REFLECTIONS AND RECOMMENDATIONS

*I cannot proclaim my liberating dream and in the next day
be authoritarian in my relationship with the students*

—Paulo Freire (1987)

The results of *Simplemente Mujer* are seen on several levels. The learning objectives were achieved during the intensive, nine-month ESL teaching, both during the papermaking activities and classroom instruction. The women developed leadership skills that were based on reflected upon experience during the planning and implementation of the art-literacy activities and performances. The women realized the strengths they already possessed and became increasingly aware of the transferability of capacities and skills to environments outside of their home. They had realized that they *could* survive. A third outcome is seen in the growth as practitioners that the executive director, the staff, and this researcher experienced during this project.

The most obvious outcomes beyond the acquisition of ESL and/or Spanish speaking and writing skills came in the empowerment of the women participants from the Domestic Violence Prevention program. Two months after the completion of the project:

- Three women enrolled in GED programs to gain the basic education needed to find a job
- Three women became volunteers in the center's women program (two of whom eventually became employed with the program)
- Two women became leaders in their children's local school councils
- Three women filed for divorce from their abusive spouses
- Five women applied under VAWA for permanent resident status.

The idea to integrate a popular art form into language learning and leadership development is not so unique as the spirit with which we did so. The strength of the project came from the idea of making paper from the "debris of our lives" and to let this paper become the bearer of our stories in the form of a paper poem quilt. There is much to the metaphor in terms of showing ourselves that the remnants of our everyday existence can birth new beginnings. The sharing of our personal narratives, the creation of our spoken work performance piece, and the writing of stories and poems on those paper squares were more than techniques to learning language and leadership. In each of these creative processes we reinvented ourselves as we spiraled back to build our knowledge, increase our skills, and recognize our capacities. The art activities helped us learn about our strengths in a non-threatening setting; our learning community gave us the support to strengthen our spirit and self-efficacy.

In follow -up interviews with the participants of *Simplemente Mujer*, the executive director and I, three years after the project, learned how the women had transferred their learning to action in other areas of their lives. We could not identify and categorize a particular way in which the women learned; but rather the way in which they choose to collaborate, construct knowledge, reflect on their experiences, and acknowledge change. During the project, we encouraged group communication so that any woman could take on a leadership role at different moments. It meant to those of us, who had more experience in facilitating the learning process, that we had to hold back during discussions. Yet, we always openly stated to the entire group when and why we chose to make space for voices other than our own. As educators, we gave up control over the teaching and group discussion processes. We trusted that we were moving toward the goals, and we acknowledged that members of the group shared the responsibility to get us there.

As we collaboratively conducted this project, we combined peer education, empowerment, and leadership development among women in a cross-cultural setting within a set of beliefs and commitments grounded in liberatory education. It was extremely challenging to maneuver in the mazes and paradoxes of society's prevailing structures of education programs. It was difficult to acknowledge the depth with which we reify—wittingly or unwittingly—positionality inherent in our roles as teacher, student, victim, survivor, and simply woman. It is not easy to let go of doing what we claim to know best as community workers and educators.

Engaging women in participating in developing and implementing the project's activities was not so difficult so long as we, the trained educators, recognized when to be directive, when to be non-directive, and when to become a strategic partner (Strohschen & Elazier, 2007) in the learning process. The openness with which we acknowledged what we were doing (i.e., the demystification of the educational process) was key in the criticaldialectical model we adopted. It was not as easy to remain true to a critically reflective stance when it came to examining our attitudes and beliefs in the moment. The executive director, the artist, the center staffers, and I had to remind one another many times that we had something to learn from all women. We learned to do this with sincerity only after we were told that we guided the group proceedings with an air of pedagogical correctness about us. In time, all members of the learning community reminded us when we moved too strongly into the teacher role. This decentering of control and our ego- checking eventually "took" and we suggest it is because we stated our beliefs and commitments, visibly, to the group. More importantly, we had given ourselves the tasks and permission to call one another out when needed. On this level, our practice and adherence to liberatory education principles greatly improved during the project.

Finally, *Simplemente Mujer* brought fourth the transformational power of relationships that can be build across a group of women of diverse backgrounds in a learning community. *Simplemente Mujer* taught us that understanding self and being open to change are essential to the success of not only collaborative literacy-leadership programs but to any communal learning endeavor that values interdependence, critical reflection, and critical-dialectical discourse.

NOTE

1.   The translation of this book is *The Fear of Freedom* (author's translation). Interesting to note is that the English version of the book is titled, *Escape from Freedom*.

REFERENCES

Centro Romero Homepage—History (2008). Retrieved August 12, 2008, from http://www.charityadvantage.com/CentroRomero/HomePage.asp

Brookfield. S. (1995) *Becoming a critically reflective teacher*. San Francisco: Jossey-Bass.

Freire, P. (2001). *Pedagogy of the oppressed*. New York: The Continuum International Publishing Group, Inc.

Fromm, E. (1990). *Die Furcht vor der Freiheit*. München: Deutscher Taschenbuchverlag GmbH & Co. KG.

HR 3355. (1994). Title IV, sec. 40001-40703 of the Violent Crime Control and Law Enforcement Act of 1994 HR 3355 and signed as Public Law 103-322 by President Bill Clinton on September 13, 1994. Retrieved November 21, 2008, from http://www.ncjrs.gov/txtfiles/billfs.txt

Krishnamurti, J. (1967). *Commentaries on living*. Third Series. Wheaton, IL: The Theosophical Publishing House.

Lee, S. (2003). Building cities and towns as a learning communities In *Online Proceedings*. Canadian Association for the Study of Adult Education. Retrieved on July 12, 2008, from http://www.oise.utoronto.ca/CASAE/cnf2003/CASAEEpgm2003-3%20.html

Mezirow, J. (2003). Transformative learning as discourse. *Journal of Transformative Education, 1*(1), 58-63.

Newman, M. (2007). *Maeler's regard: Images of adult learning*. Retrieved on October 3, 2007, from http://www.michaelnewman.info. (Originally published 1999 by Stewart Victor Publishing)

Strohschen, G., & Elazier, K. (2007). The 21st Century adult educator: Strategic and consultative partner. *Assumption University Journal, 1*(1), 42-53.

Tisdell, E. J., Strohschen, G. I. E., Carver, M. L., Corrigan, P., Nash, J., Nelson, M., Royer, M., Strom-Mackey, R., & O'Connor, M. (2004). Cohort learning online in graduate higher education: Constructing knowledge in cyber community. *Educational Technology & Society, 7*(1), 115-127.

CHAPTER 39

VOICES FROM THE EARTH

Pottery and English Experience for Hispanic Farm Worker Women, Orleans County, New York

Linda Redfield Shakoor and Deborah Wilson

Combining language learning with creative arts activities has been a winning combination for Hispanic farm worker women in New York State. We have developed an approach that engages marginalized women in a multi-faceted manner, enabling them to gain greater skills in English and to discover new avenues for creative expression.

BACKGROUND

Orleans County is a largely rural county halfway between Rochester and Buffalo, N.Y. and bordered on the north by Lake Ontario. It is home to many fruit and vegetable farms, dairy operations, and other agricultural enterprises such as hydroponics. A chronic lack of local labor has

Empowering Women Through Literacy: Views From Experience, pp. 301–310
Copyright © 2009 by Information Age Publishing
All rights of reproduction in any form reserved.

attracted a significant number of Hispanic workers, mostly from Mexico, to the area over the past two decades or so.

Typically, Mexican workers have come to Orleans on the migrant basis, or on short-term contracts, remaining only long enough to finish the seasonal harvest before moving on to warmer climates. However, over the past 10 years there has been an increasing tendency for entire families to live in the country all year round. Their children attend a specially funded agricultural workers' day care and then enter regular public school. While both men and women work in the fields, barns, and farm enterprises, the men in general have a greater likelihood of acquiring English skills, either on the job or through evening programs. Because of their domestic duties and child care responsibilities, the women have been less likely to attend language programs regularly.

Lack of language skills isolates women from regular community life. Many have had very little formal education in their first language, some having left school as early as Grade 3. Few have finished high school. The women's inability to fully communicate in stores and offices, and with physicians, lawyers, and their children's teachers, leaves them living on the margins of the local community. There is an ever-greater need for programs which serve the language needs of these Hispanic women and their children, if the goal is for them to gradually become full members of society.

World Life Institute (WLI), a private non-profit education center located at Waterport, New York in northern Orleans County, has developed several programs over the past five years to address the needs of the Hispanic farm worker population. Initially, the center received support from state funds to run ESOL, GED, and citizenship education classes in Waterport, as well as in less formal classes in migrant worker camps and private homes. Many of the women expressed their strong desire to participate in the ongoing pottery classes offered to English-speaking American students. The seed of an idea began to germinate. Why not merge the women's natural interest in handcrafts with their need for English skills, and create programming that would address both?

Building Support

After running a short, largely un-funded pilot program in the winter of 2002, World Life Institute approached the Genesee Orleans Regional Arts Council (GoArt!) for $2,500 to fund Pottery Experience for Hispanic Farm Worker Women during winter 2003. WLI received a very positive response, especially since this program aimed to provide creative programs to an underserved population. Orleans-Niagara Board of Cooperative Educational Services (ON-BOCES) also took an interest in this program, as it has a special focus on attracting and retaining Hispanic women in their continuing language programs. Additionally, special literacy funding available through a Title III Research Grant based at SUNY Brockport came on board with support starting in 2005. WLI's pottery and English programs for Hispanic women have grown remarkably, so that in fiscal year 2008 more than $15,000 in grant and state support was received. Even during the sad days of 2007, when authorities hauled dozens of undocumented workers off to detention/deportation centers, WLI had its largest and most dedicated group of women ever, along with the resources to hire an assistant who worked separately teaching pottery skills to the Hispanic children while their mothers/aunts were engaged in creative work in the pottery studio.

Over the five-year period the language development element of the program has expanded significantly. Women must learn specialized studio pottery vocabulary on their first visit to the studio, in both spoken and written form. After that, on each class day participants spend a few minutes completing worksheet activities before entering the studio, where pottery instruction is given in English largely without translation.

The Arts and Self-Esteem

The Hispanic women are not unique in describing clay as a material that absorbs their attention, transports them away from their daily cares, and in the end gives them a sense of pride in creating work of beauty which has strong decorative and functional value. But perhaps, in the context of rural life in Orleans, they have a stronger need than the general population to be engaged in an activity that brings them these benefits. Following a brief introductory period where they learn basic hand-forming techniques, many women who were initially extremely uncommunicative or shy, come to the studio bursting with ideas about projects, shapes and forms they want to attempt. In this process they begin to overcome the language barrier, and the first tentative steps toward direct conversation with the English-speaking pottery teacher occur.

Students are invited to try a variety of projects, both decorative and practical. For those on very limited incomes, making jars, cups, bowls, baking dishes and platters for home is a strong attraction. Often being in the studio opens the floodgates of memory and women begin to create objects based on items they remember from back home. Our program supports and encourages the women to delve into their roots, by providing reference books as well as images gleaned from the Internet. Not all students have an interest in traditional pottery but rather tap into their innate creativity and make unique products from their imagination.

One constant over the five years of working with this population is that the scale of the pieces is much grander than the pieces made by typical American students. Serving bowls hold enough food for 20 adults and casseroles are maxi sized. One of our funders observed that the scale of the work "shows how big the women's dreams are." Use of color is also distinctive, with surprising combinations and vibrant hues galore.

As we cannot feature each of the dozens of women who have passed through the studio doors over the past several years, we have selected a few of the many highlights:

Our student Cristina pioneered the creation of ceramic flowers in her work during the winter of 2005, by cutting and rolling small strips of clay in a spiral formation, then opening the edges to create petal-like forms (Figure 1). This idea caught on and soon she was teaching the others to make their own, or sometimes doing it for them. Even after she moved to New Jersey, an array of bowls, vases, cups, wall planters, and plaques incorporating floral elements appears at our studio every season.

Gloria, who only went as far as third grade in Mexico, has brought a fine sense of style to all her work. One of the most notable projects is a traditional Mexican crèche which she built during the pre-Christmas period. She formed a miniature house with peaked roof, its façade covered with flowers and vines. An outer porch provided space for small fig-

Figure 39.1.   Flower Dish by Cristina: Photo by Deborah Wilson.

ures of the Holy Family (not made from clay), and miniature urns for candles or small live plants.

As some of the women have become more proficient technically with their hand-forming, they have delved even more deeply into their sources of inspiration. Rosa Diaz is unusual among our students, being one of the few who completed high school before leaving Mexico. Nonetheless, she has lived the difficult life of an agricultural laborer since arriving here. Rosa was inspired by the traditional sun faces she saw in one of our reference books, which typically hang on the walls or fences of outdoor patios. She progressed to transposing the symbols from a Mayan calendar found on the internet into a design sketched with ceramic pencil onto a simple bisque-fired plate she had made from scratch. Glazed in earthy tones, this very striking piece has brought her a lot of positive feedback.

Rosa's drive to communicate more about her experience led her to create a series of garden fountains in the winter and spring of 2007. At the end of class one day, she asked to take some clay and a few tools home. A few weeks later, she brought her project back: the sculpted figure of a woman (about 20 inches high) carrying a water jar on her shoulder; it was formed so that a small pump inside the hollow structure allows water to pour from the jar. It was a moving moment when Rosa witnessed the finished sculpture being lifted hot from the kiln, and said aloud to a small group of American students gathered in the studio: "This fountain represents the indigenous Mexican Indian, a person who doesn't have any rights, and she is only able to work very hard, to attend the children, most of the time these women suffer a lot." She created two additional versions of the sculpture in the ensuing months, one a younger woman in a fancy apron (still with the water jar on her shoulder), and the most recent a pregnant woman carrying on her head a basket of flowers for sale.

After her year of being deeply immersed in expressing herself through clay, Rosa determined to further her education and has become one of the first Hispanic women in our region to enroll in community college. She completed her first year successfully. Many of her English assignments, both within our program and after she began at college, focused on her interest in pottery. When she learned of preparations for this book chapter, she wrote:

> The Mexican pottery traditions are very important to me because most women (have) grown up using (pottery) every day. What is very important to me to remember about the history of ceramics in the beginning until today (is) that most(ly) women are (making) the ceramics. What I remember most was my grandmother used a lot of utensil(s) to cook every day in her kitchen, also my mother and my aunts too. I was surrounded with all those beautiful pieces of ceramic during my childhood but I (did) not have the opportunity to learn how they (were) made in Mexico. Thanks to (the

instructors in this program) I was able to make ceramics like a plate or a cup. In the end I made different objects I never (thought) I will be able to do. In the pottery class all the women learn ceramics but in the same time learn English too. Most of the time the women don't have the opportunity to see (each other) very often (but) during the class had the opportunity to talk and had wonderful conversation with all the students who attended the class. I also have the opportunity to meet a different kind of people. I had the opportunity to create different kinds of projects like a big fountain.

To the assembled Board of ON-BOCES she described how she had found the artist in herself through this program.

Rosa's work inspired a flurry of activity in the fall and winter of 2007-2008. Several students began the season by making garden fountains that took many work sessions to complete. Elva, who had moved to the U.S. as a young teenager, stated in past English classes that she had no interest in her Mexican heritage. Yet, during the winter of 2008 she spent more than a dozen studio sessions creating her interpretation of a female figure. The glazing process alone took several weeks of painstaking effort—since, much to our surprise, each color she used had to be exactly right to represent the traditional dance costume of Oaxaca.

Guadalupe gave up her dreams of going to art school when she married at a young age. She told us that on the day of her wedding her father even offered to pay to send her to Art College if she would postpone her marriage, but it was too late. On many winter mornings in Waterport Lupe learned English while she painted elaborate roses and vines of her own design onto oversized platters she had formed by hand. She lovingly created a large wall piece featuring a glazed brontosaurus in high relief, with hand-sketched ferns and foliage filling in the background, to be hung on the wall of her little son's bedroom.

Community Recognition

An important element of building self-esteem among the participants has been to provide them the opportunity to exhibit their work to their families, supporters, and the public at large. One of the most successful language-building activities had the women keeping a written journal regarding their studio experiences. After each pottery class, our ESOL specialist encouraged them to record in Spanish (or English, depending on their proficiency level) their recollections, their questions, and their reflections on what had occurred. Selected sections of these journal entries later on became the material we published in a bilingual newsletter which the women dubbed "Creative Women with Miracle Hands" (Mujeres Creativas con Manos Milagrosas).

The following are a few excerpts of the material.

I learned to make something I had never dreamed of. This class was a great help to me with regards to new learning...I think I did well because every day I learned more and more because I was able to understand the instructions of the artist. (Ana Maria)

It is very beautiful when I am making something because I am concentrating on what I am making and forgetting every other thought. I met many new people ...and this is one the strongest reasons I want to make an effort to learn English. When I finished each pottery class I had to write something about what I learned, first in Spanish and then translate it into English. For me that was very difficult but nothing is impossible. (Silvia R. R.)

Rosa R. reflected, "It was a diversion for me when I could go to class and forget about the work I had to do all day." "I am very happy, each day learning something new. I never wanted these classes to end so soon" wrote Maria D. "Hispanic women have the opportunity after a whole day of work to forget about the work and concentrate on something else ... it can help women very much" Maria T. added. "The pottery class was a very beautiful experience because I felt something new and I realized that you can give form to your imagination," Roselia R. affirmed.

At the end of each program season our program recognizes and honors the students' achievements with a fiesta that includes presentation of certificates, food for the whole family, and an exhibition of finished work in our own building. Over the years we have observed that the husbands and children of our students make a strong effort to attend the graduation event. Most years each woman has at least one immediate family member in attendance to witness her accomplishments and praise her success.

Funders, media, and other supporters have also spurred us on to exhibit the best of the finished work in public venues. Early on, the women put their work on view in the foyer display case at our local public library. Since then, the GoArt! Gallery has featured a display each spring. Starting in 2007, we also received encouragement to begin marketing the pottery at local fairs and craft shops. This has become a source of pride, as the women have arranged to put a percentage of proceeds back in the program. This helps buy supplies and directly contributes to keeping the program going for more weeks every year.

Many of these Hispanic farm worker women, who have a tenuous relationship with the larger community around them, are deeply moved by the fact that their work is appreciated and valued by the public. Cristina's journal documented the depth of her experience:

For me entering the gallery where my finished work was displayed was the most extraordinary experience that I have had. It is a privilege that an opportunity was given to me to demonstrate what I have achieved, and I appreciate the opportunity to say "this is my work"… to see how simple clay without any form had transformed to a vase, a fruit bowl, a platter, a bowl. It is unimaginable until you experience it personally.

Rosa R. wrote "The day of the exhibit was very beautiful because they displayed all our pieces that the women from the morning and evening classes made and also because everyone who donated to the program came and that was very beautiful." Brenda added "Please continue to help and teach Hispanic women so that they may feel pride in themselves."

Among the many achievements are the publication of three consecutive annual bilingual newsletters chronicling their experience while using computers for the first time; being invited to exhibit finished work at several galleries in the region; selling sculptural and functional pieces at several fairs and conferences; and inviting one of the advanced pottery students to participate in a presentation of her work at the Nazareth College ESOL Teachers Consortium in Rochester, New York.

Literacy Teaching Strategies within the Program Context

We structured the class schedule so that there is programming three days a week, two days for ESOL and one day for pottery. To begin literacy instruction we use graphic organizers, an idea taken from teaching English to children. We extrapolated this method specifically for women with low literacy to introduce English in an undemanding way which would build self-esteem while highlighting their experiences with pottery. These consist of simple graphs using 4 boxes on an 8 by 11½ sheet, with each box separately titled. One set of boxes that has worked well for pottery activities is: *Something I like to do, Something I want to learn, Something I know how to do and Something I don't understand.* The instructor models phrases in English to complete the boxes, using terminology the students learned previously. Then each woman shares her phrases orally in small groups. After this, students use the material to write simple phrases in their journals.

Another graphic organizer employs sequential ordering. Worksheets feature arrows to write the steps of, for example, how to make a vase or platter from start to finish, again using pottery vocabulary students had already learned. As the class progresses, we add an information gap chart that includes how long the women lived here, what they like about America, their favorite color (used on pottery), and so forth. Teachers often learn from the women's graphic organizers what the students want to learn next, and can prepare accordingly for upcoming classes. One woman expressed in writing that she wanted to understand more about the grant that supported the pottery program.

In a 2005 group, Hispanic teacher aides who had jobs in a bilingual day care center where they had regular classes with an ESOL teacher, joined the pottery classes at our center. We observed that they gained significantly more poise about writing, in Spanish and English. Journaling about their experiences in pottery gave them the confidence to advance in their workplace. At the day care, they gained the confidence to begin writing weekly reports that inform parents about the progress of their children. This included documenting the development of each child's motor kills and language. ESOL instructors will appreciate how astonishing it was that combining literacy activities with art, then journaling the experience, ultimately improved the women's ability to do their paid jobs. Hispanic women with very little education in their first language no longer dreaded having to write.

Conclusion

Our findings and observations over the years of running this program have been almost entirely positive. Women gain valuable language skills

Figure 39.2.   Rosa with Voices of Earth Pottery Exhibit 2007: Photo by Deborah Wilson

while learning a craft which excites and inspires them. Rates of attendance, and retention of students over a longer time period, are measurably higher when compared with classroom ESOL activities alone. Our region and community gain a greater awareness and appreciation of the contributions these humble farm workers are making to cultural life in their new land.

As Cristina so eloquently put it, "simple clay without any form" can speak the dreams and imaginations of the students, so that everyone can hear their "Voices from the Earth" (Voces de la Tierra).

SOURCES OF INSPIRATION AND TECHNICAL ADVICE

Atkin, J. (2005). *Handbuilt pottery techniques revealed.* New York: Barron's Gardners Books.

Clark, K. (1986). *The potter's manual.* London: Quarto Publishing Ltd.

Ellis, M. (2002). *Ceramics for kids: Creative clay projects to pinch, roll, coil, slam and twist.* New York: Lark Books.

Espejel, C. (1975). *Mexican folk ceramics.* Barcelona: Editorial Blume. (Out of print but used copies available online. The is the single most often used book in our program—wonderful full-page photos documenting pottery and pottery-making in each region of Mexico).

Hogan, E. (Ed.). (1973). *Ceramics, techniques and projects.* Menlo Park, CA: Lane Magazine and Book Company.

Muller, F., & Hopkins, B. (1979). *A guide to Mexican ceramics.* Mexico City: Editorial Minutiae Mexicana.

Sellers, T. (Ed.). (1996). *Ceramic projects.* Westerville, OH: The American Ceramic Society.

Trimble, S. (1987). *Talking with the clay: The art of Pueblo pottery.* Santa Fe, NM: School of American Research Press.

Vincentelli, M. (2004). *Women potters: Transforming traditions.* New Brunswick, NJ: Rutgers University Press.

Wasserspring, L. (2000). *Oaxacan ceramics: Traditional folk art by Oaxacan women.* San Francisco: Chronicle Books.

MEET THE CONTRIBUTORS

Dr. Dawn Addy directs the Center for Labor Research and Studies (CLR&S) at Florida International University. She teaches in and directs the academic certificate program in Conflict Resolution and Consensus Building for CLR&S, serves as Prison Coordinator for the Alternatives to Violence Project (AVP) Miami, and represents prison population interests on the FIU Internal Review Board. She conducts a variety of workshops and seminars for adult learners both nationally and internationally, specializing in community building and conflict resolution. She earned her doctorate in Work, Family and Community Education from the University of Minnesota in 1997. She has coordinated prison programs in Florida for over twelve years.

Ujju Aggarwal, Priscilla González, Donna Nevel, and Perla Placencia are collective members of the Center for Immigrant Families, which is a collectively run organization for low-income immigrant women of color that organizes to transform the conditions of injustice we face and their multi-layered impact on our own lives and that of our communities.

Mary Alfred is an associate professor of adult education in the College of Education and Human Development at Texas A&M University. Her research interests include the scholarship of teaching and learning among members of the African Diaspora, welfare reform as it relates to women's economic development, and diversity issues in education and the workplace. Her work provides a platform for marginalized populations to speak about the issues that affect their lives and to offer their recommendations to alleviating these exacerbating conditions. It provides a testament of their experiences and of their power and knowledge to create plausible futures.

Patricia Anders, University of Arizona, College of Education, Chair of Department of Language, Literacy and Culture, major professor of Heidi, followed by Edie and Laura; became more connected to the adult literacy work in the community through the graduate students and their projects.

Beatrice Arrindell has earned 70 credits toward her bachelor's degree in the Marymount Manhattan College program at the Bedford Hills Correctional Facility in Westchester, NY. She maintains a GPA of 3.8 and expects to earn her bachelor's degree before her release in 2016. This essay was written as one of the assignments for a course entitled Social Justice through Children's Literature taught by Jane Maher, a long-time member of WE LEARN. As a volunteer tutor and mentor in the college program, Beatrice helps other students adjust to and succeed in college, particularly those students in the Pre-College program who need help in developing their academic skills and in increasing their confidence and self-esteem.

Geraldine Cannon Becker is an assistant professor of English and Creative Writing for the University of Maine at Fort Kent, leads reading circles for the Maine Humanities Council at The MSAD #27 Center and Home-based Instructional Program for Parents and Youth (CHIPPY) and is an advocate for literacy. She has been involved with *Women's Perspectives* at WE LEARN for a couple of years and also publishes her own work under her maiden name, Geraldine Cannon: *Glad Wilderness* (Plain View Press, 2008).

Elite Ben-Yosef earned a PhD in Literacy Studies with a focus on marginalized groups of learners. Her goal in teaching is to allow equal learning opportunities for all students by focusing on the learner's strengths and literacies. She is a professor of literacy since 1999 and, on a voluntary basis, teaches literacy at a recovery home for women, and to youth at a juvenile detention facility. Her publications include: "Raising voices through the arts: Creating spaces for writing for marginalized groups of women," *Perspectives: The New York Journal of Adult Learning,* 6(2), 2007-2008; "Students finding voice in a college classroom: Reflections on a teaching/learning journey." *Curriculum and Teaching,* 23(1), 73-88, 2008; "A pedagogy of fusion: An educational response to diversity and complexity." *The International Journal of Diversity in Organizations, Communities and Nations,* 5(5), 167-172, 2006. http://

www.Diversity-journal.com; "Respecting students' cultural literacies." *Educational Leadership*, *61*(2), 2003.

Jane E. Bennett is currently the Head of Center at the University of the West Indies (UWI), Open Campus, Belize. She is also a Lecturer in Human Resource Management (HRM) and Organization Behavior & Management with UWI, Belize and conducts training in professional development in Belize on behalf of the UWI. Mrs. Bennett is Program Director of Eglah's Training Center for Women in Belize City, and facilitates literacy classes in Adult Basic Education as well as in life skills including computer literacy and English as a Second or other Language (ESOL). She is a trained teacher as a graduate of Fordham University with a Master of Science degree in Adult Education and Human Resource Development. Her special interests include: strengthening the family unit through women's education programs which are geared towards empowering women to alleviate their poverty level and to achieving their financial independence. She founded a non-profit organization in Belize City, Belize that works hand in hand with the Belizean community for the betterment of its women. She chairs the Board and is the Program Director for this organization.

Dr. Carrie J. Boden is an associate professor and the Coordinator of the Master's Degree in Adult Education at the University of Arkansas at Little Rock. Dr. Boden holds a PhD with an emphasis in Adult Education from Kansas State University, a MFA in Creative Writing from Wichita State University, and a BA in English Language and Literature from Bethel College.

Dr. Boden's research focus has been on adult learners, specifically on the connections between epistemological beliefs and self-directedness. Most recently she has presented her findings at national and international conferences in Milwaukee, Wisconsin, Montego Bay, Jamaica, Granada, Spain, Havana, Cuba, and Detroit, Michigan. She has published several articles in international journals and books.

Delia Bradshaw has worked as an adult educator in Victoria, Australia, for over three decades in many positions, places and roles. Her particular passions are women's education, multicultural education, foundation education and e-learning. She believes that adult education can contribute significantly to the world becoming more just, compassionate, harmonious and hopeful. Delia initiated the "Women of Spirit" group and was a meeting host, writer and co-editor.

Dr. Sandra D. Bridwell began her career in education teaching Adult Basic Education in the 1970's. She is currently Professor of Education and

Founding Faculty of the Doctoral Program in Educational Leadership at Cambridge College. The focal point of Sandra's professional and academic career has been in teaching, research and community service that improves the life chances of under-served populations. She currently teaches education leadership and research methods courses. Her research focus is on women's literacy, adult learning and developmental theory. Sandra holds a doctorate from Indiana University, Bloomington in Higher Education Administration and she has completed post-doctoral studies in Administration, Planning and Social Policy at the Harvard University Graduate School of Education. She holds a Master of Arts in Teaching from the University of Louisville and a Master of Public Administration from the Harvard University John F. Kennedy School of Government.

Cindy Childress's poetry has recently appeared in *Growing Up Girl: A Manifesta, Panawoma: A New Lit Order, The Southwestern Review, Epicenter,* and *The Louisiana Review.* She served as Poet-in-Residence at the Pinellas County Girl's Correctional Facility 2002-03 and discussed that experience in a roundtable session at the Louisiana Conference on Languages and Literature in 2008. She has won the third place Christina Sergeyevna Award and the Marcella Siegel Memorial Award, both for poetry, and in 2006 she judged the Anita McAndrews Peace Poetry Prize for Poets For Human Rights. She holds a PhD in Creative Writing from the University of Louisiana at Lafayette and MA from the University of South Florida. Childress lives with her husband in Kuala Lumpur.

Dominique T. Chlup is an assistant professor of adult education and an affiliate faculty member of women studies at Texas A&M University. She received her doctorate from Harvard University. She has worked with women inmates in New York, Massachusetts, and Texas. In addition to working with and learning from her student-inmates, she researches the history of U.S. based women's corrections programs to explore how history informs contemporary practice.

Ana Bertha Diaz is an adult ESL educator with Literacy Volunteers of Westchester County & Rockland Counties, NY. She is a native of Dominican Republic, and now lives in the New York City area. As a lifelong learner she has studied business, painting, ESL, graphic arts and now is beginning an architectural engineering program as she continues to work on her painting. Her belief in the ability of people to overcome their circumstances is the basis for her teaching.

Denise DiMarzio, has been asked a lot recently why she moved to teaching at the college level from the less bureaucratic, homier world of adult education. Her flip response had been to say, "Because I can't teach the verb to be one more time." But she began to feel bad about that, feeling like she had maligned a word that had a special quality to it, feeling like she had forgotten that the smallest things often offer the most important gifts, and that what looks simple is often the most complex. She began to think about what it really means "to be," particularly as women in the world, particularly as women in a class, exchanging the role of teacher/ student. This essay is the result of that inquiry. Denise would like to offer her gratitude to the women whose stories form the heart of this essay; they are rare teachers.

Maura Donnelly worked for twelve years as a literacy educator in various New York City programs and is a recipient of New York City's Literacy Recognition Award for outstanding service in the field of adult education.

Stacie Evans is Director of Lutheran Family Health Centers' Community Empowerment Program in Brooklyn, NY. She teaches GED at Lutheran and Pre-GED at Turning Point Educational Center, also in Brooklyn. In 1996, she collaborated with poet and teacher Michael Willard to publish the Isaacs Chapbook Series, a collection written by students at the Stanley M. Isaacs Neighborhood Center in Manhattan. In 1999, she and Michael were the recipients, of the New York City Literacy Recognition Award; the first time the award was given to a team of teachers. She continues to produce student chapbooks at both Lutheran and Turning Point. She has also created a series of stories for adult emerging readers. Stacie is the author of *Black in the South*, an essay published on sonaweb.net, and *A Quiet Place*, a book of photos and reflections on Jamaica and race. She writes online at girlgriot.wordpress.com.

Sally S. Gabb, M.S. Journalism, C.A.G.S. Developmental Reading, began her career in adult education in 1971 in Atlanta, Georgia, assigned to a community school GED class. She continued as teacher, adult education director and professional development specialist at a variety of agencies in Atlanta and Providence, RI, working with basic literacy, GED preparation, and English for Speakers of Other Languages. In 2006, she made the transition to college developmental education at Bristol Community College where she is the Reading Specialist for the Center for Developmental Education.

John Gordon was Teacher-Director of the Open Book from 1985 to 2001. Since then he has worked at the Fortune Society in New York City. He is the author of *More Than a Job: A Curriculum on work and*

Society (New Readers Press, 1991) and "Welfare and Literacy" *(Literacy Harvest,* 1995).

Tzivia Gover is the author of *Mindful Moments for Stressful Days* (Storey Books, 2002). Her articles and essays have appeared in numerous publications including *The New York Times, The Boston Globe, Creative Nonfiction* and *The Christian Science Monitor.* In addition, she has been published in over a dozen anthologies including *Literary Nonfiction: Fourth Genre* (Prentice Hall), *Family: A Celebration* (Petersons) and *Home Stretch* (Alyson). Her poems have appeared in *Lilith, The Bark* and *The Berkshire Review,* among others. Gover received her MFA in creative nonfiction from Columbia University. She has worked extensively teaching creative writing to adult and young adult new readers and taught poetry to teen mothers in Holyoke, Massachusetts for eight years.

Kit Gruver teaches reading, writing and math at the King County Correctional Facility in downtown Seattle. She has a Masters in Adult Education and has been teaching literacy for over 8 years. She has worked with people in poverty since 1992 in a variety of projects in Seattle, Alaska, and Swaziland. She lives on Vashon Island where she and her husband are raising two boys and building their home and garden on 5 acres.

Laura Holland is a single 37-year-old who resides in Randallstown, MD. She is an adjunct faculty with the Center for Adult and Family Literacy at the Community College of Baltimore County. In 1992, she earned her Bachelor's Degree in Sociology and Spanish from Mount Saint Mary's University. In 1997, she earned her Master's Degree in Counseling Psychology from Bowie State University. In 2006, Ms. Holland began providing GED instruction at the South Baltimore Learning Center. Currently, Ms. Holland is providing daily GED instruction to inmates at the Baltimore County Detention Center. Ms. Holland's overall commitment to the academic achievement of her students makes her a valuable asset to any program. She possesses the ability to relate to her students' life experiences and personal sentiments. The poem *Frustrated* written by Ms. Holland is a reflection of her personal interpretation of the feelings and concerns of her students.

Jenny Horsman is a community-based educator and researcher with many years experience focussing on the impact of violence on learning: carrying out research, presenting, leading workshops and teaching. She has written extensively, including the books: *Too Scared to Learn, Take on the Challenge,* and *Something in my Mind Besides the Everyday.* She is developing an interactive multi-media Web site www.learningandviolence.net.

Jaye Jones, MA, MSW has been an adult literacy volunteer at Literacy Chicago for four years. She is currently a PhD student in Social Work at the University of Chicago with research interests that focus on developing innovative literacy interventions to promote healing among women.

Edie Lantz-Leppert, PCAE colleague, teacher of several of the students who participated in the women's group; currently completing her master's at the University of Arizona with Patricia Anders.

Susan Makinen, BS, continues to write poetry—and to take post-baccalaureate college courses. An active volunteer, she is currently working on an online poetry collection to benefit her church.

Lynne Matheson has worked in secondary schools, adult and community education centres and currently, in a vocational education institute (TAFE) in Victoria, Australia. A member of the executive committee of VALBEC for eight years, she is committed to the field of adult literacy and the provision of advocacy, support and professional development for adult literacy and numeracy teachers. Lynne's involvement with the "Women of Spirit" group has been influential in the development of her professional identity, both as an educator and as a writer.

Karen Milheim earned her doctorate in Adult Education from Penn State University at Harrisburg and is currently a part-time faculty member with Walden University. Karen's work focuses on adult basic and literacy education, particularly on strategizing and working towards accommodating students who possess challenging life barriers. Karen is a former instructor and course developer for literacy and workforce development programs in Pennsylvania, taking time off to finish graduate school and be a stay-at-home mother in recent years. This chapter was a result of her personal experiences in the field, and past life experiences, all which led her to develop a desire to continue working with individuals who have been through life's toughest challenges, but still find a way to empower themselves through education.

Gail Wood Miller, PhD, is Professor of English at Berkeley College, West Paterson, New Jersey. Her research interests include learning styles and learning differences. Among her publications is *How to Study: Use Your Personal Learning Style* (2nd ed.) (Learning Express/Random House, 2000).

Laura Porfirio, PCAE colleague, served as a co-facilitator of the focus groups; currently a graduate student at university of Arizona with Patricia Anders.

Dianne Ramdeholl was an instructor at The Open Book from 2000-2001. Her doctoral dissertation, from National Louis University in Chicago, chronicled the history of The Open Book, partly through participants' voices. She is the Adult Basic Education Coordinator at The Department of Youth and Community Development in NYC.

Cheryl Reid has been an adult literacy worker in Ontario for more than 16 years. She is known for encouraging learners to bring their whole selves to the classroom. For the past eight years, Cheryl has facilitated a women's literacy program in the culturally diverse neighborhood of Regent Park in Toronto. She also enjoys leading workshops and trainings for learners and educators. Cheryl draws on her Gestalt Therapy and Yoga Training to assist others in awareness, risk taking, acceptance, stress reduction and overall well-being.

Lorna Rivera, PhD has been an adult literacy teacher, program director, and advocate for improving access to and the quality of adult basic education. Lorna is a founding board member of WE LEARN. She currently serves on the Board of Directors for the Massachusetts Coalition for Adult Education and is the director of the Latino Leadership Opportunity Program at UMass Boston.

Lisa Robertson is the Adult Basic Education Coordinator at Windham Adult Education in Windham, Maine. In addition to her administrative duties, she teaches reading, mathematics, and GED preparation classes. Lisa has other published works pertaining mainly to evidence-based reading strategies. She is especially interested in adult education professional development and is actively involved in such for her program, school district, and state.

Linda Redfield Shakoor has a Masters degree in Bilingual Education from SUNY Albany and has worked with the community of migrant workers, children to adults, for over 30 years. She is an ESL adult teacher/trainer for Orleans Niagara BOCES focused on needs of Hispanic migrant workers. To address the lack of self-esteem, cultural marginalization and lack of English skills among women agricultural workers, Linda utilizes a unique non-textbook style which wins the hearts of her students. She and her colleagues successfully initiated the program discussed in this article, in which English is taught in the context of an artistic pottery experience at World Life Institute Education Center, Waterport, New York.

Sharon L. Shoemaker began working in adult education and literacy as a volunteer tutor, and was offered a job after a year of tutoring. She taught in Macon and Independence, Missouri for nine years. Instead of giving temporary help to students, she feels she has given them a way to earn a living for the rest of their lives. She liked to create community in her classrooms. Believing community begins with respect, she modeled respect to all who entered. They usually repaid her with the same. When she sent these poems to WE LEARN, she didn't know that she'd be leaving the classroom in order to assist the adult education director. The poems she has written are much more poignant as she begins her new position.

Maria Tereza Schaedler is a Brazilian actress and singer with a BA in International Relations. Maria came to the United States in 2004 to study at the American Musical and Dramatic Academy in NYC. She recently graduated from her Masterís in Intercultural Relations from Lesley University. She is currently working as an English teacher for adult immigrants and as an acting teacher for children in different schools in the Boston area.

Heidi Silver-Pacuilla conducted participatory action research with women literacy learners with disabilities at Pima College Adult Education (PCAE) in Tucson as dissertation research for the University of Arizona; currently at American Institutes for Research in Washington, DC.

Tanya Spilovoy is a teacher, writer, and mother. She graduated from Hamline University with a MAEd in Education with an Emphasis in English as a Second Language. Tanya has taught at grade schools, high schools, and universities in Beijing, PR China, Minnesota, and is currently an English Instructor at United Tribes Technical College in Bismarck, North Dakota. Her publications include a bilingual Hmong/English children's book collection, a Hmong culture curriculum, research on changing Hmong female gender roles, and other short stories. She lives with her husband Scott, son Dakota Sky, and cat Mocha.

Gabriele I. E. Strohschen, As an immigrant to the United States, first became engaged in community education and empowerment issues as a learner in one of the many basements where volunteers teach English. A decade later, she developed a tutor center for immigrants in Chicago. She earned a doctoral degree in Education, focusing on adult education and leadership development, at Northern Illinois University.

Strohschen now works at DePaul University-School for New Learning and embraces Liberatory-Popular Adult Education as a means to make a better world. Her teaching, study, and service are shaped by interdependence in communities of practice. Her fieldwork spans design and delivery of programs; resource development; teaching and mentoring; and building action networks with educators at *global* levels in intercultural, cross-community, and international Adult Education settings.

Deborah Wilson trained at Sheridan College School of Design and apprenticed with potters in Toronto 1975-1980. In New York State Deborah has been working to provide creative opportunities for Hispanic farm worker women residing in Orleans County. She received four Arts in Education grants 2002-2007, from the Genesee Valley Council on the Arts, and the Coalition of Arts Providers for Children, Buffalo. As a volunteer for Project Life War Orphans Program she has taught pottery classes to more than 100 international war orphans who understand little or no English. Deborah offers pottery classes to adults and children. In April 2007 she received a Community Arts Award from *GoArt!* honoring her work with diverse populations. She and her husband direct CivicaUSA, a company that provides creative and communications services to non-profit organizations. She also creates and sells an array of pottery items, from stoneware bowls to custom-glazed buttons for fabric projects.

Women from the Focus Groups: voices from participatory action research conducted with 17 women literacy learners with disabilities at Pima College Adult Education (PCAE) in Tucson, AZ.

Özlem Zabitgil is originally from the Mediterranean island of Cyprus. She has Turkish origins. She is a writing tutor at the Earth and Mineral Sciences Writing Center at the Pennsylvania State University. She completed her Masters degree as a Fulbright Scholar in Applied Linguistics/ TESL (Teaching English as a Second Language) at the Pennsylvania State University where she anticipates graduation with a PhD in Adult Education in May 2009. Özlem has a minor degree in Language and Literacy Education. Her research interests are literacy campaign analysis, adult education and social change, literacy and social justice as well as qualitative research which utilizes life-narratives and auto/ethnographic inquiry. Her recent projects include studying the experience and impact of grief in adult learning settings.

ABOUT THE EDITORS

Mev (Mary Evelyn) Miller, EdD, founder and director of WE LEARN, holds a doctoral degree in Critical Pedagogy from the School of Education, University of St. Thomas, Minneapolis, MN. As a trainer, educator, feminist/lesbian activist, and facilitator in a diverse array of community and ABE projects, she has many years of experience with participatory practices and leadership opportunities. She also has 20+ years of experience in the feminist/independent book industry.

Her interests in connecting spirituality, social justice, and education reach back into the early 1980s when she read Paulo Freire (*Pedagogy of the Oppressed*) while studying liberation theology for a Masters in Divinity (M.Div.) from Yale Divinity School, and coming to an understanding of women's spirituality practices. Mev infuses (com)-passion in her quest as an educator for social justice and human dignity. She recently built a labyrinth in her back yard as a way to continually re-center her theory/practice, mind/heart, and action/reflection. One common thread holds these pieces together: her passion and commitment to use literatures and literacies foundational to lifelong learning for such purposes as personal enrichment and enjoyment, community building, and pursuits of justice and social democracy.

Dr. Miller also worked for several years doing ABE professional development with SABES (System for Adult Basic Education Support) in Southeastern Massachusetts. Her long list of publications includes the co-edited volume *Women and Literacy: Moving from Power to Participation*, Women's Studies Quarterly Special Issue Spring 2004 published by The Feminist Press at CUNY, and Educating with Mind, Heart and Spirit. *Field Notes*, *15*(3), (2004). She has also edited and produced several ABE student-writing publications.

Kathleen P. King, EdD, is professor of adult education and HRD at Fordham University's Graduate School of Education in New York City, and former director of the university's RETC Center for Professional Development. She is also president of Transformation Education, LLC. King's major areas of research include transformative learning, professional development, distance learning, and instructional technology. Most recent endeavors continue to explore and develop learning innovations and opportunities to address equity, access and international issues. She has lead the development of numerous local and global innovative adult learning projects some reaching over 4.3 million learners through technology; most of these efforts have been underwritten by corporate, federal and state grants.

Dr. King is the author of 15 books and numerous published articles and research papers. Recent books authored and co-authored by Dr. King include, *Bringing Transformative Learning to Life* (2005), *Effective Faculty Development Using Adult Learning Principles* (2nd ed.) (in press-2009, with Lawler), *Adult Education around the Globe* (2007, with Wang), *Perspectives of Evolving Research in Transformative Learning* (10th anniv. ed.) (in press, 2009), *Human Performance Models from a Global Context* (2009, with Wang), and *Podcasting for Teaching* (Rev. ed.) (2009, with Gura). Dr. King is a popular keynote speaker and presents at international and national conferences on topics related to adult learning, transformative learning, distance education, faculty development, diversity, and educational technology.

Dr. King received her EdD from Widener University, Chester, Pennsylvania. She also has a MEd in Adult Education from Widener, a MA from Columbia International, Columbia, SC and a BA from Brown University, Providence, RI. For more information about Dr. Kathy King's academic, community and consulting work visit www.kpking.com and www.transformationed.com.

Printed in the United States
143619LV00001B/27/P

9 781607 520832